The Mountains Called and We Went

The Mountains Called and We Went

The Trail Looked So Flat On the Map

by

ANGELA JAMES

Cover designed by Angela James

Printed in the United States of America

First Printing: September 2023

ISBN - 9798857174524

Dedication

This book is dedicated to my husband and our family. Without my husband and his dogged determination, we would have never attempted such a challenge as hiking the Appalachian Trail. Even though many people hike the trail by themselves I wouldn't have been able to hike it without my husband and his we can do it attitude. Our wonderful, crazy, blended family was so supportive during our adventures. Our daughters, sons and grandchildren are loved more than they know. We have all been together so long, there are no stepchildren, no yours or mine, they are all ours. They have no idea how much it meant to us that they were following our progress, helping us out when needed and providing much needed support along the way.

Disclaimer

This book describes the author's experiences while preparing and hiking various backcountry trails including the Appalachian Trail, it also reflects her interpretations and opinions. Names and details that may identify individuals have been changed to protect their privacy.

Table of Contents

Chapter 1 - Lots to Learn 1

Chapter 2 - Getting the Right Equipment 15

Chapter 3 - Let's Just Do It 20

Chapter 4 - The Trail Starts at The Top 24

Chapter 5 - Wet, Dry, Repeat 29

Chapter 6 – Cheeseburgers 36

Chapter 7 - Smoky Mountain, Rain and COLD 45

Chapter 8 - Hot Springs is Not So Hot 54

Chapter 9 - Goodbye Trail Hello New World 58

Chapter 10 - Where are the Blueberries? 62

Chapter 11 - Llama Trains, Hurricanes and Moonbows 64

Chapter 12 - Going West 71

Chapter 13 - Glaciers & Bears 78

Chapter 14 - Fog, Rain and Snow 83

Chapter 15 - Is it Hot or What? 87

Chapter 16 - Couch to Katahdin 90

Chapter 17 - The 100 Mile Wilderness 96

Chapter 18 - Back to Civilization (Temporarily) 105

Chapter 19 - Rain, Rain, Go Away 109

Chapter 20 - Are We in The Twilight Zone? 119

Chapter 21 - The Long Trip Home 130

Chapter 22 - Here We Go Again 133

Chapter 23 – Chipping Away at It 144

Chapter 24 - Going to See Phil 150

Chapter 25 - We Will Stop When We Finish 154

Chapter 26 - Cleanup on Aisle Three 165

Chapter 27 - Virginia's Triple Crown 168

Chapter 28 - Will We Ever Get Out of Virginia?   176

Chapter 29 - We Ain't Exactly in the South Anymore   200

Chapter 30 - Rain, Rain, Rain & More Rain   216

Chapter 31 - Pennsylvania a.k.a. Rocksylvania   222

Chapter 32 - There's Bears in Them Woods   226

Chapter 33 - Where Did Mingo Go?   232

Chapter 34 - I Would Really Like a Shower That Works   240

Chapter 35 - We Met a Hermit   248

Chapter 36 - The Trail Has Gone to the Dogs   254

Chapter 37 - We Are Becoming a Tramily   264

Chapter 38 - The Final Push   281

Chapter 39 - There's No Place Like Home   287

EPILOGUE   290

Fourteen States on the Appalachian Trail   291

Our Zero Hiking Days   292

Lodging (*tenting with some facilities available)   293

References   295

About The Author   300

Introduction

When my husband, Roy, first proposed the idea of hiking the Appalachian Trail (AT) about ten years ago, I thought he was more than just a little crazy. To actually walk over two thousand miles through mountains and valleys while camping in nature for weeks seemed like an impossible task. Thousands of people hike the entire trail each year, but in addition to my husband I also thought those thousands of people were crazy. By the time we were ready to hike the AT, the odds were stacked against us. I was fifty-eight years old and my husband was sixty-four. The average hiker on the AT is in their thirties, I thought we were probably getting a bit too old to start on this journey. Only one in four people who start a thru hike of the AT actually finish the trail. Could we be two of eight to complete this trek through the mountains? The AT is almost 2200 miles of some of the most difficult hiking in the United States going through fourteen states from Georgia to Maine, or Maine to Georgia depending on which direction you hike. The average time for completion of the hike is five to seven months. That's a long time to be away from home and family. After much training and preparation, we were two very determined retirees planning to finish the AT no matter the obstacles or weather conditions thrown at us by Mother Nature. Could we even tolerate being with each other twenty-four seven for that long? This book tells of our hiking adventures including several years learning how to hike and camp. It also details a day-by-day account and the often-humorous events that occurred while hiking the AT.

"Of all the paths you take in life, make sure a few of them are dirt." - John Muir

Chapter 1 - Lots to Learn

The first time we went for an overnight hiking trip we chose a trail close to home in Mammoth Cave National Park. Sal Hollow Trail was located across the Green River from our home near Glasgow, Kentucky. The trail started at the Maple Springs Group Campground and it was about 8 miles to the backcountry campsite. We went to the visitor center on Saturday and got our backcountry camping permit. Keep in mind this was our first ever overnight backpacking trip. It was September and it was a beautiful warm sunny day. The trail led us through a forest of large deciduous trees. The leaves on the trees were still green and the forest floor was also still covered in smaller green plants. I was keeping myself entertained by looking at the different plants, trees and wild mushrooms along the trail. There was one huge Sulphur Shelf mushroom growing on a log and it was beautiful. The vivid colors of orange and yellow were in stark contrast to the surrounding forest. After a couple of hours of hiking it became apparent, at least to me, this was not going to be just any "walk in the park". The terrain was what I would consider now gently rolling, back then I might as well have been climbing the Himalayas. I was in no condition to hike eight miles much less do it with a backpack. My husband exercised every day during his lunchtime and he was in much better shape than me at that time.

Before we even got to the campsite, I told my husband to go ahead and call 911 because we were so far off grid it would take till morning for anyone to come to my rescue. I was exhausted, we had not even made it to the campsite and I was already dreading the hike back out to the car. I was also thinking if his goal was to kill me, there were quicker, more efficient ways to accomplish the task. I would come to repeat that to him many times over the course of our hiking adventures.

We finally arrived at the campsite about an hour before dark. The campsite was on a hillside in the woods and the only place to put the tent was nowhere near flat. This didn't look like a campsite to me. I was expecting maybe a tent pad, a fire ring, a picnic table or anything to indicate it was a campsite. This was my first-time backcountry camping and I really didn't know what to expect. But there was a sign indicating we were in the right place. We put the tent up and hoped we didn't slide downhill in our sleeping bags too much. At least we had the good sense to put our heads up the hill to prevent both of us from rolling to one side of the tent.

Our water supply was a bit low even though we had found a very nice piped spring along the way, drank up and topped off our water bottles before getting to the campsite. The spring was near the top of a hill and it had crystal clear cold water running from a pipe. Our bodies required more water during the hike than anticipated due to the weather being so warm. At that time, we only carried one liter of water each. We drank the water we carried and refilled our bottles with spring water. The cold water actually fogged our water bottles when we filled them. We could have probably consumed the water without treating or boiling but we didn't want to take a chance on it. When we arrived at the campsite, we would boil the water or treat with purification tablets before consuming.

Roy left me at the campsite to get our sleeping bags zipped together and placed in the tent while he walked down a path to see if it might lead to the river. If we were close enough to the river our water problem would be resolved. The path was overgrown with green weeds on either side and it looked like a fairly well traveled game trail. *We were not using the FarOut app with GPS at that time, we would discover the benefits of that later in our hiking careers.* He came back a few minutes later saying we were nowhere close to the river. We even considered going back to the spring we found earlier, but it was too far to back track, and it would have been dark soon. We proceeded to cook what we packed with us for supper, which was a dehydrated soup mix. The soup required quite a bit of water. The package of dehydrated chili contained eight servings and we decided to cook half of the package. When we halved the package, the seasoning was apparently not evenly divided. The chili was terribly salty but we didn't bring any other food for supper so we ate it. We were running extremely low on water, after cooking we only had enough water for a cup of coffee the next morning. Not long after eating we bedded down in the tent. Shortly after we got in the tent Roy's feet started itching terribly and he was terrorized by itching all night.

Roy's feet were itching, we slid downhill in our sleeping bags, both of us were thirsty due to the salty soup and we had limited water. Needless to say, neither of us got very much sleep. It's amazing how thirsty you get when you know the water supply is limited.

We got up shortly after daylight, made a little coffee with the remaining water and packed our equipment, more than ready to hike back to civilization. On the way back we took a different trail, Buffalo Creek Trail as it was only about 5 miles back to the car. This was still a long way for me to hike but at least it was a shorter trail. We didn't get very far until it was apparent the hike out was not going to be any more fun than the hike in, and we had no water. The farther we went the thirstier we became and I was looking everywhere for puddles. I have never been so thirsty in my life! At this point in our hiking adventures, we were carrying water filters called Life Straws. I was seriously thinking about drinking out of a puddle, if I could find one. There was one puddle of water in a stream that was otherwise dry, it was in rocks but it was stagnant and had insects in it. I thought the LifeStraw would make it okay, but Roy kept telling me we were not that far from the car. I passed on the water and again accused him of trying to kill me.

It was another warm day and by the time we got to our car we were absolutely parched. The closest place to get a cold drink was back across the river at the campground camp store near the Mammoth Cave National Park Visitor's Center. Thankfully the ferry taking cars across the river was running and the store was open on Sunday. I went in and bought two one-quart bottles of sports drink. We drank the first bottle in about two gulps each and slowed down to sip the second bottle. I never knew a cold Powerade could taste so good!

When we got home, we found out why Roy's feet itched. Turkey mites! His feet were covered in tiny little bites. We had both heard horror stories about turkey mites but had never experienced anything like it first-hand. The turkey mites are not mites at all, they are actually the early developmental stages of ticks. His ankles and feet were covered with what looked to be hundreds of bites. We tried everything we could think of to quell the itching to no avail, he was in misery. Cold water, tea tree oil, hydrocortisone cream, calamine, Benadryl, baking soda, bleach, and probably some things I don't remember were all tried without success. We considered seeking medical care, I'm not sure what a doctor would have done that we had not already tried except give him steroid medications and/or a shot. Roy was definitely not on board with going to a doctor and not willing to take a chance on the possibility of getting a shot. He suffered through it and the worst of the itching was finally over in a couple of days. He's a lot tougher than I am, I would have probably been in tears.

When we got home from that hiking adventure, we both were exhausted and fell asleep in the living room that evening. It was Sunday and we had to get some rest before returning to work on Monday. There were a lot of lessons learned on this trip. First, never, ever, ever, underestimate the importance of water. Second, don't ever go down a path with green weeds without having sprayed with insect repellant, preferably one with a high percentage of DEET. Third, don't eat salty food especially when water is in limited supply. Fourth, don't pitch your tent on a hillside if there is any way around it. And fifth, we needed a lot more planning for the next trip, if there was going to be one. I don't think anyone would have blamed me if I never went hiking again!

I don't know how much time passed before we decided to hike and camp overnight again, but we eventually did. We went for more backpacking overnight or day hikes to Mammoth Cave National Park, Kingdom Come State Park, Cumberland Falls State Park, Natural Bridge State Park, Land Between the Lakes, Daniel Boone National Forest and Cumberland Gap in Kentucky. We also went to Tennessee and hiked in The Great Smoky Mountains National Park, Big South Fork National Recreation Area, Rock Island State Park, Fall Creek Falls State Park, Virgin Falls State Natural Area, Burgess Falls State Park, Cummings Falls State Park, Pickett State Park and Frozen Head State Park. We really enjoyed seeing the waterfalls in eastern Tennessee and visited some of these places more than once. I found I have a special affinity for waterfalls. They are amazing and each one large or small is unique and beautiful. I'm sure I left some places out, but nevertheless, we did a lot of backpacking, hiking and camping. Each time we went camping we saw beautiful sights not visible from the highway while traveling in the car and we were always looking for the next unique location to plan a trip. We learned something new or had the opportunity to fine tune our equipment each time we went.

One of the hikes that comes to mind is a trail at Cumberland Gap, on the Kentucky-Virginia border, that goes up to Hensley Settlement. Hensley Settlement is on Brush Mountain and it is a part of the Cumberland Gap National Historical Park. The settlement began in 1903 and the last resident left the settlement in 1951. One hundred people lived there at one point in time. The school and forty-five other structures were restored in the 1960s. There were two routes we could have chosen to hike up to the settlement. One of the trails was over five miles and the other was a little over three. We decided to hike the three-mile trail since it was shorter. It started out pretty easy, but gradually became steeper. It went up what appeared to be an old road bed. This was early in our hiking career and the steepest terrain we had encountered. I would literally take three or four steps and stop to rest. I was relatively sure over the years people, mules and other animals died trying to climb this mountain with a pack and I felt like I was going to be one of them. There were rocks, roots, large areas to step or nearly crawl up and it was very slow going.

There were multiple false summits. You would think you were at the top, but the trail just kept going up. *False summits are a hiker's nemesis. We would encounter false summits countless times while hiking in the mountains. We met a hiker in New Hampshire who described false summits best. "You think you are at the top, but you are at a false summit and the trail keeps on going. You are sure your legs won't carry you any further, but the trail keeps on going. You start to completely give up, but the trail keeps on going. You start to lose faith in humanity, but the trail keeps on going. There are so many false summits you start to lose faith in God before you finally reach the actual summit of some of these mountains".* Many times, on this hike I would think we were at the top but the trail would turn and there would be another steep incline ahead. False summits were such a disappointment.

Before we got to the top of the mountain at Hensley Settlement the wind started to blow, clouds were rolling in, and we heard thunder in the distance. We hurried as much as we could to get to the top of the mountain before the rain came. We finally popped out of the woods at the top of the mountain in a grassy area near one of the log cabins just as the downpour started. We ran to the porch of the cabin to get out of the rain. The roof on the porch leaked in a few places but a leaky roof was better than no roof. We stayed there until the rain stopped. Not long after the rain stopped, fog started rolling in. We could see the fog actually moving across the fields. It was an eerie sight, like something you would see in a scary movie. The old deserted cabins, barns and outbuildings on top of the mountain only enhanced the creepy atmosphere. I half expected to see the ghosts of the settlers who lived in this area years ago to come walking out of the cabins. But thankfully it was just fog.

That night we camped on top of the mountain and actually built a fire after the rain. We built the fire on a large rock and used twigs from up in the bushes and trees that were off the ground to start the fire. The ends of the twigs were dried just enough by the wind for us to use them as tinder. Larger pieces of wood were laid next to the fire to dry, added little by little and we were able to keep the fire going. It was nice to have the fire, the weather was cool and we sat near the fire until it was time to crawl into the tent for the night. *We didn't know it then, but being able to build a fire when everything was wet would serve us well in the future.* We snuggled down in our tent, slept well and stayed toasty warm in our sleeping bags despite the cooler temperatures.

The next morning, we were hoping to see what was supposed to be a great view from White Rocks, an outcropping of rocks at the top of the mountain, but we couldn't see due to the dense fog. *We would find as we hiked in the mountains on various occasions, we were disappointed because we were deprived of the views by fog, but we were also frequently rewarded with gorgeous views so I guess it all balanced out.* We bypassed the trail leading to White Rocks as it was also further away than we realized at the time, and made our way down the mountain.

The trail downhill was as bad or worse than going uphill! My legs were sore from climbing uphill the day before and it was as difficult if not more so hiking downhill. We were really glad to get to our car and head for home. When getting out of the car after getting home it became apparent my muscles were going to be sore for a couple of days. As usual, we had to recuperate on Sunday before work on Monday. Lessons learned on this trip. First, the shortest route is not always the best route, pay attention to elevation loss and gains. Second, you can build a fire after a rain when the ground is wet, you just have to be creative. Third, hiking steep uphill and downhill trails is extremely difficult on the legs. Fourth, fog will sometimes steal the view.

We backpacked and camped in Hawaii when we went there on vacation in September of 2019. The first hike was Diamond Head near Waikiki, on the island of Oahu. We had to get up early to be in line waiting to enter the park when it opened. When we arrived the line to enter the park was already backed up, there were a lot of people who wanted to see the sunrise and hike early in the day. A trail of vehicles was lined up to enter the park and their red tail lights were shining in the dark. We were a couple of hours early and there were probably thirty vehicles ahead of us. We passed the time watching the sunrise over Oahu, it was fiery red and more than worth getting up early to witness this miracle of nature. The hike to the top of Diamond Head was not a difficult hike, only 1.6 miles roundtrip, the summit is 760 feet elevation and we were not carrying packs. Diamond Head is an extinct volcano and a very distinct landmark. The trail to the top was built in 1908 by the U.S. Army and used for decades as part of Fort Rugur military base. There were remnants of cement bunkers and observation decks on the summit of the crater. A lot of people were on the trail that morning and we were glad we went as early in the day as possible. The 360-degree view from the summit was breathtaking. We had better than a bird's eye view of Oahu and Waikiki Beach. The multiple colors of blue in the ocean from this vantage point were gorgeous. What a colorful canvas the ocean provided for our viewing. The hike up Diamond Head was definitely one of the highlights of our trip.

While on Oahu we also toured Pearl Harbor. The destruction and death that occurred there on December 7, 1941 is unimaginable. Visiting the Arizona Memorial was a very moving experience. Seeing all the names of the servicemen on the wall inside the Arizona Memorial made me realize the magnitude of the loss of life during the attack on Pearl Harbor and this wall only contained the names of the men lost on the Arizona, not the numerous people lost on other ships and other areas affected by the attack that day. Seeing the oil in the water, seventy-eight years later as it still bubbled up from the battleship Arizona was surreal. Many people visiting the memorial were moved to tears and I understand as I also felt a lump in my throat. I have been aware of the history of the attack on Pearl Harbor my whole life but being there and seeing the area made it more real for me. The history of our great country is truly amazing and the sacrifices made for the freedoms we enjoy should never be taken for granted.

We took a drive around the island and found ourselves at the Dole Plantation where pineapples are grown. The fields were full of pineapple plants and the visitor center at the plantation had gifts, foods and refreshments for sale. It reminded me a lot of Jackson's Orchard back home. Best I can recall there was a restaurant, gift shop, train ride, pineapple maze and gardens. We of course got Dole Whip, a soft serve frozen pineapple dessert and we quickly decided it was definitely something we both loved.

On the island of Kauai, in the town of Lihue, we went to the Hawaii State Parks Office to get our backcountry camping permit. We really wanted to hike the Kalalau trail but found it must be scheduled months in advance. The Kalalau trail is a very popular trail along the Napali Coast. It is reportedly one of the most beautiful and dangerous hikes in the United States. Part of the trail is on extremely high and narrow cliffs. YouTube videos of the hike show loose rock and staggering heights. I have a healthy fear of big heights and was a bit concerned about hiking this trail. Roy kept telling me the videos just made the trail look worse. I decided I would just take my time and do it. I won't lie, I was a little relieved when we couldn't hike this particular trail. But on the other hand, we missed some beautiful sites. Kauai was where part of the movie Jurassic Park was filmed. The high cliffs and waterfalls on the island could be seen from several places along the road and were unbelievable. But hiking to them and seeing them up close would have been a monumental experience.

We were told of several other hikes and chose to hike the Kukui Trail down into the Waimea Canyon. The campsite was on the Waimea River, only 2.5 miles from the parking area but it was also a 2000 feet descent into the canyon. The canyon was beautiful, it reminded us of the Grand Canyon with the layers of brown, orange and green color. There were wild goats in the canyon and we heard them several times. *We heard wild pigs on another island and saw goats (and chickens) on every island we visited.*

As we were at a particular narrow section of the trail with a big drop off on the left side, Roy stumbled and leaned really hard to the left. I was behind him and I saw him stumble and recover his balance. It really scared me, there was a huge drop on that side of the trail. If he had fallen, he would have been killed. Of course, he downplayed it but it made us both more aware of the need to take care with every step when hiking in places like this.

We passed a campsite on the way and saw a dog. He was very friendly but it appeared he had been on his own for a while because he was really skinny. I thought he was a mixed breed wire haired terrier of some sort, he was about knee high and had such a sweet face. He was very friendly and allowed us to pet him. He was glad to see us but it was apparent we were not the people he wanted to see. He stayed there and we went on up the trail to our designated campsite.

Our campsite was on the Waimea River and we forded the river back and forth several times on the way there. There were plants resembling the ones we have at home but they were huge. The ferns, elephant ears, cane and milkweed were a few I could readily identify. When we arrived at the campsite it quickly became apparent it was a mosquito haven and they were as big as

9

hummingbirds. Even with insect repellent they were still able to get in a bite every now and then. The air was thick with mosquitos. After eating a quick supper, we crawled in the tent to get away from them. We had planned on staying there two nights, but decided to hike out of the canyon after one night of camping. In addition to being a mosquito's buffet, we didn't feel there was anything to do or see for a whole day down in the canyon if we stayed at the same campsite two nights. There were other things we wanted to see and do in Hawaii. As we passed back through the campsite where the dog was the day before he came out again to greet us. I thought if we could get him to follow us, we would take him to the local humane society, at least he would be fed there. He acted like he wanted to follow us but he wouldn't leave the area. We finally decided the least we could do was feed him. We had a package of chicken for supper that evening but it wouldn't be needed so I opened it and fed the dog. If we had been in Kentucky, I would have tied a rope on him and led him out, maybe even taken him home with me. I really hated to leave him. We talked to some people later that thought the dog probably belonged to a goat hunter since they do sometimes use dogs while goat hunting. We just hoped his owner would find him before too long.

We didn't know it at the time but goat hunting in Hawaii is a big thing. Goats are not a native species and they do a lot of damage to the landscape. There is a regular hunting season, kind of like hunting deer at home.

Hiking out of the Waimea Canyon was the hardest uphill we had ever encountered while hiking. Hensley Settlement looked good compared to this uphill. I was thinking the whole time on the trip down to the campsite it was going to be difficult going back up but had no idea! I truly had to take two or three steps, stop, rest and repeat on most of the trail. It seemed like it took forever to climb out of the canyon. The hike would have been difficult without a backpack, but with a backpack it was brutal. There were several areas where the trail went up huge sandstone rocks without steps and at a very steep incline. Loose rocks also added to the difficulty of the trail. To say we were exhausted when we reached the rental car was a gross understatement of the fact. We did good to put one foot in front of the other.

We managed to get back to the town of Lihue to find a room for the night. With soreness already setting in we exited the car and went inside to book a room. We had decided on the way there we would need to stay there for a couple of nights. It would probably take that long to recuperate from the hike. The hotel was gorgeous, had a fantastic pool, was right on a beach and the landscaping was beautiful. I had only seen the flower called Bird of Paradise in pictures or in artificial form. *I knew the old Little Jimmy Dickens song, "May the Bird of Paradise Fly up Your Nose." Of course, way back when I heard that song as a child, I thought the Bird of Paradise was really a bird.* Seeing the flower growing for real was awesome, we certainly don't have plants like those in Kentucky. When we checked in the lady asked us if a second-floor room was ok. We laughed because we had just climbed out of the canyon. At this point what was a little more up? But I would have taken a ground floor room. We hobbled up the steps with our packs. *This was just a taste of the "hikers hobble" as we would come to know it.*

After we got into the room, we showered and got ready to go eat at a nearby restaurant. If going up the steps to our room was bad, going down was twice as bad. Our calves were sore and cramping up and we more than hobbled going down the stairs. After dinner that evening and the next day, we were more than happy to soak our sore legs in the pool. Lessons learned on this hike, first, the shortest trail is not always the best. Second, you have to take elevation loss or gain into consideration. *We should have already learned these two lessons but we had forgotten about Hensley Settlement at Cumberland Gap. It had been a few years since that hike, we apparently needed a reminder and boy did we ever get one.* Third, insect repellant can be as almost as important as food and water.

We also camped in Volcanoes National Park on the big island of Hawaii. As our luck would have it there was no visible lava in the park when we were there. It was the first time in many years there had been no lava. We went to the park office to get our camping permit and decided to go to Apua Point. The campsite at Apua Point, was 6.6 miles across the lava fields where previous eruptions had created a very unique landscape. The trail was right along the ocean and it was a beautiful hike. The rock formations made from lava were very unusual and the waves crashing against the rocks were beautiful. The trail was close enough to the ocean to feel sea spray a couple of times. There was even a place where the lava had left a stone arch up high at the water's edge and it was the perfect place for a photo. The lava rocks had taken on different characteristics as the lava flow cooled. Some of the rocks had beautiful brilliant orange or yellow colors and either bubbles or swirling patterns while other rocks even looked like ropes all twisted together. *The last volcanic eruption at this location was in the early 1970's. I sure wouldn't want to be there if it happened again, yikes!*

We got to the designated campsite in the early afternoon and pitched our tent under the one coconut tree on the beach. We quickly put on our swimsuits and went wading in the tidal pools to cool off. The water was refreshing after hiking across the lava fields. We had to be careful, the rock in the tidal pools was of course volcanic rock and we didn't want to get all scratched up. The waves crashing into the area were strong. There was no way we would have taken a chance on swimming in the ocean there, wading the small pools was just fine. The one tree didn't provide much shade and we went to the only structure in the area. It was a small building used by park staff who were doing turtle patrol. Thank goodness it had a water catchment system to contain rainwater and we were able to get plenty of fresh water although we still filtered it. When we registered for the campsite, we were told there may or may not be water at the "turtle hut" and we packed extra water with us but it would not have been enough to comfortably get through the hike. The turtle hut as it was called, also had what looked like a little carport on it and it provided much needed shade. We were sitting at the hut drinking water when two girls, who were park staff, arrived. They told us they were conducting turtle patrol. They had stayed at a different location the night before and had hiked nine miles from that location. They would be camping on the beach and getting up every hour all night long with their red headlamps to search the beach for nesting sea turtles. So far there had been no turtle nests found at this location, but we were told it was early in the nesting season. If there had been any turtles nesting at that time, they told us we could have gone with them to see the nests, if we had red lights, which we did. It would have been awesome to see the turtles on the beach laying eggs or seeing the hatchlings trying to make it to the ocean. We had only seen things like that on TV but to see them first hand would have been a once in a lifetime experience. At least we met the girls and talked with them about their experiences of working for the national park service.

We settled into our tent at dark after we ate our supper. We didn't get much sleep even though we were tired from the day of hiking and the heat, there were ants in our tent! Thank goodness they didn't bite, but you couldn't sleep for them crawling on you. If you searched for them with your head lamp you really didn't see but maybe a couple. We would think it was okay, about the time you would be drifting off to sleep, an ant would run down your arm or leg. The turtle girls carried a large piece of plywood out to where they were staying that night. They had put their cots on the boards so they were not sinking into the sand. I bet they knew about the ants and didn't have an ant problem. I don't remember if we tried insect repellent or not, if not we should have. As soon as it was light enough to safely travel, we hiked out to the rental car. Needless to say, we got a nice room with an early check in as soon as we got to the nearest town. We showered and took a three- or four-hour nap before going to dinner. The hike in the heat was exhausting, not to mention the lack of sleep due to ants!

Even though the campsites in Hawaii were not ideal, we enjoyed seeing the Waimea Canyon, Waimea River, lava fields, the coastline, swimming and meeting the turtle girls. These sites were beautiful and unusual and not accessible from a road or even a day hike for us. We were glad we hiked the backcountry in Hawaii, for us it was a once in a lifetime experience and we made some wonderful memories. We also learned a lot about hiking in very challenging situations.

During our earlier hiking adventures, we found out, through trial and error, what equipment worked well and what didn't. Roy still would frequently mention hiking "The Trail" and I still thought he was crazy. I couldn't wrap my head around hiking almost 2200 miles and I really couldn't see us doing it. It seemed like it took me a day or two to recuperate from a 5- or 6-mile hike. Both of us were still working and retirement was a faraway place we would not be visiting any time soon. We had too many obligations, the trail would have to wait. Besides, we still had a lot to learn about hiking before we tackled the AT. Thankfully not every hiking trip turned out to be like Sal Hollow, Hensley Settlement or our hikes in Hawaii. The trips became more enjoyable as we continued to research hiking, made adjustments to equipment and streamlined our process of setting up camp. We also learned more survival skills and felt more confident about being out in the back country and off grid. There was no cell service in a lot of the areas we hiked and we needed to be prepared for anything. We had been at this hobby for a few years, were we ready for the AT now? Hiking the AT was a hike like no other and we had to be fully prepared before setting out on the journey.

"To walk in nature is to witness a thousand miracles."
- Mary Davis

Chapter 2 - Getting the Right Equipment

Roy researched camping and backpacking equipment focusing on the weight and durability of the items. He purchased a Sierra Designs tent for two when we first started hiking and strategically measured the footprint to be the exact size of two NeoAir inflatable mattresses. We then purchased two of the NeoAir mattresses and two L.L. Bean twenty-degree Downtek sleeping bags. He assured me this set up would be comfortable and it wouldn't be like my idea of roughing it while tent camping. I thought the set up was a clever way to encourage my participation.

Over the next few years, we went on overnight camping trips, when my husband could convince me to go. I had to admit our tent and sleeping set up was comfortable and we learned how to pack and set everything up. I told myself we were not really roughing it that much. In addition to planning for our weekend overnight trips my husband was actually covertly preparing me for "The Trail".

I too eventually started to research equipment and realized I wanted to see as many unique places as possible. Hiking to these places would also be a great way to get some much-needed exercise. I was still working and my office job and it didn't allow for very much activity, so I became pretty much a weekend warrior. I did little things throughout the week to try and keep myself in better shape. I parked as far away from the entrance of my office building as possible to get in a few extra steps each day. I also walked longer distances between parking lots and other facilities to attend meetings. I don't think it was really enough to make a difference but I felt like I was at least putting forth some effort. I just didn't think I had the energy to exercise before or after work each day after being gone for ten hours plus. If I didn't have the strength to exercise each day, how would I ever be able to hike long distance trails?

I purchased my first backpack after much consideration of pricing, reviews and female specific features. I chose a women's Osprey Aura 65. The weight of my backpack itself is just under four pounds, it fit me well and I was able to carry everything necessary for a long-distance backpacking trip. I was happy with my purchase even if it did set me back about two hundred and fifty dollars at the time. There were newer ultralight backpacks available that weighed less. I had even gotten another backpack before hiking the AT and it weighed about two pounds. The newer pack just didn't fit me and was not comfortable. But my Osprey backpack worked and it didn't hurt me while I carried it. I decided to stick with it and I'm glad I did. The Osprey packs have a lifetime guarantee which was also a great selling point. Roy also purchased an Osprey men's backpack; his pack was actually more lightweight than mine.

Not long after purchasing my first pair of trekking poles I decided I needed something more user friendly. The poles I had were adjusted by turning the shaft of the pole so the length could be adjusted as it telescoped to the desired length. I found it was extremely hard to adjust them if they were twisted too tight or my hands were wet or sweaty. If the poles were not tightened enough, they would collapse while hiking and potentially cause me to fall. Roy had Black Diamond trekking poles and he was very happy with them. I decided on Black Diamond poles also and they were much more user friendly. We would find out later this was one of our better purchases and we depended on them greatly while hiking over rough terrain. Trekking poles can help immensely when climbing up and down steep hills. Going uphill they allow you to pull with your arms a bit so your legs are not doing all the work. Downhill they take some of the pressure off your knees and help you maintain your balance. Not all hikers are sold on using trekking poles but we found them to be invaluable. We also found that most of the older hikers usually used trekking poles. Even though we did have several falls during the course of our hiking trips, the trekking poles would save us from many more.

Our GSI Halulite Dual Minimalist cook set included a cook pot with a strainer lid, two insulated bowls with sip lids, two regular bowls and two telescoping sporks. All the items could be nested into the small stuff sack. The sack itself could be used to hold about a quart of water and it came in handy several times. The only problem we encountered with the set was the plastic sporks. They had handles that telescoped out and even with being careful your fingers more often than not would get pinched when trying to extend or reduce the handle length. The sporks had to be collapsed to fit into the set. Other than the sporks, the cook set was perfect for two people. We replaced the finger pinchers with titanium sporks. Problem solved. We used this cookset on all our hiking trips. It is still in good shape if we want to use it again.

Our headlamps required a couple of tries to get right. The first purchase was a little heavy and not very user friendly. The second time we opted for Black Diamond headlamps and they were exactly what we needed. They were lightweight, waterproof, allowed for multiple adjustments of brightness and they also had a red light. The red lights don't attract as many insects, help you maintain your night vision and are also good when you don't want to disturb others with your light.

It also took us a couple of tries to get the right water filter. The first ones we got were too hard to drink from and you couldn't filter water through them. We also experimented with water purification tablets and decided we had to wait too long for them to work and they gave the water a horrible taste. We did a little more research and decided on the Sawyer Squeeze Water Filtration System. The filter has a screw top that will fit on any standard plastic bottle. You can opt to drink from the filter or filter the water into a bottle and drink from the bottle. We more often than not filled our bottles with available water and drank through the filter as it saved us quite a bit of time. Many hikers spend several minutes each day filtering water. We found one hiker who drank water without filtering just because it looked good. We were not that trusting and always filtered the water we collected anywhere in the great outdoors. If fresh water was available, we rinsed our water bottles and filled them with fresh water. It was easier to drink without the filter but we didn't mind using the filter, especially if it prevented us from becoming sick.

Choosing shoes was the most difficult part of getting the right equipment and we both went through several pairs of boots and various athletic shoes before we both eventually settled on Hoka trail runners before hiking the AT. Shoes must be comfortable and fit well. They should be at least one half to one full size larger than you normally wear. This will allow extra room for thicker hiking socks, swollen feet from hiking long days, prevention of blisters and the extra length keeps your toes from pushing into the end of your shoe when hiking downhill. Many hikers have horrible blisters, lose or lost toenails, develop plantar fasciitis or Achilles tendinitis or other foot ailments that take them off the trail. We sure didn't want to be plagued with foot problems. I also found that men's athletic shoes fit me better than the women's shoes. They were just a little wider and although not as sleek and attractive as women's shoes they were more comfortable for me. I wasn't going for style; I definitely needed the comfort. We did some of our winter or early spring hiking in boots but we wore trail runners on the majority of hikes.

In addition to shoes, socks were a major consideration. We hiked with cotton socks, sock liners, wool blend socks, wool socks before we finally settled on Darn Tough wool socks. Darn Toughs come with a lifetime guarantee. If your socks wear out go to a store that sells the socks or mail them back to the company for a replacement pair. The socks were comfortable in hot or cold weather and we felt they made a big difference in how our feet felt at the end of a day of hiking. The twenty dollars plus we paid for each pair of socks would more than pay themselves during our hiking adventures.

Comfort and blister prevention took the right combination of socks, shoes, tape and foot care. Even with the right socks and shoes I was still a tender foot. Apparently, the way I walked caused additional pressure on the side and base of my right big toe. I found through using Band-aids and different tapes, kinesiology tape stayed on the best. The way I used it was not its intended use but it worked for me. I just cut it to fit the painful areas and I eventually used it to tape both feet on the side and base of my big toes. My fourth toe on each foot is crooked and they also started to rub on the underside so I just included them in my taping routine. The tape would usually last about three days unless I got my feet wet. The tape stuck really tight and I sure didn't want to lose skin by pulling it off so I would wait until it loosened enough to pull off without pulling the skin. I finally developed calluses on my feet and was able to go without taping. Every evening before snuggling down in our sleeping bags we did foot care. I carried Desenex foot powder and we removed our socks and used it every night, even with the tape on.

Another thing that helped with our feet was to avoid having wet shoes if at all possible. Lots of hikers just plow through no matter the mud or puddles. We avoided them, it may have slowed us down a little but if we had developed blisters or another foot ailment that took us off the trail for a few days we would definitely lose more trail time than walking around all the puddles.

Rain equipment was a riddle that was not to be solved. After trying several different types of rain suits and ponchos we found that no matter the rainsuit, if it rained long enough you were bound to get wet. If the rain did not soak through your raincoat from the outside, the sweat would make you wet from the inside. The rainsuits were actually very hot when hiking. I finally tried a hiking umbrella and it worked well if the wind was not blowing too much. It also came in handy to provide shade from the sun. The hiking umbrella attached in the front on my pack straps near my chest and it was hands free.

Roy became obsessed with ultralight backpacking. Ultralight backpacking is packing very lightweight equipment and the least amount possible. Serious hikers weigh the items in ounces or grams. One of the tips to reduce weight is to even cut the handle on your toothbrush! A shorter handle equals less weight even if it is less than gram. Those items that weigh less than an ounce or gram can add up to pounds if you are not careful. I purchased a small kitchen scale and we did weigh our items in efforts to keep our pack weights as low as possible. The goal was to keep our base weight around twenty pounds. Base weight is the weight of your pack without food or water. We had read about hikers who carried as little as fifteen pounds total. Some hikers only carry a sleeping bag and stay in the shelters every night or have a hammock with their sleeping bag on the AT. We knew sleeping every night in a shelter was not something we wanted to do. We also were not sure about hiking the long distances between some of the shelters so the tent was a must. Keeping the pack weight

19

down was going to be a challenge. We would never get our pack weights that low, we enjoyed our tent, air mattresses and sleeping bags. They were however among the light weight options available at the time we got them. Numerous times during our hiking trips we would be more than glad we had them with us even if they were extra weight.

A lot of hikers would not have carried the pack weight we carried. What suits one person may not suit the next so there is a lot of individual preference when it comes to equipment. For us, all the research, test runs, trial and error using various equipment more than paid off. We spent about $3500 on our hiking equipment including our shoes and clothing, good equipment is expensive in any sport. But our equipment held up well throughout our hiking adventures and we could continue to utilize it for future trips. The equipment we selected may not have been right for everyone but it was right for us. All the prepping we did before we first started hiking and the constant fine tuning of our equipment on weekend hikes and vacations prepared us well for the challenges of the AT.

Believe you can and you're halfway there."
- Theodore Roosevelt

Chapter 3 - Let's Just Do It

The discussions regarding hiking the AT continued off and on throughout the years. Roy researched hiking the trail and watched countless YouTube videos. He was absolutely obsessed with the AT. Finally in December 2018 I told him we just needed to do it, hike the trail and get it over with. We had saved enough money, there was no reason we couldn't quit work and just go hike the trail. We finally agreed we would both retire and hit the trail in February of 2020.

We took our trip to Hawaii in September 2019 for our twenty fifth wedding anniversary. When I returned to work, I gave my resignation effective January 31, 2020. I gave the notice for January 31 because my insurance would remain in effect throughout the month of January. I also gave my notice well in advance in hopes my position would be filled before I left. Our department was extremely busy and I was hoping to minimize the impact of my leaving on my co-workers. My last day of work was actually December 19, 2019 and my co-workers surprised me with a small retirement party. You couldn't have asked for a better group of people to work with, I would not miss the work but I would definitely miss the people.

With all the vacation time I had, even with the trip to Hawaii and the holiday pay I had vacation time remaining. The time was paid out to me at the end of my employment. Health insurance was available through the Affordable Care Act for both of us. I had all my ducks in a row and I was just waiting for Roy to close his business.

Roy owned and operated his electronics shop for over forty years. Closing it was a huge step for him. Working in one place for forty years and being your own boss does not exactly make you adapt to change very easily. I kept waiting for him to close the shop but he just kept going to work. During January and February 2020, I walked nearly every day at home. I knew I needed to get myself in better physical shape and get my head in the right place before hiking the AT. This was also when I cleaned our house from top to bottom in preparation for being gone for several months.

While cleaning, I moved a large basket and in doing so I strained my back. For a couple of days, I did well to hobble around the house. I did try to go for my usual walk but only made it a short distance in our subdivision before I had trouble getting back to the house. What a time to hurt myself when I was trying to get in shape for the AT. I only missed walking for three or four days before I was able to resume my normal daily walks but it took a few weeks for my back to heal completely.

It was winter and I tested different layers and types of clothing for varying temperatures. I had wool base layers and knew at what temperature they were needed after playing with how to dress in different temperatures and conditions. I literally walked through rain, sleet and snow. I bet our neighbor, Pete, thought I had lost my mind. I saw him one day when the weather was fair and he asked me about being out there when the temperature was twenty degrees or when it was snowing or raining. I explained our plans to hike the AT and I'm sure he didn't understand the magnitude of the hike but I know he thought we must be crazy and I was thinking he was probably right.

During our trail preparations we discussed trail names and Roy said his trail name should be Hey Bear. Our kids and grandkids all thought it was funny when he told them about seeing a bear when we were hiking in The Great Smoky Mountains National Park. He held up his hands and yelled, "Hey Bear", before the bear ran away. Just for the record, I didn't get to see the bear that day. Everyone we met on the trail would ask if we saw the bear and of course Roy would say he did. I was apparently the only one who didn't get to see it. We had never seen a bear in the wild and were cautiously excited about the prospects of seeing one. I was pretty aggravated that it ran away before I got to see it, but I guess if it took a step toward Roy like he said, I would forgive him for scaring it away. He did say he was a little torn between telling me to hurry and catch up to take a picture or scaring the bear. Christi, our daughter, even got him a coffee mug with a picture of a bear and Hey Bear written on the mug. He also suggested my trail name should be BooBoo. BooBoo was the name of the first dog I ever remember having as a child and Roy talks like Yogi Bear and calls me BooBoo. *I thought, why not be called BooBoo? But if I was BooBoo shouldn't he be called Yogi? We would have that question posed several times.* A lot of hikers wait to be named by someone on the trail but probably as many names themselves.

Our kids and grandkids thought we were crazy but knew if we set out to do something we would more than likely do it. They were in awe of our plans and would follow us closely while hiking the AT. A couple of them got AT wall maps and monitored our progress. Our family members and friends would also be able to follow us via a Facebook group I created. I planned on posting pictures and news of our progress along the way.

My sister was worried about us being eaten by bears. She mentioned bears every time I talked to her. She said she would never forgive my husband if he "got her sister eaten by a bear". I told her that lots of hikers hike the entire AT without seeing a bear and we would definitely be on the lookout for bears. Besides, there are lots of people on the AT and the bears would usually avoid people. *I actually really hoped to see at least one since I had never seen one in the wild. I had missed seeing one in the Smoky Mountains the day everyone saw the bear except me and it still ticked me off.*

We had our equipment packed and ready to go, just waiting for the right time. We monitored the weather and tied up loose ends. Finally, on February 26, 2020, Roy decided he was finished at his shop and he wanted to start the trail on his birthday, February 28. So, on February 27 we got our son-in-law, Jamie, to go with us to Amicalola Falls State Park in Georgia and drop us off there to start the trail. When we arrived, we went to the check in point to register, received our AT hang tags and participated in the AT base camp instruction. Jamie was very interested in what we were doing and he stayed with us while we registered and went through the base camp. He took pictures and video to document the beginning of our journey. The basecamp was pretty much what we expected. *We met Ray and his son Kyle at basecamp, we would leap frog with them for much of the trail between Springer Mountain, GA and Hot Springs, NC.* Jamie left us at the Amicalola Falls State Park Lodge where we stayed the night in preparation for hiking the approach trail the next day. After talking about it for all these years we were finally doing it! The mountains were calling.

"Because in the end, you won't remember the time you spent working in an office or mowing the lawn. Climb that mountain." - Jack Kerouac

Chapter 4 - The Trail Starts at The Top

Amicalola Falls, a large cascading waterfall, is Georgia's tallest waterfall at 729 feet. It is located near Dawsonville, Georgia and in the Amicalola Falls State Park. *If you are a waterfall lover like me, it would definitely be worth the trip to see it.* We had been there once before and hiked some of the trails in the park a few years before our AT hike. Our twin grandsons Kyle and Cody were with us and we also hiked up and down the 600 stair steps at the falls. I was a bit slower on the stairs than my husband and the boys. It was really sweet how the boys took turns hanging back with me and asking if I was okay. At that time, I was not exactly in the best physical condition for hiking and I was slow but it was worth the hike to see the falls up close and I managed to make it up and down the steps. They were among the most beautiful waterfalls we had ever seen and we really enjoyed being there and sharing this experience with the grandkids.

The AT approach trail goes from Amicalola Falls to the beginning of the Appalachian Trail at the top of Springer Mountain. The approach trail is 8.5 miles and does not technically count as part of the trail, but you can't get to the start of the trail without hiking to the top of Springer Mountain, either from the lodge side or from another trail on the other side of the mountain.

February 28, 2020 - We left the lodge at Amicalola Falls State Park Lodge and hiked the approach trail to the Springer Mountain Shelter. *Happy Birthday to Roy, he got what he wanted for his 64th birthday! We didn't start at the base camp and up the stairs on the falls, some hikers hike the stairs but it is not a requirement. I was in a lot better shape than the last time I hiked at Amicalola Falls but I still didn't want to carry my heavy pack up the 600 steps. We sure didn't need to hurt ourselves right off the bat by trying to get up the stairs with our heavy packs. I thought it was just weird that the AT started at the top of Springer Mountain and you had to hike to get to the start. The "approach trail" we hiked, over eight miles, didn't even count toward the nearly 2200 miles. But I sure felt like it should have counted.*

The hike up the mountain was pretty much what we expected and we covered the distance without a problem. The weather was pleasant, not too cold and perfect for hiking. The trail, though mostly uphill, was a fairly easy path through the forest. We arrived at the Springer Mountain Shelter and met several other hikers also beginning their attempts at hiking the entire AT. I signed our names, Boo Boo & Hey Bear in the log book at the shelter. *Each shelter usually has a log book for hikers to sign. The signatures document the hikers who have passed through and can assist rescuers in locating a missing person on the trail. It may also be useful to see if someone you know has gone ahead on the trail. Due to Covid we signed less logs as our hike progressed along the AT. We avoided the shelters for the most part and we didn't want to handle something everyone else was handling.*

We met a ridge runner that evening at the Springer Mountain Shelter, her trail name was Foxie. She talked to all the hikers, giving tips and answering various questions about hiking the trail. Ridge runners and trail ambassadors patrol the trail to ensure hikers don't need help and to educate them on leave no trace principles. Most of the leave no trace principles are common sense; plan ahead and prepare, travel and camp on durable surfaces, respect wildlife, dispose of waste properly, leave what you find *(not always the case as we would find out later),* minimize campfire impacts and be considerate of others. She also told us to always cover our pot when cooking so it would boil faster and use less fuel and to always sleep with your head away from the walls in the shelters because mice run the walls and this will keep them from running over your head. *I think I will be sleeping in the tent for the most part, thank you very much.* She advised to put your damp socks or clothing in your sleeping bag at night, it will help them somewhat dry and they will be warmer when you put them on the next morning. *We did this a lot and it really helped.* She also talked about how to attend to things when nature calls by digging cat holes and using natural materials to wipe. *Just for the record, I can get along with digging a cat hole, but I want Charmin and wet wipes and I am more than willing to carry them. You would be surprised what people do that does impact the trails like leaving trash or not staying on the trail. But we did find those folks were not the seriously dedicated hikers, long distance or thru hikers who seemed to be a lot more respectful of nature.*

We had not slept in a shelter before, all our practice runs had been sleeping in our tent. Believe it or not we had never camped out more than one or two nights in a row before starting our journey on the AT. Camping out on the trail night after night would definitely be different. The weather was cool and there was a light dusting of snow on the ground with more snow in the forecast, therefore we made the decision to sleep in the shelter. *Keep in mind, the shelters are like a shed. They have a roof and three walls and they are built from wooden planks or logs like a barn.* There was a guy and a girl who also slept in the loft with us. Both of them were starting the trail by themselves. The girl didn't look a day over eighteen and she was a tiny little thing, we didn't catch her name. She bedded down between us and Pete who was from Louisiana, he was in his thirties. He smoked pot, but was very polite about it. He asked if we minded and he stepped away from everyone so as to not blow smoke on them. *Oh well, to each his own. Better he was polite instead of being a butthead about it. It was not the last time we would see marijuana on the trail.* We put our Tyvek ground cloth down in the loft, to protect against anything that might put a hole in our air mattresses. We laid our mattresses side by side and our two sleeping bags were zipped together to make one big one. *The next day we found out the mercury dropped to twenty- three degrees that night but we stayed plenty warm, fully clothed and in our twenty-degree down sleeping bags.* There were ten people in the shelter, four in the loft and six on the ground floor, thankfully there was minimal snoring and we slept well.

That evening as we snuggled down in our sleeping bags, I pondered why anyone would hike the AT by themselves. I definitely felt better having a partner to share the adventure. *As time went by, we met a lot of people who were hiking by themselves and I never really got a clear answer to the question. Most hikers who are alone eventually become members of a tramily (trail family). Some of the tramilies are two or three hikers and some are several. It just depends on who is hiking at the same speed and who you see and talk with every day.*

February 29, 2020 - There was about two inches of snow on the ground that morning. We boiled water to make coffee and after we ate a little breakfast, we stowed our gear and started to actually hike on the AT. Snow had to be brushed off of the Springer Mountain sign in order to get a picture of it. We met Captain Marvel and Wild Rabbit at the beginning of our hike and swapped taking pictures of each other at the plaque marking the southern terminus of the AT. They lived near Boston and each of them would be sixty years old by the end of their AT thru hike. *We would later see lots of mature hikers on the trail, most were early retirees like us with aspirations of hiking the AT in order to mark it off their bucket lists. We would hike with Captain Marvel and Wild Rabbit off and on over the next few weeks.*

Pete from Louisiana was up and ready to go that morning. The shoes he wore looked like low cut casual tennis shoes without much padding, support or tread for traction and of course no insulation or water resistance. The tread left a funny looking honeycomb footprint. That morning he had his feet wrapped with plastic bags over his socks and had put his shoes on over the bags in an attempt to keep his socks dry. I couldn't see how he was going to hike the trail in those shoes without sliding all over the place but he didn't let them slow him down. We saw his distinctive footprints in the mud and snow and laughed to each other about being able to track him anywhere.

It snowed for the first hour or so we hiked. The snow was in big fluffy flakes like feathers, very wet snow and it melted quickly. The weather was pleasant after the snow stopped and we just enjoyed the day. After so many years of talking about hiking the AT we were doing it! We made it to the Hawk Mountain campsite and decided not to hike ahead 0.7 miles to the shelter so we set our tent up. We were ready to crawl in our tent by 5:30 p.m. It gets dark very early in the winter and we were exhausted after hiking 7.2 miles.

After eating supper, we hung our food bags in a nearby tree. *We each carried waterproof food bags and hung them up in the trees* or used the bear cables at the shelters to keep bears from eating our food. The bear cables were usually easier to use unless they were broken or tangled. At times we would have difficulty finding the right tree. The bag was supposed to be hung with a rope, over a small tree limb (too small to hold a bear up) six feet from the tree and suspended at least twelve feet off the ground. It was also supposed to be about two hundred feet from your camp. These measurements vary depending on the source. Trees were too big, too little, too high but we usually could find one just right if we looked hard enough. Although I must admit we did skip hanging the food bags a few times when the rain was relentless. We also used bear proof food storage boxes found at many of the shelters when they were available. Thankfully we never heard of anyone losing their food because of a bear while we were hiking on the AT although we were definitely in bear territory. We crawled in our tent that evening after securing our food and slept soundly after being out in the cold all day.

I'd rather be hiking in the rain, than sitting inside at a desk on a sunny day." - Unknown

Chapter 5 - Wet, Dry, Repeat

March 1, 2020 - We continued to hike northbound or NOBO. The weather was beautiful, the temperature was in the sixties. The weather was perfect for hiking. We crossed or walked along several small streams beside the trail. *In addition to being in awe of waterfalls I really like small streams that flow through the forest and we got to see and hear them off and on throughout the day.* It was fairly easy hiking and the day was pretty uneventful, we just hiked and covered the miles. We camped that night in our tent at the Gooch Mountain Shelter campground after hiking 8.3 miles. Again, we turned in early after eating our supper and slept soundly.

March 2, 2020 - It was cold and it rained all day. It was hard to find the beauty in hiking through the forest with rain and fog stealing the views. We met a trail ambassador named Joe that afternoon and we asked him about bears. He told us they almost always run away when they see you and a little noise will make them run away. But there was one bear that pretty much played peekaboo with him. It was behind a tree and would peek at him, he said he thought the bear thought it was hiding from him. He wanted to run the bear away from the trail and this one didn't go as easily as others but it was not aggressive. Trail Ambassadors and Ridge Runners want to ensure the bears run away when they see people to minimize the chances of negative bear-human encounters. I was hoping to see a bear in the wild, but I did want it to run away after I got a good look.

Trail magic was waiting for us at Woody Gap. *Trail magic is when a hiker gets something that is totally unexpected, usually in the middle of nowhere and given by someone who gives and expects nothing in return. Trail magic can be food, a ride, or any act of kindness. A lot of the people who provide trail magic have hiked the trail before and understand the needs of the hikers.* The trail magic we received was in a Styrofoam cooler setting by a sign at the trailhead. Someone had written Trail Magic on the cooler with a marker. When we opened it we found Snickers and Cokes, a pleasant surprise! We each took one Snickers and shared a Coke and left the remainder of the cooler's contents for other hikers. We had only been on the trail three days but the Snickers and Coke sure tasted good. It was nice to have a little magic in the rain and fog.

We set our tent up in the rain at Lance Creek after hiking another 8.3 miles (same mileage as the day before). We were camping in the only semi-flat spot we could find which was in the red mud and it was still raining. The tent site was on a slope and we set up so our heads would be uphill. I hoped we didn't slide downhill all night. We noticed Pete from Louisiana had set up his tent there also, he had gotten there before us (we saw his footprints in the mud) and his campsite was in a little better spot. I could not see how he was going to stay dry, it looked like he had just a tarp stretched out and he was under it with all his gear. We set our cookpot just outside the tent and was able to heat water for our supper while sitting in the tent when the rain slacked up for a bit. Roy, me and all the gear in the tent, it was pretty crowded but we were thankful to get out of the rain for the night and we stayed dry in our tent despite the rain. We were in the tent well before dark.

March 3, 2020 - *In addition to dark coming early this time of year, the daylight comes much later. The sun was not up before 7:00 a.m. That meant we would sometimes spend fourteen hours, or more, in the tent. For some reason we didn't mind sleeping most of that time. At home we usually slept seven or eight hours but, on the trail, we would sleep much more, probably because we were exhausted at the end of each day.* We packed up our muddy wet tent and got back on the trail by about 9:00 a.m. It rained all day long, again. We hiked over Blood Mountain and the trail was sloppy the entire way. We walked through sections of the trail that were more like a creek. I saw a pair of Darn Tough socks that were orange and gray, at first glance I thought they looked like the socks I had seen Pete wearing. They were sopping wet and I didn't really need them or want to pack them so I didn't pick them up.

There was a stone shelter on top of Blood Mountain. A sign indicated it was built in 1937 by the Civilian Conservation Corps (CCC). *Later we googled the CCC and found it was part of Franklin D. Roosevelt's New Deal. The program ran from 1933 to 1942 and was dissolved due to drafting of men during World War II. The program employed over 3 million young men over the nine years it was in existence. Bridges, roads, park structures, fire lookout towers, foot trails, dams, landscaping in campgrounds and picnic areas are just a few of their activities. The CCC was a brilliant program introduced to help with the high rates of unemployment during the Great Depression. We would see many structures and improvements built by the CCC all along the AT.*

There should have been great views from the top of Blood Mountain but it was fogged in and we couldn't see anything. We kept pushing on to get to Neels Gap. We ran into the trail ambassador Joe again. *I don't know what makes these people keep hiking the same sections of the trail, but apparently, they enjoy doing it.* I thought Joe would have picked a better day to hike but he evidently didn't mind the rain. We spoke to him briefly and he recognized us from the day before. We finally made it to Neels Gap on US route 19. *Neels Gap is known for a tree hanging full of hiking shoes. Apparently southbound hikers take their shoes off and throw them up in the trees to celebrate the near completion of the trail. I thought hikers got thirty miles from Springer Mountain heading northbound and after going over Blood Mountain said screw it, threw their shoes up in the tree and went home! At that point, I wouldn't have blamed them if that's what they did.* The shoes hanging in the tree were an eerie sight, in the fog and rain, but also a welcome sight since we planned on going from there to a nearby town. Mountain Crossings was the outfitter at Neels Gap that sells shoes, and there was also a hostel conveniently located there but we opted for the chance to stay in a motel since leaving Springer Mountain four days before.

We shared a ride to Blairsville, GA with a hiker from Raleigh, NC. I didn't get his trail name, but he was wearing a hat with a large brim and he also looked forward to getting out of the rain. We got a room at the Seasons Inn. It was right on the square in the middle of town. Not the fanciest room we ever stayed in but it was warm, clean, convenient and best of all dry. It was wonderful to have a hot shower and a bed to sleep in after being so cold and wet. We spread our gear all over the room in order to get it dried out. There was a clothesline out back and we hung our tent out to dry. Our shoes had to be propped over the heating unit with air blowing inside them. *Waterproof shoes and rain jackets are not truly waterproof if it rains all day and you walk through two to three inches of water most of the day. Our gear was spread all over the room and at first glance it looked like we had trashed the place. But we just had to repack everything the next morning and we would leave the room in pretty good shape for a couple of wet dirty hikers.* There was a $6.99 pizza buffet across the street, we ate there that evening and thoroughly enjoyed the food. *They may have lost money on us because we made several trips to the buffet and ate like horses. It's amazing how good food can taste after hiking for just a few days.*

March 4, 2020 - We got a ride back to the trail. The weather was nice and hiking was much more pleasant than the past couple of days. Most of the day was spent hiking with Wild Rabbit and Captain Marvel. We leap frogged with them but we were all together when we arrived at Tesnatee Gap. There was trail magic in the parking area and it was early lunchtime. Grilled burgers, hot dogs, chips, desserts and soft drinks. The two guys who set it up just wanted to say a prayer with us before we ate and wouldn't accept money when we offered. It was hard to believe people do this for hikers. We left there feeling blessed with full hearts and full stomachs. We were energized by the good meal and fellowship. Trail magic appeared a second time later in the afternoon at Hog Pen Gap. A woman who had hiked the AT before had her vehicle loaded with soft drinks, beer, oranges and apples. We each took a beer and a piece of fruit. *Fruit on the trail is hard to come by, it's definitely too heavy to carry and it's not available in most of the small resupply places on the trail.* After our second trail magic it was getting later in the afternoon, it would be dark and colder in a couple of hours. We hiked on up the trail to find a place to camp for the night after hiking a total of 8 miles.

March 5, 2020 - It was another cold, rainy, miserable day. We had to keep moving to stay warm. Despite the rain we hiked 10 miles and made it to Blue Mountain Shelter. Pete was there and had set up his sleeping quarters in the shelter. He and a couple of other guys were enjoying taking it easy and smoking a joint. They told us to set our tent up in the shelter but we opted for setting our packs in the shelter while we set up our tent outside. We quickly got our tent set up and changed into dry clothes. Not long after we set up Wild Rabbit and Captain Marvel arrived. They were soaking wet and nearly frozen. They had hiked with their puffy jackets under their raincoats. *Raincoats will not keep you dry after being in the rain all day, we knew this and never hiked with our puffy jackets under our raincoats.* Their jackets were soaked, they managed to get a tent set up and were able to get some warm food down. Thankfully their sleeping bags were dry. They planned on leaving first thing in the morning and going to Helen, GA to get dried out. *Another lesson learned, definitely don't ever get your puffy jackets wet or down sleeping bags either for that matter. They lose all their insulating capabilities and it takes forever to dry them. If the weather is too cold this could get you in real trouble.*

March 6, 2020 - When we got up that morning Captain Marvel and Wild Rabbit were already gone. We hoped we would see them up the trail somewhere after they got dried out. It was cold and windy all day but at least it wasn't raining. We hiked 11.7 miles, our best day for mileage so far. We made it from Blue Mountain Shelter to Swag of the Blue Ridge and we camped in the tent. It was cold and I guess we made better mileage because we again had to stay moving to stay warm.

March 7, 2020 - We hiked 7.4 miles. The plan was to go to Hiawassee, GA and get a room for the night and of course to dry out our gear again. *Carrying wet gear only added to the weight of our packs.* We had no phone signal to call ahead, but we ran into a hiker named Metro on the trail and he was able to use his cell phone as he had a different carrier. He helped us to get a room reserved at the Budget Inn in Hiawassee and agreed to share his ride with us if we could make it to Dick's Creek Gap for the pickup. We decided we would make it if we had to run, Metro was a much faster hiker, he told us he could hike two miles per hour. We were not able to hike that fast but hiked as fast as we could. *Roy says if you say there is a room or food up ahead, I will always hike faster, I think he is probably right.* When we got to the parking area it was across the road and Metro was on the other side motioning for us. I thought the ride was there and we needed to hurry but was pleasantly surprised when I discovered there was trail magic again. Don and Deb had chili, cokes, chips and snack cakes. We ate before getting in the van for our ride to the motel, the driver who arrived not long after we got food actually waited for us to finish, he encouraged us to eat and didn't rush us. *The people who provide trail magic are so giving. If everyone in the world was as friendly and supportive as they are on the trail the world would be a better place. I would say this several more times before we finished the trail. No wonder the folks that provide trail magic are called Trail Angels.*

We got to the Budget Inn and had to wait outside as our room was not yet ready for us to check in. The sun was shining and we sat outside with Metro to warm up and soak up some of that wonderful sunshine we hadn't seen in a couple of days. We pulled out our phones and took advantage of the Wi-Fi while we waited. The motel was dated to say the least but it was clean and it had a hot shower and a warm bed. We again spread out all our stuff to dry in the room and popped our tent up outside. *Seems we were always getting wet, drying everything out just to only get wet again. Wet, dry, repeat was becoming a pattern and I hoped this would not continue although I was not about to bet on it.*

There were several places within easy walking distance, we resupplied at the local Ingles grocery and got a few things at the Walgreens. *We would find that Walgreens and CVS usually had several useful food items we could use for resupply.* We ate supper at Daniel's Steakhouse, it had an all you can eat buffet and we made several trips to fill our plates. After we ate, we returned to our room to get our gear together, watch a little TV and rest before returning to the trail the next morning.

March 8, 2020 - We got a ride back and resumed the trail at Dick's Creek Gap. The weather was fantastic, it was a little warmer and there was abundant sunshine. The sunshine was a definite boost for our morale. We crossed the GA/NC border that afternoon. *It didn't seem like we would ever get out of Georgia. Looking back now it didn't take long at all in the grand scheme of* things. But we were more than happy to be out of Georgia and we could cross it off the list of the fourteen states on the AT. We camped at Bly Gap just across the GA/NC border after hiking 9 miles.

There were several people camped in the area and I found it difficult to find a private place to pee. I decided to use my peanut butter jar. Yes, peanut butter jar. When we were prepping for the trail, I watched an older woman on YouTube who was giving her tips for the trail. She advised female hikers to get a medium sized plastic peanut butter jar, wash it out and use it to urinate in your tent when needed. Well, I have to go often and it sounded like common sense. If you're in your tent, it's raining and you gotta pee, use the jar. If you gotta go really bad and you're in the tent at night, use your jar. If there are too many other tents around, just use your jar. It actually worked well and I came to refer to it as Granny's pot. I didn't use it every day, but it did come in handy several times.

"After a day's walk, everything has twice
its usual value." - G.M. Trevelyan

Chapter 6 - Cheeseburgers

March 9, 2020 - *Happy Birthday to our daughter, Christi!* We met a man from Fountain Run, KY. Just down the road from home! Nobel actually started the trail three days before us and was four years older than my husband. I was impressed with our ability to have caught up with him. He was taking a break and talked about how badly his foot was hurting so there went my thinking we were going faster he was apparently just going slower. We sat with him and talked about home for a while at the Standing Indian Shelter where we stopped to use the privy. There was another hiker who had blonde dreadlocks who stopped in at the shelter for a break also. When he learned of Nobel's foot pain, he offered him a joint, he said it really helped with pain. Noble thanked him but declined the offer, he said he had pain medication. I seriously wondered if he would be able to continue much less finish the trail due to his foot pain the way he was talking. We left him and hiked on ahead, it was just too early in the day to stop for the evening. *We later saw on trailjournals.com where he skipped around and hiked a lot of the trail, he even submitted Mt. Katahdin. He didn't hike the entire trail but he did a lot more than we thought we would be able to do.*

Roy kept getting far ahead of me and I was having trouble hiking up the mountain. I had difficulty hiking the trails without rocks or roots and going steeply uphill, I actually did better hiking up steps. I hiked alone for what seemed like hours before I finally caught up with him. *I don't mind him hiking ahead, but if I had trouble, I wanted to at least be able to yell and be heard. Besides, I could be attacked by a bear or a person up to no good and he would never know. Maybe this was one more way he was trying to just get rid of me. I kept telling him there were quicker ways. I was not concerned about hiking the distance, but I was concerned about keeping a fast enough pace to keep up. Thankfully he never got that far away from me again for the rest of the trail, he would either slow up or stop and wait for me pretty often. I also gradually got in better physical condition and was able to keep up better. By the time we finished hiking the trail I would most usually be right behind him.*

37

We finally made it to Standing Indian Mountain, elevation 5478 feet. No wonder I was having so much trouble climbing the hills! There was a beautiful view at the summit. This was the highest elevation we had hiked thus far and it seemed as though we were on top of the world looking down on the other mountains. There were no leaves on the trees and we could see for miles. We pitched our tent not far from the top in an area where hikers had camped before. We hiked 9.2 miles that day before we stopped for the evening.

It was cold and windy at the top of the mountain. This was one of the very few times we actually started a campfire. The wind was so strong we were afraid to build a large fire, but it did provide us with warmth for a little while. *Most of the time we were so tired when we stopped for the evening there was no need for a fire. We just wanted to lie down and would fall asleep in a matter of minutes after eating and securing our food for the night. We used our cook set and pocket stove to cook so there really was no need for a campfire.*

Once we got our tent set up and supper finished that evening we bedded down before dark as we knew it would probably get colder. It also became so foggy at the top of Standing Indian Mountain; you could only see a few feet. Roy got out of the tent to use the bathroom; he had a flashlight but it didn't help because of the thick fog. If he lost sight of the tent and got turned around, he could be lost in the fog or could walk off a bluff before he could see it. I talked to him until he got back to the tent. I stayed in the tent and was thankful I could use my peanut butter jar.

March 10, 2020 - This day was our best hiking day so far. We hiked 14.8 miles and were exposed to our first bit of hand over hand climbing when we climbed up and over Albert Mountain. The climb required going over rocks, getting on knees and even taking the pack off once or twice to put it up and over the rocks, trekking poles were of no use. I was definitely not a fan of rock climbing. We later learned there was a bad weather bypass around Albert Mountain that we could have taken, but Roy wanted to stick to the original trail. As usual he was ahead of me and he was waiting at the base of the fire tower on top of the mountain when I arrived.

There were several old fire towers along the AT, some of them you could go up and see fantastic views but this one was locked. We found a spot on the trail that day where someone had made a 100-mile marker with sticks. We thought it was unreal to have actually hiked 100 miles and took a picture, we were so proud of our accomplishment. *Only 2100 miles to go! At this point I felt like we had already been through the wringer and I couldn't imagine what it would take to get to the finish.*

It rained off and, on all day, but we made it to Long Branch Shelter. *I thought it was a shame this Long Branch wasn't Miss Kitty's place from the old western TV show Gunsmoke. We could have bellied up to the bar for a sarsaparilla or beer.* The shelter was a fairly new large double decker shelter and it had plenty of space.

We met Curveball at the shelter, he had long dark dreadlocks, he had hiked the trail before and was hiking agai*n. I wondered why anyone would want to hike the AT more than once. I believed if I could get through once, it would be more than enough for me. We later found out about a man from Mountain City, Tennessee, Warren Doyle who hiked the trail eighteen times. That's a total of over 39,000 miles not counting any side trails. No wonder he was inducted into the Appalachian Trail Hall of Fame in May of 2020. I don't know what motivates these people.*

Curveball told us he hiked around thirty miles per day. *How in the world could anyone hike thirty miles a day? We hadn't even been able to do half that much. Besides the physical aspect of hiking that far each day, how would you have time to actually stop and enjoy the sights? We would never find out because we would never complete thirty miles in one day.* Curveball was camped in a tent nearby and came to the shelter to cook his supper. *Hikers usually go to a common area to cook and eat when camped near a shelter. In order to minimize the chances of encountering a bear, food should not be cooked or consumed in your tent.* Curveball cooked his supper and hung out at the shelter for a while, we also noted he liked his weed. He was another polite pot smoker and I couldn't help but think maybe the weed helped him hike those thirty miles a day.

Several people were camped in tents and hammocks around the shelter. We decided to sleep in the shelter, there were only five of us who wanted to sleep there and it would be dry. We took the loft and a guy and two women took the main floor. The shelter was large enough for eight to ten people, there would be plenty of room. One of the women was an older lady who spoke with a British accent. She had previously hiked with her husband; he had died and she was intent on finishing what they started. The other woman was fortyish, retired military and had a husband and kids at home. The guy was probably in his thirties. All of these hikers were hiking alone. The guy informed everyone that he snored and he even offered earplugs to those who wanted them but no one accepted his offer. We all bedded down for the night when it became dark. It would have been a good night except for the incessant snoring. It was not just a subtle snore; it was loud and would have rattled the windows had there been any to rattle. If you made a little bit of noise, he would stop for one or two breaths then snore even louder. I had my own earplugs and had put them in but they could in no way drown out the relentless snoring. It was going to be a long night.

March 11, 2020 - The guy who kept us awake all night inquired about his snoring and the woman with the British accent told him he was a, "champion snorer". The way she said it with her accent was hilarious. I think she was just being polite but this guy snored like a freight train! We would be on the lookout for him in the future. *I forgot the names of the hikers who slept in the shelter, with all that noise I was not able to think about anything else.*

We met a guy on the trail at Winding Stair Gap, he gave us pins and bracelets declaring Franklin, NC to be a trail town on the AT near mile 110. He said Franklin wanted to be known as a hiker friendly trail town and he was helping to promote it. We kept the trinkets as mementos. After hiking 7.2 miles we arrived at the highway and got a ride to Franklin from a man named Johnny. He spoke with an accent and told us he was born in the Alps. He told us repeatedly that it was cooler in fog and it was three degrees colder for every 1000 feet in elevation gain. He had a wealth of information on the local area and he kept telling us to be safe. He took us to the Budget Inn in Franklin to get a room. We checked in and showered then of course went to find food. We ate cheeseburgers and fries at the Kountry Kitchen restaurant, the food was wonderful! *It was one of the best cheese burgers I have ever had, or maybe I just had true hiker hunger.* We went to the Ingles grocery to purchase supplies and we also purchased two 24-ounce beers.

When we got back to the motel, we saw Noble from Fountain Run who had caught up with us. We were really surprised to see him; he was still complaining about his foot and I thought he would have left the trail by now. He had been looking for us and asking everyone if they had seen a couple from Kentucky, but he couldn't figure out where we went after leaving him a couple of days ago. He apparently missed us when we went to the summit of Standing Indian Mountain. He had gone ahead of us to the next shelter and we passed the shelter the next morning before he left. Roy gave him one of our beers (for his foot) and he gladly accepted. We shared the other beer. We did laundry, put some of our equipment out to dry and set up our tent in the parking lot so it could dry out, again.

There was a hiker box at the office at the motel. I found a pair of women's North Face rain pants. I took them because I didn't have an extra pair of dry pants and I could definitely use them. *A hiker box is where hikers will leave items they don't need or don't want to carry. The items may be picked up by other hikers that can use them. Many useful things can be found in a hiker box. Sometimes you could find things like shaving cream, new razors in a package where someone only used one, partial large bottles of shampoo or body wash (I would use out of them and return them to the box), sometimes people would even leave food items such as ramen noodles or tuna packets. A couple of times we even found cans of fuel for our cookstove. It became a habit to check the hiker boxes because you never knew what useful thing you might find.*

March 12, 2020 - Our shuttle driver, Johnny, returned us to Winding Stair Gap to resume the trail. Again, he told us about it being colder in fog and higher elevations and repeatedly told us to be safe. He was a kind man and it seemed as though he really enjoyed talking with hikers.

We saw a rock lookout tower; it was really neat but it was too foggy to see anything from the top so we didn't climb it. Thankfully it wasn't too cold. There was rain early in the day, it was foggy and just felt damp all day. We camped at Wayah Bald, elevation 5337 feet after hiking 11 miles. The fog had cleared for a bit and we again had gorgeous views of the mountains from up high. We were more than glad to climb in the tent and bed down after a long day of hiking mostly uphill.

March 13, 2020 - There was rain and high winds most of the night before and neither of us slept very well. It was going to be another long day. It seemed like we hiked uphill most of the day. In reality we went up and down through several gaps and streams and traveled 10.6 miles. There was a huge open observation deck at Wesser Bald and we climbed it. The 360-degree view of the mountains was amazing. We were really glad to get the tent set up at Wesser Bald and eat our supper. We crawled in the tent with hopes of sleeping better and having better weather the next day. We were also excited because we knew we would be staying in a room the next night.

March 14, 2020 - We hiked 5.9 miles and arrived at the Nantahala Outdoor Center (NOC), elevation 1727 feet by about 1:00 p.m. This was the lowest elevation we had seen on the trail. Downhill to the NOC was on lots of steep rocks, the worst downhill we had encountered thus far. If Albert Mountain gave us a taste of uphill, down to the NOC was our worst (or best) example of downhill. We went really slow and took our time knowing one bad fall with an injury could jeopardize our hike, not to mention our lives. *Falling with a heavy backpack strapped on would send you totally out of control, there would be no way to manage the additional weight if it got off balance. The pack will literally throw you down, and stomp you. We would experience this several times before our hike was finished, it was usually when you had let down your guard and when you least expected it. Thankfully our falls were on fairly level ground.*

When we arrived at the NOC, we got a couple of tall beers and a room for the night. There were several other hikers there, we saw Ray, Kyle & Pete. We went to the restaurant and had cheeseburgers and fries. *Yes, cheeseburgers again. How can the best cheeseburgers on the trail be determined if you don't eat them everywhere?* They were awesome, probably a tie between the NOC and the Kountry Kitchen for the best burgers on the trail, so far. The first thing we noticed was no condiments on the tables. We were given salt packets and ketchup packets as part of Covid precautions.

We watched TV and caught up with the news. We had only been gone two weeks but it seems the world has gone crazy over toilet paper and hand sanitizer! Kids were not going to school; church services and NCAA basketball games were all canceled due to the virus. We talked to family and they were encouraging us to scrap the hike and come home. We assured them we would take precautions and monitor the news for further developments.

I washed our clothes at the NOC and while doing the laundry I met a woman named Bluebird. She started at Springer Mountain on February 21. This made me feel good, we started a week later, we were faster on the trail even though I had thought we were really slow hikers.

March 15, 20202 - We hiked 8.1 miles. The trail was pretty much all uphill from the NOC. We left the NOC at 1732 feet elevation. When we stopped to camp that night, we were at Cheoah Bald, elevation 5062 feet. Needless to say, there was lots of tough hiking. The view from our campsite was unbelievable. I never knew the mountains could be so beautiful even in the winter or the sky could be so blue. If the leaves had been out the mountains would have been green, but we would also have had our views obstructed by the leaves in a lot of areas. We were able to set up our tent and warm in the sun for a little while before it set. We met an older woman on the trail earlier in the day, Mama Dog who was planning on staying the night near Sassafras Gap. Cheoah Bald was 1.2 miles ahead of her and again I felt like we were excelling in our hiking abilities. After we set the tent and ate supper, we climbed into the tent thoroughly exhausted. Of course, it was getting colder as the sun was setting and as usual, we were more than ready to snuggle down in our sleeping bags for the night.

March 16, 2020 - We climbed the infamous Jacob's Ladder, it was a very steep uphill climb with few rocks or roots, my least favorite kind of trail. I believe I took three steps forward and slid back two the entire way up! I also found someone's titanium spoon/fork. I picked it up and carried it with me. I thought if I ran across anyone who had lost it, I would give it to them. *You run across all kinds of stuff that has been either left by mistake or dropped. No one is coming back for the stuff. If you need it or can use it you might as well keep it unless you happen to run across the owner. Roy found a Sea-to-Summit pack cover worth about $40. For several days we asked everyone we saw if they had lost it, but we never did find the owner.* I was glad we finally made it to the top of Jacob's Ladder. *I sure wouldn't want to climb that one again.* We hiked 11 miles and set our tent up at Cody Gap. We thought of our grandson Cody when we saw the name of the gap. Hiking with Ray and Kyle also made us think of our grandson Kyle. The name of the gap and Ray's son Kyle were just a couple of the reminders of home and what we left behind to hike the trail.

Ray and Kyle were camping there also, they had hammocks and had a lot more flexibility on where they could camp than we did but we were able to find a good spot to set our tent. Pete from Louisiana, we met at the Springer Mountain Shelter was there with his hammock also. He had met Ray and Kyle and had been hiking with them. We also met a woman with her 13-year-old daughter who was hiking the trail. The mother was homeschooling the daughter as they were hiking. The daughter was learning Spanish from her mother and said she had learned more while on the trail than she did at school. *We found out later through some AT news article, the mother and daughter completed the entire trail in August of 2020. What an accomplishment! Most of these hikers were far faster than us but we were slow and steady and hiked more hours. They sometimes took zero days (days where you don't hike) and we didn't.* They had all zoomed past us earlier in the day. They would start later in the morning, zoom past us about midday, then stop early. We would often get to the same place by the end of the day. It was kind of like the tortoise and the hare. *There were a few hikers like the mother and daughter that we only saw a couple of times and they continued on ahead of us.*

That evening we saw the snoring fellow from the Long Branch Shelter, we watched and waited to see where he put his tent before setting ours up. We sure didn't want to listen to him all night again! *We would continue to be on the lookout for him to see where he set his tent before pitching ours if we were in the same area.*

March 17, 2020 - It rained most of the night and off and on until about noon. Most of the hike was downhill over a slick muddy trail and we had to be extra careful not to fall. We made it to Fontana Dam after hiking 8.7 miles. We got a room with a king-sized bed at the resort and I had a hot soaking bath. Fontana Dam had a shelter called the Fontana Hilton which was supposed to be the best shelter on the entire trail. *We passed on the Hilton, who wanted to stay in a shelter when you could stay at the resort?* We put our gear out to dry, again.

We had a great dinner although we had to order it and take it back to our room. Due to Covid, precautions the dining room was closed. We had fish, fries, chicken tenders and onion rings. Yum! *Looking back at that meal we must have been in a fried food deficit. I didn't get a cheeseburger that time but I would continue my quest later for the best cheeseburger on the trail.*

"Tough times never last, but tough people do." - Robert H. Schuller

Chapter 7 - Smoky Mountain, Rain and COLD

March 18, 2020 - We hiked 7.4 miles this day. Someone had told us the next thirteen miles from Fontana Dam, 1685 feet elevation, was all uphill and I believed it. The highest point on the entire AT is at Clingmans Dome, elevation 6612 feet, and we were headed that direction. We left Fontana Village, walked across the Fontana Dam and entered the Great Smoky Mountains National Park. Camping permits for the Smokies were required before entry on the AT and we were able to get them online while we were at the resort. The camping permits cost twenty dollars per person. In the Smokies you were supposed to stay in the shelters, if they were full you were allowed to pitch your tent nearby. Due to Covid, the park service was telling everyone to avoid the shelters and use their tents. *This was more than alright with us. We liked our tent much better anyway.*

We saw the Shuckstack fire lookout tower at 3993 feet elevation. Roy was excited to see the tower and wanted to climb up it and see the view. I was exhausted from the big uphill climb that day and I told him to go ahead and I would sit this one out. He climbed the tower and the snoring guy climbed the tower with him. Roy told me the tower was dilapidated, the windows were broken and there were boards missing in the floor, but the views were fantastic. I was really glad just to rest for a few minutes.

The wind started to blow and we could tell rain would be moving in soon. We only had about 1.3 miles to go to the place where we planned on camping for the night. We made it to the Birch Spring Tent Sites about 3:00 p.m. just as it started to rain, imagine that. We learned how to set up the tent, throw backpacks in, inflate mattresses and get sleeping bags out all with us both in the tent. Close quarters but we made it. *Unfortunately, this would not be the last time we had to set the tent up in this manner. We refined the procedure as we went and though it was crowded, we learned by doing everything in the proper order it wasn't really all that difficult.*

March 19, 2020 - After hiking 11.4 miles we made it to Spence Field Shelter. This was a neat area with lots of grass, a few smaller trees and lots of blueberry patches. Of course, there were no blueberries at this time of year. *We later heard about the Spence Field shelter being closed and no camping in the area due to bear activity. I'm sure they were gorging themselves on blueberries. Glad we were not sleeping in their breakfast bowl!* We cooked and ate at the shelter. We talked with Ray, Kyle and Pete and a girl from Maine. We had been leap-frogging with all of them since beginning the trail. During the course of discussion Pete said he lost his titanium spoon/fork. I told him I found one at Jacob's Ladder and I gave it to him, he was glad to get it back. He also said he had lost a pair of orange and gray Darn Tough socks. I told him about seeing them on Blood Mountain but I didn't pick them up. *That was early in our AT hiking adventure and we had been told to leave what you find. We would come to find out this meant natural things like plants and rocks.* I guess he was lucky to get his eating utensil back.

The girl from Maine looks to be in her mid-twenties and is hiking the trail by herself. She said she did it for her physical and mental health. She kind of adopted us and checked in with us every morning to ask how far we were planning on hiking. When we got ready to set up tents at the end of the day she was usually nearby and we would talk with her again. She was very knowledgeable about camping and I felt she was wise beyond her years. We didn't even know her real name at that time and she didn't have a trail name yet. I was ready to call her Grasshopper because of her bright green tent. Ray, Kyle and Pete didn't have trail names either. We were meeting and hanging out with this group a lot, we were becoming somewhat of a tramily.

March 20, 2020 - The morning was beautiful. We actually crossed Rocky Top at 5422 feet elevation. *You know, "Good ole Rocky Top, Rocky Top Tennessee", from the song!* I found myself singing the song and being thrilled with actually being there. *Yes, it is a real place and it is beautiful.* I took several pictures before it started to rain. You learn how quickly you can don the rain gear when you see it coming in fast. The rain continued off and on for the remainder of the day. We got to the Derrik Knob Shelter in the early afternoon and it was crowded with people trying to get in out of the rain. The shelter reminded us of our son Derik. This is where

Roy got the trail name, HazMat. He was wearing his bright yellow rainsuit and when he entered the shelter one of the kids in the shelter called him HazMat. It did look as though he was wearing a HazMat suit. *I had called him Big Bird, Big Banana or Gordon's Fisherman, but I hadn't thought of HazMat.* The rain slacked up a bit and we decided we could hike more miles so we decided to continue on the trail. It was just six more miles to Silers Bald Shelter. We hiked a lot of uphill but still managed to get in 11.8 miles. It was a long day and we were both tired. As usual it didn't take long for us to go to sleep after getting in the tent.

March 21, 2020 - We finally made it to Clingmans Dome, the highest point on the entire AT, an elevation of 6612 feet. *It's strange that the highest point is in Tennessee and it is not above the tree line.* The hike up was exhausting but I was mesmerized by moss covering the trees and rocks in the forest. It made me think of the description of an enchanted forest in fairy tales. The weather was good, but it was foggy at the top with no view. At least we didn't really miss anything, we had been to Clingmans Dome several times over the years when visiting the Smoky Mountains. We hiked 7.3 miles and camped at Mt. Collins Shelter. Clingmans Dome is at the 200-mile point. *Wow, 200 miles done, only 2000 more to go which still seems impossible. These 200 miles have taken a lot of determination.*

March 22, 2020 - After only hiking 4.9 miles we arrived at Newfound Gap. *Hiking a short day is called a nero. We would often hike neros on the day we got into towns instead of hiking zero for the day.* From Newfound Gap we got a ride to Gatlinburg. We left Ray, Kyle and Pete at Newfound Gap, hoping we would see them up the trail somewhere. Ray had arranged for a delivery of supplies at Newfound Gap and there was no need for them to go to town. A guy from Germany rode from Newfound Gap to Gatlinburg with us. He was leaving the trail due to Covid and trying to figure out how to get back to Germany. He was hoping to find a way to Knoxville, TN and then to Atlanta, GA. *With all of the travel restrictions due to Covid I was sure glad we were not that far away from home. I can't imagine what that poor guy went through trying to get home.* We booked a room at the Econo Lodge Inn & Suites for two nights. We had stayed there before and knew it was a good place and conveniently located.

We ate pizza at the Mellow Mushroom and it was delicious. *Pizza is food hikers love for some reason. Maybe because it's high calorie, high fat and tastes so good.* Of course, they had Covid precautions in place. The tables were spread out farther than normal and there were no condiments on the tables. It seems the world has gone crazy; Gatlinburg was to be closed at midnight that night due to Covid. The streets were deserted. *We have been to Gatlinburg many times and the streets were always crowded with people. It was an eerie sight to see the streets so deserted.* The people we did see appeared to be in a hurry. Everyone was trying to get what they needed before the place closed. There were only a couple of restaurants planning on staying open to do take out only but most places were closing, period. We didn't know how long we could stay on the trail. We were able to get supplies in Gatlinburg and intended to at least get through the Smokies at this point. We talked with family members and were informed about all the changes at home related to Covid and encouraged to come home. We felt being on the trail was one of the safest places to be as long as we could continue to get supplies and stay away from people. We were also monitoring the recommendations from the Appalachian Trail Commission (ATC).

March 23, 2020 - Our first zero day. We stayed in Gatlinburg and watched it rain most of the day. Luckily, we didn't have to hike through the rain this time. It did clear off long enough for us to walk to a bank to get cash just in case we needed more. The inside of the bank was closed so we walked through the drive thru, Covid precautions. We did a load of laundry, got our gear dried again and got everything ready to resume the trail the next day.

We watched a movie on TV and ordered takeout from Calhoun's for supper, the food was delicious. All news was about the virus. There were so many differing stories it was hard to figure out what was true. We still felt we were safe as long as we had very little close interaction with other people.

Our son in law, Jamie, got in touch with us to let us know about someone who was interested in renting Roy's shop building. We got the paperwork via email and Roy did an electronic signature to agree to the deal. Jamie and our son Derik were going to work on cleaning out the shop and moving the stuff to storage. *What a time for this, but thank goodness we have the boys to help us.*

March 24, 2020 - We called for an Uber to take us back to Newfound Gap. It was a miracle we even got a ride. A man from Asheville, NC had brought someone all the way to Sieverville, TN and he just happened to see our request. He had decided he would go through from Gatlinburg, TN to Cherokee, NC on his way home and Newfound Gap was on his way. Newfound Gap is about 13 miles uphill from Gatlinburg so hiking back to the gap was not something we wanted to do. We did hear about some other hikers who did hike back to the trail from Gatlinburg because of being unable to get a ride, but thankfully we were lucky. Our Uber driver was quite the character. He was retired from a corporate job of some sort but had worked for a while at Biltmore in Asheville, NC because he said he had to do something besides sit around the house. He talked about Biltmore in detail and was a fountain of knowledge on the place. *We visited Biltmore a few years ago and were in awe of the place. I can't imagine having the money to build a place like that!*

We finally made it back to the trail and it started to rain within an hour. So much for getting dried out again! We went through the area near Cherokee, NC called Charlies Bunion but didn't take the side trail to it, visibility was impossible due to fog plus it was raining and cold, so we stayed on the main trail. The wind and rain were relentless. At one point it started raining harder and was blowing sideways. We were near Laurel Top when we stopped at a spot out of the wind in hopes the rain would settle a bit before going further. It didn't. I had put on my raincoat when it started to rain but had not put on the pants. I put the pants on while we were stopped and very quickly, we decided to push on. If we didn't continue to hike, we would get much too cold.

We hiked 10.5 miles that day and made it to the Pecks Corner Shelter. The shelter was full of other hikers and someone yelled out, "Hey, HazMat" and waved at us. Seems like that trail name has stuck. The hikers at the shelter were trying to get a fire going and smoke filled the air. We were cold and wet but didn't want to add the smell of smoke to the mix. Besides, we didn't want to be in close proximity to too many people, all the talk of Covid was making us more aware of our actions. It was still raining and with both of us being sopping wet we were extremely cold after we stopped. While we were hiking the cold had been tolerable. After we stopped, we were both shivering.

We set the tent in the only flat spot we could find; it was barely large enough to accommodate it. Backpacks were thrown into the tent and we crawled in. Cold didn't even begin to describe how cold we were, we were both freezing. This was hypothermia like we had never experienced before. *Thankfully we never got that cold again on the entire trail.* After crawling in the tent, the first order of business was to change into dry clothes before setting up our mattresses and sleeping bags. Changing out of wet clothes in a tent with wet gear was definitely a challenge but we managed. After getting everything set up, we ate a little bit of food that didn't have to be cooked. Cooked food would have probably helped us warm up more quickly, but it was still raining. We ate in our tent and no food bags were hung up that night. *Any bear in his right mind wouldn't have been out in this weather, would he? We were so cold and it was still raining, we just couldn't get out and look for a tree.* We snuggled down in our sleeping bags after getting everything set up, it seemed like it took forever to get warm. We used a disposable hand warmer to help get our hands warmed. *This was the day we both remember well as the most cold, wet, miserable day on the entire trail. The saying is, "never quit on a bad day", but if they were all like this, I'm not sure I would be able to abide by that saying. We have both had positive attitudes and found ways to get through any situation encountered thus far. But these type situations have a way of really bringing you down.* We thought with a good night's sleep we would surely have a better day tomorrow. Once we finally got warm, we fell asleep and slept like babies. *It's amazing how well you will sleep after being out in the cold all day.*

March 25, 2020 - It rained all night and was still drizzling when we broke camp. It finally cleared off and stopped raining after lunch. It was still cold and windy in places, if you were on the wrong side of the mountain. Our gear dried out some after the rain stopped. We hiked 13.1 miles and camped at Cosby Knob Shelter. *We have heard of Cosby Knob Shelter several times since staying there. It has been frequently listed as closed due to bear activity the same as Spence Field.* We had seen no bears at this point, we had been told that many hikers complete the entire trail without seeing a bear. *I really wanted to see one, just not too close.*

March 26, 2020 - *The sun shined all day, thank the Lord. The weather had really been bad the past couple of days and we really needed the sunshine.* We hiked 9 miles and completed the AT through the Smoky Mountains National Park. We were lucky to even get through, the national parks and national forests were closing due to Covid. We saw a posting in one of the national forests saying it was closed and those who entered could be fined $500. *Wow, we were not even supposed to hike outside because of Covid? The theory was if long distance hikers became ill, Covid could be spread from town to town up and down the trail. Also, due to the small trail towns being in more remote areas, access to medical care would be seriously limited.* We were planning on continuing to hike, not stay in shelters and maintain our distance from people in town.

Roy had been having a problem with his right Achilles tendon for over well over a year. He did see a doctor for it once. Prescription medication and physical therapy didn't seem to help, he just kept going despite the pain. *I was concerned when we started on the trail, I knew he would never complain unless it was really bad.* It was really starting to bother him worse the more we hiked. I really don't know how he stood the pain as long as he did. I knew when he agreed to take medicine it was bad. *He doesn't like taking medication of any sort and he doesn't ever complain of any physical ailment. I have always thought this could be a blessing or a curse depending on the situation. I was just afraid he would have something major going on and he wouldn't tell me.* He finally took the medication I offered. I gave him 800mg of Ibuprofen (hikers call Ibuprofen Vitamin I) and we continued to hike. We hiked a little slower which was alright with me, at least I could keep up with him.

We could have probably made it to Standing Bear Farm but thought it was best to stop early.

I carried my own homemade first aid/medication kit on the hike. I had over the counter cold and pain medications. I also talked with my doctor in preparation for the hike and had two different antibiotics in my kit. I carried various Band-aids, tape, safety pins, ointment and of course foot powder. Roy joked that I had a portable pharmacy. My kit came in handy and we used most everything except the antibiotics.

Less than a mile from I-40, we set up camp near a stream to help drown out the noise from the road. We washed our socks in the creek because they smelled worse than bad! *Much like rain gear, waterproof shoes are not waterproof if you are walking in rain for hours. Plus, they are very difficult to dry once they are wet. If you did put on dry socks, they would only get damp from the shoes. Our wet shoes and sweaty feet were becoming a bit ripe. Nothing stinks as bad as wet hiking socks, except maybe a skunk. I told Roy we should tie our socks in the stream overnight. My Daddy told me a long time ago about skinning skunks. If an unskinned skunk carcass is tied in a creek, the running water will wash away the smell by morning, then it can be skinned without the odor being an issue. This was apparently an old fur trapper trick. Made sense to me that it would work for stinky socks too! We didn't leave them in the creek but we probably should have.* We used our food bag rope as a clothesline to hang some things out to dry since we had lots of sunshine.

March 27, 2020 - The weather was sunny again and warm thank goodness. We arrived at Standing Bear Farm and saw the girl from Maine leaving as we were getting there. She had stayed there in her tent the night before. We stopped there long enough to wash and dry some clothes and get a few supplies. It's a neat place, we took several pictures and wished we were staying there but we needed to move on because it was so early in the day. We crossed Snowbird Mountain and saw the FAA (Federal Aviation Administration) VOR (Very High Frequency Omni-Directional Range) Station at 4263 feet elevation. *These stations are ground based navigational systems. It was definitely a unique site to see up close. Roy, being a private pilot, was especially interested and we took several pictures at the station.* We camped that evening at Groundhog Shelter, elevation 2897 after hiking 8.5 miles. *We were sure hoping for more days like this and hoped we could put the rain and cold we endured behind us but unfortunately there was still more to come.*

"If you believe in yourself and have dedication and pride - and never quit, you will be a winner. The price of victory is high but so are the rewards." - Bear Bryant

Chapter 8 - Hot Springs is Not So Hot

March 28, 2020 - The hike was mostly uphill. *Seems to me we go more uphill than downhill, but maybe it's just me. Haven't you heard about those people who walked to school, uphill both ways? I now understood how they could say that!*

We went over Max Patch, elevation 4629 feet. Max Patch is maintained as a bald. *The whole mountaintop was cleared and sown in grass for cattle many years ago.* There was a 360-degree view of mountains and the views were breathtaking. The weather was sunny and warm, a big change from a few days ago. There were a lot of people at Max Patch taking advantage of the gorgeous views and weather. Max Patch was another unique place and the AT goes right over the top or you can drive to a parking lot and walk to the top. We stopped there, had lunch and took a few pictures. I wanted to come back and see this place again when we have more time.

We pitched our tent at Roaring Fork Shelter that evening. There was a creek nearby and we both washed our hair with Dawn dishwashing liquid. *We carried a very small bottle with us while hiking and it came in handy. We washed our hair in COLD WATER, talk about brain freeze! But at least we had clean hair. This was the fifth night since leaving Gatlinburg, I guess the hair was due for a wash.* The remainder of bathing would be accomplished in the tent with baby wipes.

News on the trail has been that Hot Springs, NC, normally a busy trail town, is essentially shut down. News travels fast through the trail grapevine. Few if any motels or hostels were open due to Covid. There was also supposed to be a Dollar General with good resupply options. It looked like Covid was really starting to be an issue for the trail.

March 29, 2020 - There was light rain in the morning but we were able to get the tent and other equipment packed before it started. A couple of hours later the rain cleared and the weather was beautiful. Thank goodness, we were most grateful to not be hiking in the rain. We hiked 14.7 miles; the trail was not as much uphill. We hiked most of the day with the girl from Maine. We camped at the same place the night after we left Standing Bear and we have been hiking with her since. We were looking forward to getting to Hot Springs the next day and hoped to be able to get a room and of course a hot shower.

March 30, 2020 - We only hiked 3.2 miles, mostly downhill, before we arrived at Hot Springs, NC about 10:00 a.m. Hot Springs could be seen from quite a distance away and it seemed like it took forever to get there. *The town is on the French Broad River and any time we crossed a river it was at a lower elevation, this one was 1336 feet. Hot Springs, NC is a very popular town for hikers and the AT goes right through the town.* The trail is marked by markers inset into the concrete on the sidewalks. There is usually everything a tired, hungry hiker might need, but not so much during Covid.

The first thing we saw was the Smoky Mountain Restaurant, we didn't pass up the opportunity to eat there. There were hikers all over the porch eating and backpacks were lined up on the ground in front of the porch. We set our packs well away from the other hikers and kept our distance as best we could. The dining area of the restaurant was closed, but you could put in your order and they would hand it to you out the door. *Covid precautions. Ugh!* But thankfully they were open and serving hungry hikers. The food was excellent! Roy had pancakes and of course I had a burger and fries. *How can the best burger on the trail be determined if you don't keep eating burgers?* Everyone was thrilled with the food and it was excellent. We even saw one hiker who ordered two dinners. One of his dinners had the largest chicken fried steak I had ever seen. Based on the taste of the food we had I bet it was delicious. *Of course, we thought anything other than trail food was delicious at this point.*

After eating we walked down the street to the Dollar General to get supplies and ran into Ray, Kyle and Pete. They told us rooms were limited since the hostels were closed but they had stayed at the Iron Horse Hotel in town. They were heading back there and would tell the manager about us. We also found out they had gotten trail names since we last saw them. Ray was Direction, Kyle was Wild Bill and Pete was Captain Jack. Pete did look a lot like

Captain Jack Sparrow. This was the last time we would see this crew. *We would hear later that Pete went back to Louisiana. Ray and Kyle continued on the trail despite Covid and finished at Mt. Katahdin later that summer. We saw several people who had saved money and taken time off work to hike the trail. Covid messed up plans for many hikers causing them to scrap the hiking and return home. We were so glad we were retired and didn't have to worry about having the time to hike the trail*

At the Iron Horse we knocked on the front door, a lady came to the door and we told her we needed a room for the night. She said she would allow us to stay if we had been on the trail for a while and hadn't been sick. We told her we had been on the trail since February 28th and neither of us had been sick. We had not been in a room since leaving Gatlinburg nearly a week ago. She said for $100 she would do one load of laundry for us, have our supper at 4:30 p.m. and breakfast with coffee in the morning. I was digging for my money before she finished the last sentence. She gave us the code to a door at the side of the building and told us she would meet us at the top of the stairs. The room was great, it had been remodeled and had a nice private bathroom. She gave us a laundry basket and told us to put anything we wanted washed in the basket. The Iron Horse was an old hotel and it faced the railroad tracks in Hot Springs. It had lots of antiques and was beautifully decorated. There was a restaurant, bar, gift shop and hotel. The owners were exceptionally nice. *I think with the Covid impacting their business they were just doing what they could to keep their business going. I looked up their Facebook page, it was apparent they catered to locals, vacationers and hikers alike and apparently had a good business before Covid.* The only portion of the business open was the hotel and they were only renting a few of the rooms to hikers like us.

We spent the evening sitting out in the common area talking with other hikers. There were no TVs in the rooms. All news would have been about Covid anyway. Terrapin from Clearwater, FL, was quite a bit older than us and was just taking his time hiking the trail. He talked about his wife driving up and meeting him in Gatlinburg where he had stayed a few days. He also had been at the Iron

Horse a couple of days and talked like he was going to stay a couple more. We got the room Ray and Kyle had the night before. The girl from Maine came in after us and she actually shared a room with Terrapin, it had bunk beds. She had no trouble crawling into the top bunk and he stayed out in the common area with us while she used the shower. Pete had roomed with him the night before and he hooked her up with Terrapin to share the room. If not for Pete's help, she may not have gotten a room at all. She called home to talk with her family that evening and made the difficult decision to leave the trail. Her boyfriend was going to come get her. He would leave the next morning for the eighteen-hour drive from Maine. Her family was concerned about Covid and insisted on her coming home and she reluctantly agreed. We would definitely miss seeing her and talking with her every day.

Hot Springs would have been a lot of fun with all the facilities open. There were restaurants, bars, outfitters, hostels and other businesses that were normally very busy, but they were closed. The only things we found open were the Smoky Mountain Restaurant, Dollar General and Hillbilly Market. We also went to the Hillbilly Market and picked up a few supplies. It was the local quick stop for gas or groceries. Covid was sucking the fun out of everything in the town for everyone. *There is no telling the financial impact Covid had on these small trail towns. Unfortunately, a lot of small businesses would not survive.*

"Walking is a man's best medicine." - Hippocrates

Chapter 9 - Goodbye Trail Hello New World

March 31, 2020 - We said goodbye to the girl from Maine and finally found out her real name was Kristina. We left Hot Springs not knowing how long we could continue before we too went home. Roy had been monitoring advisory bulletins from the Appalachian Trail Conservancy (ATC) and at this point we could continue. When leaving Hot Springs, we crossed the French Broad River on a huge road bridge. The river was wide and beautiful, the trail went alongside it for a good distance before it went up a hill. A rocky outcropping called Lover's Leap Rock about a mile from the river crossing had great views of the river and the town of Hot Springs below. To say the least it was a tough climb coming out of Hot Springs.

After hiking 10.8 miles we stopped at the Spring Mountain Shelter. The shelter was full of younger hikers, I said they looked like a litter of puppies piled up on top of each other. They were apparently not worried about Covid. No way were we staying in the shelter with all those people, we found an area dedicated for tent camping up the hill from the shelter. It was raining lightly and getting colder. We got most of our tent set up just before it started raining harder and we had to crawl in to finish. We ate a cold supper in the tent.

We had good cell phone service for a change and it allowed us to check emails. Roy received an email from the ATC saying we needed to get off the trail. There had been suggestions to cease or postpone hiking the trail before but this was a definite directive to get off the trail. They had decided to grant extensions to the 2020 hikers who complied with their direction. It didn't matter if you hiked 5 miles or 500 miles, you could get credit for the miles you hiked, restart whenever you wanted, complete the trail within one year from your restart date and still be considered a thru hiker. If we didn't get off the trail, they wouldn't give us credit for the nearly 300 miles we had completed thus far. We decided this direction could actually be to our benefit, it would give us extra time to finish the remainder of the trail. That did it, we were going home. Thru hikers complete the entire AT within twelve months and section hikers complete the trail in sections over time. Roy really wanted to be classified as a thru hiker so we decided to follow the directive.

April 1, 2020 - We called our son in law Jamie and asked him to pick us up at the TN/NC state line on North Carolina Route 208 at Allen Gap. We would hike 3.4 miles to the pickup point. Our tent was iced over that morning but we had stayed warm and dry in our sleeping bags. We broke the ice off the tent as much as we could and packed up our dirty wet gear one last time. The weather was gloomy, extremely foggy and it sleeted or snowed on us as we hiked down the mountain to the road. We sat down beside the road and waited for our ride home.

To say we were glad to see my white Kia coming into view with Jamie behind the wheel was an understatement. We had only been waiting about forty-five minutes when he arrived but it was starting to feel colder. He said we looked like a couple of hobos sitting on the side of the road. Roy had socks on his hands because his gloves had gotten wet. Hobos don't wear $20 Darn Tough socks on their hands! Lol! To say the least this had been an experience we wouldn't soon forget and we got a lot of practice for the remainder of the trail. We each had gradually assumed our separate responsibilities in setting up our camp and we could get our tent set up quickly when necessary. We actually didn't have many snafus. Our only trouble during this time spent on the trail would come from learning how to deal with the rain but we were handling that too. We just needed to keep our heads in the game in order to finish what we started. In Greenville, NC we stopped at McDonald's for a dose of fast food before getting on the road home. I never knew a Big Mac and fries could taste so good.

When we got home it was like a different world, schools closed, no concerts or sporting events, the six-foot rule, one way aisles in Wal Mart (*boy was that a joke*), demands for hand sanitizer, toilet paper and masks. Gas prices had dropped by a dollar and everything on TV revolved around the pandemic. The whole issue was politicized and there were people who believed it was all a government conspiracy. It was all the President's fault for not handling it correctly, people refused to wear masks, people who wore masks were shamed, people who didn't wear masks were shamed and each day this situation became more and more bizarre. Anti Vaxxers were protesting vaccinations and mask mandates were challenged because, "you can't tell me what to do with my body". For every person who refused to treat the situation seriously there was someone who went overboard with precautions and they all let each other know about it. There was no limit to the people with opinions and there was so much misinformation being spread it was hard to know what to believe. Of course, we got information from TV news, the internet and don't forget Facebook. What was true? I had been a healthcare professional for over 35 years and I was amazed at the whole fiasco. People were dying horrible deaths and folks thought it was all a conspiracy? I guess by now you can tell where my opinion lies. Back in the early 1900's an influenza pandemic killed millions of people and it took years without the benefit of modern medicine for that pandemic to subside. Not to mention other influenza pandemics, smallpox, cholera, plague that also killed millions of people. I guess there are people out there that thought that those were a conspiracy also. I could only hope this pandemic would be over sooner since we did have vaccinations and treatment in development and hopefully enough people who would take appropriate precautions. All we could do was to take appropriate precautions for ourselves and our families, wait and pray the pandemic would blow over.

Hiking the trail would have to be put on hold until the ATC could figure out how to manage it during the pandemic, or wait until it was under control or resolved. When we were able to restart, we would have to consider the seasons, weather and our one-year window to complete the trail as thru hikers.

After getting home we washed all our gear and put it on the back deck and out in the yard to dry. It looked like we should have been having a yard sale. Roy got a much-needed haircut at home due to Covid. Most people got Covid haircuts or just let their hair grow. We tried to wrap our heads around what was going on with all the Covid stuff and tried to adjust to a new way of thinking about visiting family, traveling and even going out in public. A lot changed in the few weeks we were gone; it was a whole new world and it was going to take some major adjustment.

"Life is about 10% what happens to you and 90% how you react to it." - Charles R. Swindoll

Chapter 10 - Where are the Blueberries?

We went for walks at home nearly every day to try and stay in shape. We had both lost about twenty pounds each during the thirty-three days we were hiking on the trail. Hiking was apparently better than a crash diet. We thought it would be easier to hike when we returned if we could stay in shape and keep the weight off, we still had plenty to spare. We went for a few short hiking adventures when we could safely manage considering Covid.

In August of 2020 we decided to hike to Gregory Bald in the Great Smoky Mountains. In late July and early August blueberries are supposed to be plentiful if you get there at the right time. We had been close to the area when we hiked through the Smokies. The trail to the top of Gregory Bald was a little over 6 miles and it was a moderately difficult trail. It reminded us of many of the trails up the mountains on the AT. There were lots of rocks, roots and steep uphill ascents. When we arrived at the top, we were in awe of the fields of blueberry bushes. The whole top of the mountain was covered in blueberry bushes and maintained with rows mowed to allow access to the blueberries. The whole time we were there we kept thinking about how this was probably a bear's dinner table and how we were on their turf but thankfully we didn't see any. Had it been June we would have been treated to an awesome display of azaleas in bloom. Colors reportedly range from fire red, wine red, orange, salmon, yellow, white, pink and even multicolored. This would definitely be a reason to hike here again.

Our climb up was also rewarded with an unbelievable view of Cades Cove from the top of Gregory Bald. Cades Cove is a huge valley in the Great Smoky Mountains National Park. The valley was home to settlers before the park was formed. It is the most popular destination for visitors to the park. It has several well-preserved homesteads, scenic mountain views and abundant wildlife. It is common to see deer and bears during a drive of the loop through the cove. We had been to Cades Cove many times during our visits to the park.

The weather was pleasant that day, clear skies, sunshine and perfect for hiking. We saw several people at the top who had also hiked up to enjoy the views. Most of the hikers didn't camp on top of the mountain that night. There was a camping area and it was just the two of us and one other camper nearby who were brave enough to stay. Most everyone mentioned bears and asked if anyone had seen any that day. No one we talked to had seen bears, but everyone was on high alert. We ate our supper and settled in for the evening, as usual we slept well after a day of hiking, despite the talk of bears.

The next morning, we hiked back to our car with about two cups of blueberries to show for our efforts. We would have been allowed to pick one gallon per person per day and we carried plastic gallon bags with us just in case, I guess we were overly optimistic. But it would be another good reason to come back at a later date. We estimated we were probably a week or so past the peak of blueberry season. That could have been why we didn't see any bears, they had probably eaten their fill and moved on to the next bear food that was in season. We managed to get enough blueberries to make a few muffins when we got back home. I made homemade blueberry muffins with a lemon glaze and they were very tasty.

"Climb mountains, not so the world can see you but so you can see the world." - David McCullough,Jr.

Chapter 11 - Llama Trains, Hurricanes and Moonbows

In September of 2020 we hiked the hike and bike trail from Park City, Kentucky to Mammoth Cave National Park. We parked the truck in Park City on Saturday and would return to it on Sunday. The trail was a little over 8 miles through the forest and alongside the roads. It was a relatively easy trail for us. The weather was mild and it was a sunny day which made for an enjoyable hike. There were several signs along the way describing the notable areas. It was interesting to learn a little more about the history of the land before it became part of the national park. There were several markers and signs along the route that told of the railroad, a general store and a hotel in the area.

My paternal grandparents once lived in an area called Dennison's Ferry, which is now part of the Mammoth Cave National Park. They had to move when the park service took the land to be part of the national park. My Dad was born at Dennison, Kentucky which no longer exists. There is a town called Denniston, in the northeast of Kentucky, but it is not the place he was born. Dennison's Ferry is a place by the Green River, but there is no ferry as well as no town, there is just a gravel parking lot where people park while fishing, canoeing or kayaking on the river. Every time I have been there, I get a feeling of nostalgia thinking about my ancestors living in the area. My Dad was born near there in 1926. However, the area we were hiking was not close to Dennison's Ferry I was sure we would visit Dennison's Ferry again sometime, just not on this trip.

We got a campsite at the Mammoth Cave campground and pitched our tent. We walked to the campground store to get ice cream, cooked hot dogs for our dinner and played cards at the picnic table at our campsite until it was time to turn in. We crawled in our tent as the evening got cooler and snuggled down for the night. The next morning, we hiked back to the truck. The trip back seemed a little easier than the day before, there was not as much uphill hiking. We headed for home with another hiking trip under our belts.

Another memorable trip was the hike to Mt. LeConte, the third highest peak in the Great Smoky Mountains National Park. We hiked there the Friday after Thanksgiving 2020. We chose to hike the five-mile Alum Cave trail to the rustic LeConte Lodge. The trail started near Gatlinburg and required a lot of uphill hiking and it really challenged us but it was worth the effort to see the area.

The lodge is the third highest peak in the Smokies at over 6593 feet elevation. Gatlinburg is about 1300 feet elevation. Hiking up one of the trails is the only means of access for visitors. Reservations for the lodge are booked several months or even years in advance and the cost of lodging is pretty expensive. However, it has the distinction of being the highest inn providing lodging for visitors in the eastern United States. In addition to the lodge, there is a gift shop and several cabins available for reservation. All supplies must be brought in by helicopter or llama train. Llamas have soft pads on their feet and they don't cause damage to the trail. Several llamas are brought up from Gatlinburg by the llama wrangler three times a week via the Trillium Gap trail to pack up clean linens and other supplies, they return with soiled linens and garbage. While the llamas are at the lodge, they are served a meal of pancakes. Each llama has a name and they are one of the main attractions at Mt. LeConte.

Hiking up was a fairly difficult hike and thank goodness we planned on hiking back down the next day. Instead of staying at the lodge we registered for camping with the park service and camped at the LeConte Shelter at the top of the mountain near the lodge. We couldn't stay in the shelter due to Covid precautions but we could camp there.

The lodge had Covid precautions in place also and they were not doing their usual things including allowing guests or visitors to pet the llamas. The llamas were behind a roped off area and we watched from afar as they ate pancakes and were prepared for the trip back down the mountain. I was able to zoom in to get a few pictures. After looking around the lodge and cabins we headed on up to the campsite.

After setting up our tent we hiked to a lookout to see the sunset and got there just in time to see the sun slipping over the mountains but the views were gorgeous. We met a guy up top who said he was going all the way back down the trail to his car. We knew it would be dark before he could get very far and Roy offered to let him use his headlamp since the guy didn't have a light but he declined the offer. He left and we were still a little concerned about him when we met a couple who were also going back down. We talked with them and found they had lights, we told them about the guy who didn't have lights and they knew him and said they would probably catch up to him. When we returned to our tent, we met a woman in her early seventies who had set her tent near ours. She had hiked up one of the more difficult trails because she said she liked to challenge herself. *Wow, I hope to have her attitude and ability at that age.* We ate our supper and settled in for the night. Not long after getting in our sleeping bags Roy started snoring loudly, I woke him and told him to roll over before a bear heard him and considered him a threat. He was sounding about like the hiker we avoided while hiking on the AT earlier in the year but I had no choice but to sleep with him in our tent. My only salvation would be if he could hold it down until I could get to sleep too.

The weather was clear and cold that night on Mt. LeConte but we stayed warm. *That was one good thing about our tent and sleeping equipment, we never were cold at night and I for one was thankful. If I am hot, I am miserable, but if I am cold, I am even more miserable. I like cooler weather for hiking, just not too cold.* We hiked back to the car the next morning and headed for home. Having heard about Mt LeConte for years it was wonderful to finally get to see the lodge and the llamas even if we couldn't pet them. Dang Covid! Still sucking the fun out of everything, it even derailed us from petting the llamas of the llama rain.

In April of 2021 we hiked at Cumberland Falls State Park in Kentucky. Cumberland Falls, also called the "Niagara of the South" is 125 feet wide and 68 feet tall. We had been to Cumberland Falls many times over the years but this time we hiked a few different trails. One of the best trails we found was on the opposite side of the falls from the viewing area visited by most tourists. Seeing the falls from a different vantage point made them look totally different and my opinion even more beautiful. The Eaglte Falls trail went along the river below the main waterfalls for a couple of miles. Eagle Falls, another waterfall in the area, was a 44-foot waterfall that flows from the west bank of the Cumberland River just downstream from Cumberland Falls.

We timed our visit to Cumberland Falls to coincide with when the moonbow might be visible. A moonbow is a lunar rainbow and it occurs at night when light from the moon illuminates falling water drops. The drops may be in the form of rain or can be mist from a waterfall. Cumberland Falls is one of the only places on Earth that has a regularly occurring moonbow and it occurs during a full moon. We walked to the viewing area after dark and waited for the much-anticipated moonbow. To the naked eye the moonbow appears to be pale white. With the right kind of photography, the colors of the rainbow may be seen. My phone wouldn't capture a picture with colors but we did see the white arc from the moonbow and it was definitely an unusual sight.

We tent camped that night at the campground in the Cumberland Falls State Park. Our site was in a lower area about 50 yards down a hill into the woods and there were no other campers close by. There were lots of RV campers on another loop in the campground and we could occasionally hear them as everyone settled in for the evening. Roy went to sleep not long after crawling in our tent but I had trouble going to sleep. I decided to read for a while, I have the Kindle app on my phone and frequently use it for reading. It was quiet and as I was reading, I heard something moving through the woods, I thought it was probably a raccoon or other woodland creature. A few minutes later I heard a loud crash, I thought the sound came from the RV campsites and didn't give it a second thought.

The next morning, we discovered the reason for the crash. The garbage can up on the road from our tent had been turned over and garbage had been scattered everywhere. A Krispy Kreme donut box and Pabst Blue Ribbon (PBR) beer cans were in the edge of the woods and both had teeth marks. The can had been attached to a large flat slab of concrete to prevent it from being blown over. A raccoon didn't turn this can over, it had to have been a bear. Who knew bears would like donuts and PBR? This would become a running joke between us about how to catch a bear with donuts and PBR. We picked up the trash and reported the incident to the campground office. I believe they agreed it must have been a bear, we went back through the area later and the trash can had been removed. Hopefully they were going to replace it with something bear proof. Years ago, we never had to worry much about bears in most of Kentucky. If there were any bears they were in the far eastern part of the state. The parks in Kentucky further West are now becoming more bear aware as the black bear's territory continues to move farther East from the Appalachian Mountains.

After leaving the AT in 2020 Roy was anxious to get back to the trail as soon as possible. I however was not quite that enthusiastic. I really enjoyed being at home, having contact with family and friends even if we didn't visit as much as before due to Covid. We stayed busy with our house at Panama City Beach, Florida. We had it rented full time for almost six years and the guy moved out in February 2020 before we left for the trail. We had done just enough for it to hold until we were finished with the trail and could devote more time to it. We went to Florida several times over the next year or so. We got a new roof put on, painted the house inside and out and I also refinished several pieces of second-hand furniture to put in the house and decorated it to look more like a beach house.

We put down new flooring in the Florida house in September of 2022 during Hurricane Sally, a Category 2 hurricane that dumped 10+ inches of rain on the area. Several roads in the county were under water and local news was advising residents to shelter in place until the waters receded. While looking through the front sliding glass door, we discovered a squirrel had sought refuge from the storm on the front covered deck of the house. The house is a stilt house and the deck goes all the way across the front. The poor squirrel was sitting on the railing out front as the storm raged. The palm trees in the neighborhood were whipping back and forth in the wind like we had never seen before. The strong gusts of wind and blowing rain had the squirrel really working hard just to hang on. He saw us watching him and got spooked. He ran up and down the posts and finally scurried off the deck and under the house. If only he had known we wouldn't hurt him, he could have come inside and weathered the storm with us.

We went out to a nearby store for groceries when the rain passed and drove by the beach. We have had the house at Bid-a-wee Beach since 2000 and had never seen the ocean look so angry, it was frightening. Even though the eye of the storm was further to the west in Alabama, the storm surge caused huge waves at our beach and tornado warnings in our area. We actually went to the lower level under the house in the utility area at one point since the tornado warning was for the Bid-a-wee Beach area. We were in the outer bands of the hurricane over 100 miles from where it made landfall. I don't think I ever want to be this close to a hurricane again, and this was a category 2. I don't even want to imagine what would happen during a category 5 storm.

All this time Roy was still making plans for our return to the trail. The ATC was still not recognizing hikers who were hiking the trail. But a lot of hikers hiked the trail anyway. The only reason we didn't hike was because the ATC would not support our hike nor give us credit for the miles we had already hiked and Roy wanted us to be recognized as "2000 Milers". If you complete your hike within one year you can apply for a 2000 Miler certificate and your hike is registered with the ATC. Your name and photo are recorded in their records. It is a more prestigious recognition than the section hiker completion. But hey, if you hiked 2000 miles who cares whether it was thru hiking or section hiking? To me 2000 miles is a huge accomplishment any way you look at it.

Finally, May 11, 2021 the ATC cleared everyone to return to the trail. I was just not ready; all I could think about was the impending summer heat. Hiking is difficult in cold weather but I much prefer it to be cool when hiking. We had planned on a big road trip out west and I really wanted to keep those plans as well. We agreed to put the hike on hold for a bit and make sure our timing was right for the seasons and weather. And to ensure we could actually finish within one year without hiking too much in the dead of winter.

"Not all who wander are lost." - J.R.R. Tolkien

Chapter 12 - Going West

If you have ever been to the western United States, you know there is a lot of wide-open country. Lodging can be difficult to find unless you are willing to drive long distances at times. We were planning a long road trip and knew we would have more flexibility if we camped part of the time. This however was going to be car camping, not tent camping. We did plan to do some hiking but no backcountry camping. We set about to transform Roy's white 2003 Ford F-150 pickup into a camper. YouTube has several videos showing how people turned their vehicles into campers and we watched several of those while we researched the best way to proceed. Roy found a topper for the truck on Craig's List and we drove to a small town near Clarksville, Tennessee to pick it up. I ordered a bed frame to fit in the bed of the pickup truck, it did require a minor modification, but that was not a problem. We covered some plywood with carpet and by the time we were finished we had a place for a bed on an elevated platform in the back of the truck. A memory foam mattress with a waterproof cover and a set of sheets completed our sleeping quarters. Roy also built some lightweight drawers to slide under the bed. We had our camp stove, coffee pot and lots of supplies necessary for car camping. We would put a cooler in the backseat of the truck with drinks and food for the road.

Our itinerary was . . . we didn't have one, but whatever it was it included as many national parks as possible. Glacier National Park was a must see and we would look at other parks along the way.

June 1, 2021 - We packed the cooler and a couple of bags with clothes and food and hit the road. The first time we stopped after leaving home was at Skeeter Mountain Rest Area in Illinois. We had a ham sandwich for lunch and just covered miles on this day. We went through several larger cities, Evansville, St. Lewis, Kansas City and made it to Iowa by the time we stopped for the day. The Lewis and Clark State Park had a convenient campground. It was a very nice, quiet place. We cooked our dinner at the campsite and enjoyed a gorgeous red sunset as Canadian geese flew in to take advantage of the lake. After eating, we crawled into the Casa de James, it was very comfortable and we slept well.

June 2, 2021 - There was an absolutely beautiful sunrise at Lewis and Clark State Park. We heard coyotes last night; they were really close to the campground. Hope they didn't have goose for their evening meal. We made coffee and had a little breakfast before resuming our journey.

We drove through Iowa into South Dakota. Before we entered the Badlands National Park, we visited the Minuteman Missile National Historic Site. During the Cold War there were hundreds of Minuteman Missiles that could have been used against the Soviet Union in the event of a nuclear war. They were housed in underground silos and hidden beneath the landscape of the great plains. We watched a video and toured the visitor center there and were amazed at the history of the missiles.

Roy's America the Beautiful card got us into the park for free. He had thought the card allowed entry into the national parks at half price, but we found the camping fees were half price. The admission would have been $30, the card would save us quite a bit of money since we planned on visiting several parks. We needed to stretch our legs so we hiked a couple of short trails there. No wonder the place is called Badlands. Nothing there but sand, rocks, gullies and scrub plants. Definitely nothing for humans, as far as I could see, except to look at the unique landscape while passing through. We did see several Big Horn Sheep and they seemed content to be there. I was sure there had to be snakes and lizards living there also but we didn't see any.

We just had to stop at the famous Wall Drug in Wall, South Dakota for a buffalo burger and fries. They were really good! If you can call this place a store, it has anything you could ever dream of and at least six of each one. It is all under one roof and probably covers more than a full city block. We didn't even scratch the surface of things to see there. We were happy with the food.

We also went through the town of Deadwood. You have probably heard of Deadwood in some old western movie. We saw wagons being pulled by horses and several old buildings from one hundred plus years ago. The main street consisted of many old buildings that had been restored and were used for various businesses. It was definitely something to see.

We stayed that night at Keyhole State Park in Wyoming, another campsite on a beautiful lake. We got a prime campsite near a huge rock formation on the lakeshore with a great view. We backed the truck into the site, we would be able to see the lake from our bed. After we ate our dinner, we decided to take advantage of the showers. This was also our first experience with coin operated showers. We each had our homemade shower kit with our toiletries and towels. We got our clean clothes and headed to the showers. Roy of course got finished before me, his shower was fifty cents and mine was seventy-five, I have a lot more hair. The showers were hot and they worked fine. It just took a while to get dried and dressed with our scaled down version of towels. After dinner and taking a closer look at the lake, we settled in for the night looking forward to wherever we would go in the morning and what we might see next.

June 3, 2021 - We awakened to another beautiful sunrise over the lake, we lingered in our bed just a few minutes longer to admire the view. After making coffee and a small breakfast we continued our trek toward Yellowstone Park. We drove across Wyoming to Cody, from there we entered the east entrance of Yellowstone. There were beautiful views of the mountains and lots of them were still snow covered. We came to Yellowstone Lake not long after entering the park. It is a huge lake and the mountains reflecting in the water in all directions on the lake was awesome. We drove through the park toward the south entrance admiring the sights. The Grand Tetons were outside the south entrance and we went there to see the towering mountains over 14,000 feet in elevation. The loop toward Jenny Lake took us so much closer to the Grand Tetons than staying on the main road to Jackson, Wyoming. It was definitely worth the time to take the loop, we got more of an idea how massive those mountains really were. Snow covered mountains towering over everything in sight were a sight to behold. Pictures don't even begin to capture the beauty of the area. We got out and hiked an easy trail in the area near the base of the Tetons. It was good to stretch our legs after being in the truck so long.

We were not able to find a campsite in Yellowstone or the Grand Tetons campgrounds. I was using an app called Free Roam and several times we were able to find BLM (Bureau of Land Management), free dispersed camping sites. I found a campsite outside Yellowstone in the Bridger/Teton National Forest. There were several other campers there but the camping area was plenty big enough and it was a quiet spot. It was weird, 10:00 p.m. MST and it was still light outside, but we slept well after getting settled in for the evening. *We would later hear about Gabby Petito being murdered in August 2021; her body found in the Bridger-Teton National Forest. It was bizarre to think we had been there just a couple of months before and it was such a beautiful place for such a tragedy.*

June 4, 2021 - It was 43 degrees this morning! Yesterday afternoon it was 81 degrees. The weather has been perfect so far. I sleep better when it is cold at night as long as I have plenty of covers. We went back into Yellowstone and went to Old Faithful. We walked to the geyser and some of the hiking trails in the area. The steaming ground with all the pools and smaller geysers is an unbelievable sight. Old Faithful erupted pretty much on time and a large crowd gathered to witness this spectacle of nature.

We were waiting for geothermal activity that occurred every few minutes at a small steaming pool of water near Old Faithful when we met some folks from Panama City Beach, Florida. They have a house in Seclusion, the subdivision that joins Bid-a-Wee where our Florida house is located. The guy told us he frequently walks the beach there. We talked to the couple for a few minutes and left hoping we would see each other again on the beach in Florida. Sometimes it really can be a small world.

We headed north from Old Faithful toward Mammoth Hot Springs. There was a traffic jam and we were bumper to bumper moving at a snail's pace for about two hours. Come to find out it was because of buffalo in the road. A buffalo jam was holding up traffic! They were walking the road in a canyon where there was no shoulder on the road and steep hills up or down on either side. They moved at their own pace and no one could get around them. If they were crowded too much by a vehicle they could attack. So, everyone just crawled along and let them have their way. When we finally got to an area where cars could pass there were still dozens of buffalo walking alongside the road. I sure didn't want to challenge them for the real estate, but I took a few pictures from the safety of the vehicle as we drove by. We were relieved to find out it was buffalo causing the delay, we feared there had been an accident involving people and this was no place to have something like that happen. Because the area is so remote, medical care would be hours away.

We again had to go outside Yellowstone Park to find a place to camp. Timber Campground was outside the north entrance a few miles up Jardine Road, a gravel road uphill with a lot of washboards and potholes. Roy kept saying it was going to tear the truck up if it got any worse but we finally made it. There were only three campsites and we were lucky enough to get one of them. There was an open grassy area with large trees around the perimeter and it looked like a great place to set up camp for the night. This campsite was in the Gallatin National Forest, there were postings about bears everywhere and as we read the multiple signs, we became more aware of the possible presence of bears in the area. Also, we realized if a bear was around there was a good chance it would be a grizzly. A grizzly bear is not to be taken lightly. The saying came to mind, "People in sleeping bags are the soft tacos of the bear world". I really did not want to find out if that was true. We decided to eat something we didn't have to cook so there would be no smells to entice the bears. We were bedded down in the truck before dark. I would not go outside for anything until daylight since I didn't want to bump into a bear. I had not neglected to bring my peanut butter jar along, just in case. The topper on the truck gave us some sense of safety although, if a bear wanted in the truck, he would be able to break in without problems. At least the truck would keep the bear who was just curious at bay and we did have bear spray, if we didn't spray ourselves with it in the topper.

After we got home, we received information from Amazon regarding a bear spray recall. The recall involved certain lot numbers manufactured in a specific timeframe. Our can was within

75

the recall parameters. The instructions were to take your bear spray outside and attempt a short burst of spray. I reluctantly took it outside and attempted to spray, it didn't even sputter! Yikes! Glad we didn't encounter an angry bear! Amazon refunded the cost of the bear spray. In addition, I contacted the company and they issued a prepaid label to send it back. They sent a replacement can of bear spray and a couple of other goodies for returning the defective product. The replacement worked but I hope we never have to use it.

June 5, 2021- Thankfully we didn't see or hear any bears at the campground the night before. We got up that morning and had some coffee and breakfast before we drove back into Yellowstone at the north entrance. I had oatmeal and coffee and for some reason I dumped my oatmeal packet in the coffee. I was talking to Roy and not paying attention to what I was doing. I took a taste anyway, yuck! Maple and brown sugar oatmeal does not taste good in coffee. I had to pour it out and start all over.

Mammoth Hot Springs was our first stop and it seemed like we hiked all over it on the trails and boardwalks over the geothermal ground. The crystal-clear pools of boiling hot water were a very unusual site to say the least. There were several elk in the area, I guess they were used to the pools of boiling water. We were in awe of the whole area and I think we hiked every trail there. We also drove out to the Roosevelt Lodge on the north side of the park. On the way back we saw a black bear and a cub but they were too far away for a picture. We saw dozens of elk and buffalo in the fields on the way out and back from the lodge also, we were happy they didn't cause another traffic jam.

We left Yellowstone at the north entrance and headed to Shelby, Montana. This is truly, "big sky country". The blue skies and big puffy clouds definitely appeared different from the ones at home. The clouds look a lot bigger and a lot closer and the view of the sky is unobstructed by buildings. In other words, there were a lot of wide-open spaces that made the sky appear bigger, and it was beautiful. After driving all day, we were ready to stop for the evening and found a room at the Comfort Inn in Shelby, Montana. There was a drive-in restaurant nearby called the Dash-In and we decided to go there for supper as our choices were a bit limited. This part of the country is not as populated as the eastern United States and fast-food options are limited unless you are in a larger city. We ordered hamburgers and Roy got a milkshake made with real strawberries. The food was excellent.

"No matter how sophisticated you may be a large granite mountain cannot be denied – it speaks in silence to the very core of your being." - Ansel Adams

Chapter 13 - Glaciers & Bears

June 6, 2021 - We looked at the National Park website to determine how to get into Glacier National Park. Tickets were only online and a limited number was available each day. To request a ticket, you had to wait until 8:00 a.m., enter your request and hope it went through. I had all our information entered on the website and was waiting until 8:00 a.m. to press enter. When the clock flipped from 7:59 a.m. I hit the button. Within five seconds a message popped up, Sold Out! We would just head that way and see how to get admission to the park. We could have entered the park if we had a campsite reserved, but we had not been able to reserve a site since the campgrounds were full.

Breakfast at the Comfort Inn was great and we ate our fill before leaving. We talked to several people as we were eating breakfast and were told you may be able to get into the park later in the day without a ticket. We were also told it might be best not to stop as we went through the Blackfeet Indian Reservation on the way to Glacier National Park. Apparently, they had a great fear of Covid on the reservation and didn't take kindly to visitors. We made it through the reservation without stopping but we didn't need to stop for anything so it was not a problem.

The visitor center at the entrance to the park was open, visitors were not allowed inside but a ranger was stationed outside. We talked with a ranger, he gave us some printed information and explained we could enter the park after 5:00 p.m. without a ticket, we just had to get in line at the entrance and wait. We asked about hiking some of the trails and he explained there were some very nice trails on the edge of the park near a place called Two Medicine. We went there to spend the day sightseeing until 5:00 p.m. We hiked the Ptarmigan Falls Trail, approximately seven miles round trip. The falls were beautiful, not the biggest we have ever seen, but each waterfall has its own unique charm and this one didn't disappoint. There was actually a Ptarmigan on the Ptarmigan Falls Trail, it tried to peck us and we had to fend it off with our hiking poles. The trail was an in and out trail so the Ptarmigan also came out to harass us on the way back. *Those*

*things are aggressive and they don't back down easily. We would
see a Ptarmigan on the AT later that was even more aggressive
than this one.*

Bighorn sheep were sunning on a big flat rock above the trail.
The herd of males were a sight to see, there were about eight to
ten of them. They were about 40 yards away and seemed rather
unconcerned about hikers on the trail. The trail was fairly easy in
comparison to trails we hiked on the AT. We ran into snow on the
ground and continued on the trail for a few minutes. The trail was
not easily identified with snow on the ground and we were
following footprints of other hikers. The snow was getting deeper
and there were deep tree wells around the fir trees. We were not
equipped for hiking in the snow, our athletic shoes would get wet
and cold very quickly and we became unsure of continuing to hike
the trail so we decided to return to the truck.

We got in the line to enter Glacier National Park at 4:30 p.m.
Cars were already lined up and even though we were there thirty
minutes or so early we were about twenty cars deep in the line.
The lakes and glacier covered mountains in the park were
unbelievable! We had only gone a short distance on the road to St.
Mary's inside the park when we spotted a large grizzly bear beside
the road. He was busy eating grass and he was about 30 yards
away. We stopped to watch him and I was able to get pictures and
a video from the truck. We learned that bears eat grass and roots
when they get out of hibernation because berries and such are not
in season and they have voracious appetites. The bear looked up
at us a couple of times but kept on eating. He was concentrating
on his food more than us, thank goodness. I had been
programmed to have a healthy fear of bears and there was no way
I would have stepped out of the truck. We also saw a mother
grizzly and a couple of cubs up on the side of a mountain. We had
stopped to use the restroom and several people in the parking lot
were looking up at the mountainside. We were able to see the
bears with binoculars. We couldn't believe we had only been in the
park a few minutes and had already seen four bears.

We drove in and out of the east entrance, The Road to The Sun
(the main road through the park) was not open all the way through

because the snow had not yet been cleared off the road. We drove past numerous lakes and snow covered or glacier covered mountains. The water in the lakes was crystal clear and the reflections of the mountains in the water was unbelievable. Pictures do not even begin to show the beauty of the landscape.

After we left the park, I found a shortcut road from St. Mary's back to Two Medicine. I didn't realize it was a very narrow road high upon a mountainside. *It's a shame the map didn't give those kinds of details.* The road was in terrible disrepair and it had no guardrails! I was anxious to say the least, Roy was driving and my side of the truck was nearest the edge. He had nerves of steel but I couldn't even look. I had to stare straight ahead and really talk to myself to keep from crying. I have more than a healthy fear of heights and this was definitely testing me. We finally got through the shortcut, without me having a full-blown panic attack, and found a place to camp in the Lewis and Clark National Forest just outside the park near Two Medicine.

June 7, 2021 - We hiked two trails near Two Medicine, Astor Falls and Rockwell Falls. On the way back from Rockwell Falls we saw a mother grizzly with two cubs. We walked past without seeing them even though we had met some people on the trail who told us about them. We met five or six people coming back to see the bear and we backtracked with them to see it too. We spotted the bear; she was lying behind a large log near the tree line and when she raised her head to look at us it looked as big as a barrel. We stayed a safe distance and backed up even more to allow additional space between us. I got a couple of pictures but even with zoom the pictures were not very good. The bear apparently didn't consider us a threat because she turned her attention back to the cubs and didn't move from the area. Bear count in the park so far was seven! There was a deer that walked within two feet of Roy while we were hiking one of the trails. I was not afraid of us at all. I wondered if it had been fed by people. We also saw a little chipmunk and he skipped along up and down the path. He would stop and stand on his hind feet as if begging. It was very apparent he was used to being the recipient of a handout. We were excited to see what other animals we could see. We both hoped to see a bull moose.

We camped at Emery Bay Campground just outside the park. Luck was on our side when we checked the website, a campsite was available at Fish Creek Campground inside the park for the next night. We were thrilled to finally get a campsite inside the park.

June 8, 2021 - Apgar Lookout was a challenging 3.6-mile hike with approximately 2000 feet elevation gain, we decided to hike to the top and enjoy the view of Lake McDonald. The hike was not too bad, at least this trail had long switchbacks. There was an old fire tower building at the top, we couldn't go inside but were able to walk around on the deck outside to get a better view of the lake below. If the views from the bottom of the mountain looking up was breathtaking, the views from high up looking down over the lake were even more so. We took a short break at the top, used the privy and had a snack before hiking back to the truck. This trail was definitely worth the hike for that view.

We found a place to get ice cream after the hike and it was a more than welcomed treat. We got Huckleberry ice cream. Huckleberries are like huge blueberries and they were delicious. Huckleberry goodies were everywhere, ice cream, jam, pies, etc. I also got a picture frame and a couple of Glacier t-shirts from the gift shop where we got the ice cream. We camped that night at the Fish Creek Campground inside the park.

Glacier National Park was a place we had talked of visiting for years and we were in awe of the mountains with clear lakes, the glaciers and of course the grizzly bears. There is no way pictures could capture the beauty of it all. The size, the colors of the mountains and the skies, the clarity of the water could not be displayed in any picture. We would just have to commit most of it to memories and what wonderful memories they would be.

*"Hiking is not for everyone. Notice the wilderness
is mostly empty." - Sonja Yoerg*

Chapter 14 - Fog, Rain and Snow

June 9, 2021 - This morning it was 38 degrees! We stayed warm in our bed, but needless to say we didn't spend much time outside before getting in the truck and on the road. Mt. Rainier in Washington state was next on the list after leaving Glacier National Park. We spent most of the day just covering the miles to get there. We traveled through western Montana and discovered we were only about fifteen miles from Tom Oar's place. *If you have seen the show Mountain Men on the history channel, you know Tom Oar. He is a retired Bronco rider who has a cabin near the Idaho and Canadian borders in Montana. He became one of the most beloved of the mountain men on the show because he was so adept in the arts of hunting, trapping, tanning hides and making custom items from the tanned hides and furs. He also made knives, usually with deer antler handles. He explained details in each step of the process on the show and had a way of communicating with people that made everyone want to know more. We opted not to go to his house. He probably wasn't there anyway. (Maybe we were foxes with sour grapes!)*

There were numerous apple farms in Washington, we saw huge orchards, large trucks, and processing facilities. *Farmers started growing apples in Washington in the early 1800s and by the 1930s were marketing apples nationwide. Washington is the nation's leading apple-growing state. It was incredible to see where Washington apples are grown. Each region is known for something. I guess we missed the potato farms in Idaho, they must have been farther south.*

We stopped at a Dollar General Store (they had them there too) and bought a few supplies and ice for the cooler. After a long day of traveling, we camped at Ohanapecosh Campground in Mount Rainier National Park and cooked hamburgers for supper.

June 10, 2021- We reserved a campsite at Cougar Rock after driving up to the Paradise Inn. *The inn was built in 1916 and was designated as a National Historic Landmark and placed on the National Register of Historic Places. The lodge is set high in the mountains in the Mount Rainier National Park.* The drive there was interesting. It was snowing and it looked to me, being from Kentucky, like it should have been January instead of June. The road was closed from the inn over the mountain on the other side due to snow that had not been cleared from the road. There were markers along the edges of the road to mark the road when covered by snow, the markers appeared to be at least 15 feet high! *People at home get crazy, running out to get milk, eggs and bread because the weather forecast calls for an inch of snow.*

Because of the rain, snow and fog we were not able to see the mountains at all that morning. We hiked Eagle Peak trail, ran into snow about a half mile from the end and had to turn back. It's just not worth getting hurt walking on ice or snow. We hiked to Carter Falls instead, it was again not the biggest falls we have seen but it was very pretty nonetheless. The trees here are huge and the snow-covered mountains are almost unbelievable. The weather cleared in the upper elevations this afternoon and we were rewarded with gorgeous views of Mt. Rainer. Mt. Rainier is at 14,000+ feet elevation and is a snow-covered mountain. Thank goodness we had that wonderful view; it would have been a pity to come all this way and not even see it. Pictures couldn't begin to capture the majesty of the mountain. We stopped at a gift shop and I bought two t-shirts. We had a gorgeous view of Mt. Rainier from the gift shop and we lingered there a little longer to get pictures and enjoy the spectacular site in front of us. We were so thankful the weather cleared enough to actually see the mountain, luck was on our side, this time.

We camped at Cougar Rock Campground. The trees there were huge and when we backed the truck into the campsite it looked like a little matchbox vehicle compared to the trees. There were a couple of crosscuts on display at the campground from trees that were apparently hundreds of years old. There were little signs posted at different rings on the trees explaining what year it was at the time or what was going on. We swapped taking pictures at the crosscuts, they were much wider than we were tall.

June 11, 2021 - Last night after talking it over we decided to go to Oregon and see Crater Lake. We got up and had coffee and breakfast and prepared for the day. Going through Portland was a unique experience. There were tent cities for miles and miles along the highway. We couldn't believe the number of homeless there, sometimes we don't realize how fortunate we are.

Lots of rain, snow, fog and wind at Crater Lake. It was 35 degrees on top of the mountain and it was raining/snowing. We only got a glimpse of the lake and Wizard Island through the fog and we were lucky to even see that. Apparently, Crater Lake is in fog 80% of the time in June. After checking the weather, we decided not to gamble on waiting until the next day.

We camped at a dispersed camping area near Lakeview, Oregon and we were the only people there. We ate at a local burger place, not as good as Dash-In in Montana but we were happy with the meal. From here we planned to head toward Rocky Mountain National Park (RMNP) in Colorado.

June 12, 2021 - It rained on us during the night and it was clear and cold when we got up that morning. We drove through Nevada, Utah and Wyoming and stopped for the night at Rock Springs, Wyoming. After we checked in at the Clarion we each had a nice long hot shower and decided to eat dinner at the Mexican restaurant in our hotel. The hotel was in an excellent location with most anything you might need nearby. We watched TV and washed two loads of laundry before turning in for the night.

June 13, 2021 - We had a nice cooked to order breakfast at the hotel. We got ice for the cooler and we were off again. We spent the day driving from western Wyoming to RMNP in central Colorado. The timing for ticketless entry at RMNP was after 3:00 p.m. We got in line and entered within a few minutes of arriving. The "timed entry permit" system is a pain, but at least our timing was right this time. The timed entry was put in place to help with overcrowding of visitors in the national parks and I guess it worked but it was still a pain. We drove across the northern and western sections of the park and we saw several elk and one female moose. The snow-covered mountains are still unbelievable. I'm really glad Roy is driving, these winding roads with steep drops, no guardrails and hair pin turns intimidate me. The road was not as bad as the cut through road near Glacier National Park, but the steep drop offs still kept me on the edge of my seat. We got a campsite at the Greenridge Campground just outside the park to the south, it's a nice campground with a beautiful lake view.

June 14, 2021 - We went back to RMNP and saw a big moose but he didn't want to come out of the bushes by the creek where he was eating. He wasn't feeling very photogenic apparently. We got a pretty good look at him even though we were unable to get his picture. We went back across the north section of the park. Before returning to the park we hiked to Calypso Falls and Colburn Falls. More beautiful waterfalls! A campsite was available outside the east entrance of the campground for $6.50. Per recreation.gov campsites in the park are first come, first served. We thought all the sights would be gone since we couldn't enter the park until 6:00 p.m. this time. We wanted to see Bear Lake and were hoping to get there while the sun was still high enough to shine on the lake. The sun was fading but we were still able to get some beautiful pictures with reflections of the trees and the sky. We checked as we were leaving and a campsite was available at the Glacier Bay Campground. We decided to stay in the park and forfeit the $6.50 campsite. We had not left anything at the other campsite so it was not a problem. The Glacier Bay Campground was a nice quiet place and we slept well.

"And into the forest I go, to lose my mind and find my soul." - John Muir

Chapter 15 - Is it Hot or What?

June 15, 2021 - We left RMNP and drove south to Sand Dunes National Park in Colorado. We were amazed to see that much sand! Huge sand dunes at the base of mountains looked totally out of place. It looked like sand dunes in a desert with a mountain backdrop. It was beautiful but odd.

It was really hot and we didn't feel like playing in the sand so we chose not to hike the sand dunes. There was a shallow creek flowing between the parking area and the sand dunes and people were carrying chairs, coolers, and umbrellas like they were going to the beach. It was definitely warm enough to seem like the beach. People were sitting in the sand and playing in the water. *All I could think was they were going to get sand in places they didn't know they had. I don't even sit in the sand at the beach.* We had been in cooler areas in the mountains and the temperature being so warm there was almost a shock to our systems. There were also people there with snowboards "surfing" down the sand dunes. Wow, who would have ever thought riding a wave of sand would work? Although this place was definitely something to see, it was not the beach as far as we were concerned and we didn't stay there very long. We were glad we checked it out but we had other stuff to see.

Santa Fe, New Mexico was not too far away and we decided to get a room there for the night. Santa Fe has a lot of history, arts, crafts and other things to see. San Miguel Church is located there, it is the oldest church in the U.S. The Santa Fe Trail and the old Route 66 also pass through the area. Our room was close to downtown and we were able to walk around and see most of the things there. One of the most interesting things we saw was a deer skull with antlers in a store window. The skull was covered with silver and it was beautiful. It made us think of our grandson, Kyle. He has dipped deer skulls in various paints and they look great. We took a picture and sent it to him.

There were lots of shops with pottery and silver/turquoise or beaded jewelry displayed in the windows. There were also shops that had bronze sculptures on display. I had Roy take a picture of me in front of a huge sculpture of an elk that was sitting outside on the sidewalk. I couldn't begin to imagine where to put something like that. It was huge, so lifelike and so detailed, the artist was very talented. I could have gotten lost in just admiring all the artists' works and the displays.

There was a group of Native Americans in the town square singing and playing a drum. The songs they were singing were Native American songs and we didn't understand anything about them, but the singers were amazing to watch. It was awesome to see younger individuals participating in the singing and helping to preserve the culture. *We would find later that around the Santa Fe area, Pueblos are the local Native American tribe.* We made it back to the room after walking around for a couple of hours, it was cool and quiet and we got a really good night's sleep.

June 16, 2021 - After leaving Santa Fe we drove east toward Texas. We saw lots of windmills used to generate electricity, we don't have them back home and we were in awe of the number of windmills there. We stopped in Amarillo and ate at "The Big Texan". We didn't make Amarillo by morning but we did get there in time for a late lunch. The food was excellent and the atmosphere was great. Their claim to fame was the "72-ounce steak". If you can eat the shrimp cocktail, salad, steak, baked potato and roll within one hour it is free. I bet our grandsons, Kyle and Cody, could eat the meal without a problem (if they were not too picky about the food). We saw this place on the Travel Channel some time ago and thought it would be neat to eat there. The place is huge and they move people through quickly. After eating lunch, we were back on the road. The temperature was 100 degrees going across Texas and Oklahoma. We were sure glad the air conditioner on the truck was working! We went from one extreme to the other with these temperatures.

It was still 85 degrees when we got to the campground in Ft. Smith, Arkansas. Thank goodness for the fan Roy had rigged up in the camper part of the truck. It ran all night. We were close to an airport, apparently in the flight pattern. We thought they were landing on us a couple of times. But at least we didn't hear any planes after 10:00 p.m. We slept without cover until early morning then covered with a sheet. The temperature dropped into the 70's by morning. We got up, made coffee and left for home. We decided since there were several things to do in connection with selling our duplex, we would cut the trip short and go on home. Besides, we had thought of going to Big Bend National Park in south Texas and with the temperature being 100 degrees yesterday it would only be hotter further south. Big Bend would have to wait.

June 17, 2021 - The duplex closing is Friday, 6/18 at 4:00 p.m. We were so glad to be closing that chapter of our lives. We have both put in a lot of work at the duplex over the years. Roy's not going to miss those calls that say the heat pump is not working on Superbowl Sunday, the water heater is leaking, or the toilet is stopped up and we were out of state. When we were in Washington state on this trip, we got a call about the toilet and had to get our son, Aaron, to go fix the issue. We left Ft. Smith driving I-40 to Nashville then I-65 North. We were 63 miles from home, (just north of Nashville on I-65) when there was a traffic accident that stopped us for two hours. *No buffalo this time.* We finally got home around 5:00 p.m. I couldn't believe we traveled all those miles and the only place we were delayed, other than by buffalo in Yellowstone, was this close to home. *Go figure.*

We traveled through 18 states on this trip: Indiana, Illinois, Missouri, Iowa, South Dakota, Montana, Idaho, Wyoming, Washington, Oregon, Nevada, Utah, Colorado, New Mexico, Texas, Oklahoma, Arkansas and Tennessee. Together we have seen 37 states, only 13 more to go. We also saw 8 national parks on this trip: Badlands, Yellowstone, Glacier, Mt. Rainer, Crater Lake, Grand Tetons, Rocky Mountains and Sand Dunes. Mileage for this trip was 7257 miles.

"The mountains are calling,
and I must go." - John Muir

Chapter 16 - Couch to Katahdin

In July 2021, Roy came up with the idea of skipping ahead on the trail to Baxter State Park in Maine and hiking Mt. Katahdin. Katahdin is 5268 feet in elevation and is the highest mountain in Maine. It is the northern terminus of the AT and is considered to be an extremely difficult hike. To hike the AT, you must start (or end) at the top of the mountain. *Again, the trail starts at the top.* On the way up or down you must hike the Hunt Trail because it is the AT. There are other trails leading to the top, one of them is called the Knife Edge Trail. There are portions of this trail only four feet wide with two thousand feet drops on either side. No thank you, if this was the only way to complete the AT, I wouldn't do it. I have a healthy fear of heights thank you very much. I'm not sure I could even crawl on that trail and luckily the Hunt Trail was the required path up or down the mountain. We booked our flight from Nashville, Tennessee to Bangor, Maine, reserved three nights and shuttles to and from Katahdin at the Wilderness Edge Campground in Millinocket. We would climb Mt. Katahdin July 27, 2021.

On July 20th, I received a call from my sister. She was following the ambulance to the hospital; her husband had collapsed at home and she had called 911. Roy and I went to Bowling Green to the hospital, they would not allow us to go in due to Covid. We waited in the parking lot for what seemed like hours. My Sister spoke with the multiple Doctors who were attending to my brother-in-law. I was finally able to talk to her later after we had gone home. Her husband was in CCU and on a ventilator, visitors were allowed but had to wear a mask. I went to the hospital the next morning. After I got back home Roy and I discussed our return to the trail and I told him I just could not leave with my brother-in-law in the hospital. I didn't feel good about the outcome of his condition and I felt I really needed to be there for my sister. I had purchased protection for our reservation at the Wilderness Edge Campground, if we canceled for any reason we could reschedule at a later date. I called and canceled our reservation at the campground, the shuttles, our flights and the reservation to climb Mt. Katahdin. The mountain wasn't going anywhere, we would go when I felt better about leaving.

I went to the hospital several times over the next two weeks. I spent a lot of time talking with my sister about her husband's condition. His prognosis was very poor. He didn't regain consciousness and attempts to wean him from the ventilator had not been successful. She ultimately made the difficult decision to withdraw life support. A week or so after the funeral we resumed our plan to hike Katahdin. I hated leaving my sister at this point but I really didn't know what else to do. I would call her as often as I could and I would send her updates on our location through GPS in the FarOut app. *The app allows you to use text to send your coordinates and a link to maps. The recipient of your text can pinpoint exactly where you are. We didn't use the app the first time we hiked on the AT, but I felt it would be beneficial especially since we were going to be in even more remote areas than before.*

August 14, 2021 - After a long hiatus we were going back to the trail. We rebooked the flight, campground, shuttles and Baxter State Park-Katahdin reservations. Our son in law, Jamie took us to the airport in Nashville to catch a 7:30 a.m. flight to Bangor, Maine. We got up at 3:30 a.m. for the trip to Nashville. Our flight had a layover of a little over an hour in Atlanta then we caught the flight to Bangor. We arrived in Bangor at 1:30 p.m. eastern time. We hiked from the airport to the bus station, about 0.6 miles, with our backpacks on. The bus wasn't scheduled to leave for Medway, Maine until 5:30 p.m. We ate at the Wendy's next door to the bus station and waited while it rained. We walked to a nearby shopping center to look for camp fuel. *You cannot take the fuel canisters on a plane even in your checked baggage.* No luck, we would have to find it somewhere else.

The bus was about ten minutes late and after waiting for another bus to arrive, we finally departed about 6:00 p.m. I remembered reading somewhere to never get in a hurry or expect anything to be on time when traveling this route. I called the campground to let them know we would not get to Medway by 6:40 p.m. as scheduled since I had a shuttle arranged to pick us up at that time. We were instructed to call when we arrived. We got to

90

Medway around 7:00 p.m. and called for the shuttle. We finally got to the Wilderness Edge Campground near Millinocket about 7:30 p.m. By the time we checked in, got to our campsite and set up our tent it was 8:30 p.m. We ate some Doritos and shared a 24-ounce Miller Lite. The campground was really nice, shady and quiet after 10:00 p.m. We crawled in the tent, exhausted after a long day of traveling.

August 15, 2021 - We got up around 6:00 a.m. and walked to Millinocket, about a mile away, to get camp fuel. There was a general store and they had almost everything a hiker might need. We spent a quiet day at the campground planning our hike to Mt. Katahdin. It seemed really odd to have no car, nowhere to go and nothing to do. *We knew we would pay for this day of leisure the next day.* Our plan was to leave the campground for Katahdin at 5:30 a.m.

August 16, 2021 - We were at the campground office at 5:30 a.m. as scheduled but our shuttle driver was not. At about 5:45 a.m. I called to see where she was, she had overslept. When she arrived, it was apparent she had a horrible cold or something going on. Her nose was running non-stop and she was coughing occasionally. She said it was allergies but we were a little concerned about Covid, but she said she really felt okay other than having a runny nose. *Ugh! I hoped we didn't get contaminated with whatever she had.* We finally got on the road around 6:30 a.m. After we arrived at the Katahdin Stream campground, we went to the Ranger's Station and signed in. After going through all the planning of hiking and traveling to Katahdin we finally started the hike around 8:00 a.m.

We could see Katahdin from a distance and it looked like we would be climbing to the top of the world. The top of the mountain was much higher than anything around. The first mile and a half of the Hunt Trail was relatively easy. The farther the trail went, the more difficult it became. The trail gradually faded away and it became a rock scramble. There was no way to "hike" up Katahdin. We put away our trekking poles as they were of no use. As if the trail was not difficult enough, there were areas where rebar had been put into the rocks to allow for climbing. The rebar was not the most user friendly, but it did help. We also had to grab rocks and pull to get up, so we put on vinyl mechanic's gloves to protect our hands from the rocks. Thank goodness we had them, they also helped to be able to grip more firmly as we were climbing. We had our backpacks on but we only carried the essentials. Our packs were less than 8 pounds each and over half of that was water. I don't think I could have climbed Katahdin with a full backpack. After a multitude of false summits, we reached Thoreau Spring and I thought we were at the top. Nope, the top is still up and over another whole rock slide and across the mountain a long way. We finally reached the top of Mt. Katahdin about 2:00 p.m. Some other hikers offered to take our pictures at the Katahdin sign and we swapped taking pics with them. There were several hikers there who were finishing their hike. We could only imagine how great it must feel to complete the entire trail. We sat down and ate a snack but only stayed maybe fifteen minutes at the top. If the trip up was bad, the trip down was far worse. Much like going down to the Nantahala Outdoor Center in North Carolina, but instead of an hour to get down it was more like six and a half hours to get down. Katahdin was one rock slide after another, this was not hiking as we knew it!

The day we hiked Mt. Katahdin, Roy didn't feel well. He said his throat was sore and he drank water like it was going out of style. He sweated profusely and I feared he was diluting his electrolytes with too much water. He didn't feel well for several days when we first started hiking in Maine. We were a mile or so away from getting back to the parking lot where we were dropped off and Roy took a hard fall. He hit his knee and scraped it up terribly, but as usual he brushed it off, said he was fine and went on. *That's him.* Earlier I twisted my right knee coming down the mountain in a place where there was rebar and it was nagging a bit. *Dang it, that was my good knee.*

We arrived at the parking lot around 8:30 p.m. and we had to use our headlamps for approximately the last half mile because it was dark. *When I first booked our trip, I told them to allow us twelve hours to hike Katahdin because we knew we would be really slow. We read somewhere the average time to hike Katahdin* was eight to twelve hours. We knew we had spent too much time on the couch to hike Katahdin with any speed. The guy said, "That would put you coming down after dark, no one comes down after dark." Well, they do now! We felt confident we would hold some sort of record for the longest time to hike Katahdin. When we arrived at the parking lot we were relieved to see Kyle from the Wilderness Edge Campground waiting for us. Thank goodness he was there. We were so glad to see him. We crawled in the vehicle thoroughly exhausted. When we got back to the campground it was 9:30 p.m.

We were both more than exhausted. Earlier in the day we had grandiose delusions about taking a shower and even going to Millinocket to get something to eat. Before we finished the trip down the mountain, we knew there was no way that was going to happen. Roy looked like he was about to fall over and I'm sure I didn't look any better. We were both pretty beaten up. We crawled in the tent, ate a few bites of food and drank some water. I cleaned up his knee where he had fallen and put a bandage on it. He had also banged his left big toe pretty badly and the nail was blue. I told him he would probably lose the toenail and he said he probably wouldn't. *He later did lose the nail and it just had grown out before we started the last leg of our AT journey in February of 2022.* We had planned on starting the trail southbound the next day but we quickly decided we should postpone and take a zero day to rest. *Big lesson learned, hiking the ten miles roundtrip at Katahdin is not to be taken lightly and you shouldn't go from the couch to Katahdin.* But at least it was done and now we could cross it off the list. I don't know if it would have been any better if we hiked it at the end of the trail and finished at the top. The hike up Katahdin would be brutal anyway you looked at it.

*"We must embrace pain and burn it as fuel
for our journey." - Kenji Miyazawa*

Chapter 17 - The 100 Mile Wilderness

August 17, 2021 - The folks at the campground were not surprised when we showed up at the office the next morning asking to reschedule our shuttle and stay at the campsite one more night. We were simply too exhausted to start the trail. Roy must have been as sore and tired as I was since it didn't take much to convince him to take the day off before heading southbound through the 100 Mile Wilderness. We stayed at our campsite most of the day. We ordered pizza and a 2-liter of Pepsi, had it delivered to the campground and ate the whole thing. We got Gatorade at the camp office and drank plenty of other liquids to ensure we were well hydrated. There was a couple from Wisconsin staying in a large camper in a campsite near us. The guy talked with us and offered to take us to town if we needed anything. *We must have looked pretty rough.* He also came over at supper and offered to bring us food his wife had cooked since they had extra. We thanked him for his kindness but we had already eaten a whole pizza.

We found two pairs of Darn Tough socks that had been left at a campsite near ours. They were lying on a rock; someone had probably placed them there to dry then accidently left them. We asked at the office if they would call anyone who left things at the campground. They said if the socks were still there when they came through to check on things, they would just throw them away. *Maybe they didn't know these were expensive socks.* We went back to the campsite and I put the socks in a Ziploc bag. I told Roy I would keep them and rinse them out and wash them the next time we did laundry. *Finding those two pairs of socks was like finding forty dollars. These socks are really popular on the trail because of the lifetime guarantee.*

August 18, 2021 - We left Millinocket at 8:15 a.m. with Kyle, our shuttle driver. He took us to the Katahdin Stream Campground where we started hiking to Katahdin the day before. From there the AT went southbound out of Baxter State Park and then into the 100 Mile Wilderness. We hiked 10 miles to Abol Pines Campground. The hike was fairly flat and very easy compared to what we had experienced thus far in Maine. The weather was nice, the hike was pleasant and the trail wound around large trees and gently rolling terrain. The campground near Abol Bridge was beside the Penobscot River. *The only Penobscot I had ever heard of was Margaret Houlihan's husband Donald Penobscot on M*A*S*H. Lol!* The river was pretty and flowed by quietly. There was some very light rain that afternoon. We ate our first Mountain House meal. *Mountain House is a brand of dehydrated food which can be found at many places along the trail, it's even sold at Wal Mart. I had ordered two weeks' worth of dehydrated meals in preparation for hiking through the 100 Mile Wilderness since it's lightweight and easily packed.* We slept well that night after we got settled in our tent.

August 19, 2021 - We started into the 100 Mile Wilderness after crossing Abol Bridge and hiked 11.5 miles to the Rainbow Springs Campsite beside Rainbow Lake. We saw a trail that apparently went to a hunting or fishing camp nearby and we heard and saw float planes coming and going. Rainbow Springs ran into the lake and there was a pipe from which to get water. It was cold clear spring water and we drank our fill of water through our filter. It tasted as good as it looked. We sat at the lake for a while and soaked our feet while we continued to hydrate. The hike was exhausting and the weather was warm. It was nice to cool off at the lake before we settled in for the night. We thought the unspoiled beauty of the lake was unusual. It was really quiet, except for the occasional float plane. There were no houses and no boats on the lake, certainly not like our lake at home. This was just the beginning of the beautiful sights we would see on this journey.

August 20, 2021 - The weather was HOT. Hiking was laborious to say the least. Roy sweats so much and drinks so much water I am concerned about him. He pushes so hard and I'm afraid he won't say anything even if he is really sick. I know he is not feeling well. I seem to be holding up a little better right now.

A woman called Marmot was on the trail today, she told us about ALDHA (Appalachian Long Distance Hikers Association) in Abingdon, Virginia. She told us about the Trail Days celebration like Damascus, Virginia but their celebration has apparently less of a party atmosphere. We crossed over Rainbow Ledges and ate handfuls of ripe blueberries and huckleberries around lunchtime. They were so sweet and good. We camped at Crescent Pond and went for a swim in our underwear to cool off and wash off the sweat from hiking before crawling in the tent.

August 21, 2021 - We were both a bit tired and only hiked 7 miles. We met some interesting people on the trail. We met Buttercup, she was 73 years old and she started the trail four months ago at Harper's Ferry, West Virginia. Her husband was scheduled to meet her at Katahdin Stream campground. We also met Swamp Thing and Sugar Babe; they were from Mississippi. They are close to our ages and they have completed about 1500 miles of the trail. We really enjoyed talking with them and told them to be sure and get some blueberries at Rainbow Ledges. They were going northbound (NOBO) and we were headed southbound (SOBO), too bad we were not heading the same direction. We arrived at Nahmakanta Lake in the early afternoon and were pleasantly surprised to see another cool, clear, serene body of water.

We talked to some other hikers on the trail who told us about trail magic 0.3 miles up the trail from the lake. We dropped our packs at out campsite and decided to go find it. A guy was at the parking area and he was running support for his wife who was hiking the AT, but he was also providing trail magic. He had a Yeti cooler full of cold drinks of all sorts, chips and Dunkin Donuts. *Can you believe it, Roy didn't get a donut. I knew then he was not feeling well.* I got a Powerade, Roy got a bottle of Gatorade, and we both got a bag of chips. When we got back to the lake we went for a swim, the water was so clear you could stand chest deep in the water and clearly see your feet. The water was crystal clear and the reflections of the sky and clouds on the water were absolutely beautiful, it looked like a postcard picture. We used soap and shampoo and took a lake bath which was far better than no bath. We camped in our tent near the beach. When we saw the beach, we were in love! There were two old chairs, a small table between them and a fire ring built of rocks on the beach looking out over the water. There was a colorful sunset that evening and even though we were tired we thoroughly enjoyed the swim and sitting in the chairs just admiring the sunset.

August 22. 2021 - On the trail that day we met Halt, Go and 65 from South Carolina who were going NOBO. Some of these trail names were really funny. We have only seen one SOBO hiker and she blew past us like we were sitting still. We hiked 11 miles and camped at Antler's Campsites on Jo Mary Lake. It was a little cooler and the wind was blowing, the waves on the lake were lapping at the shoreline. It was not a good time for a swim.

When we arrived at the campsites we met Factoid, she was from Louisiana. She loved to play trivia, therefore the trail name. She had a whole cheese pizza out here in the middle of nowhere and she offered to share. *It was cold of course but who cares, it was pizza. She had apparently arranged for a resupply part of the way through the 100 Mile Wilderness and the pizza was part of the delivery. Years ago, there was no way to arrange for resupply in the 100 Mile Wilderness. It's still limited but possible now. However, we carried all our stuff without arranging for supplies to be brought to us.*

We saw a view of Katahdin from the trail, the visibility was good and even from this distance Katahdin still looked like the biggest thing around. We have hiked 56 miles in the past week, including the hike up Katahdin. *Not too bad for week one in this terrain. Hopefully we can build up to more miles each day as we go but I'm not going to hold my breath.*

August 23, 2021 - It was raining when we broke camp and was misty most of the morning. We saw several people on the trail, most were headed NOBO and would be finishing their hikes soon. A couple from New Mexico passed us on the trail going SOBO. They climbed Katahdin on 8/19 (three days after us). They wanted to get to Vermont in time to see the leaves turning. *I thought they had a good chance of making it, but I didn't think we would get that far soon enough to see the leaves.* We camped at Crawford Pond Beach after hiking 11.15 miles, it started to lightly rain again as we were setting up for the evening. *At least the rain brought much welcomed cooler air with it. It has been more than hot for the the past few days. We found out later the rain was compliments of hurricane Henri.*

August 24, 2021 - We hiked from Crawford Pond to Logan Brook, approximately 9 miles nearly all uphill. We hiked 800 feet up Boardman Mountain that morning. I had a good cell signal at the top of the mountain so I called my sister. She was glad to hear from us and I felt better after checking on her. That afternoon we climbed 1200 feet up. We were both pretty tired that evening and we found a campsite near a stream that had ice cold water. We sat for a while on rocks at the stream and it felt like air conditioning. It was a very welcomed relief after being hot all day.

August 25, 2021 - We hiked up White Cap Mountain and picked blueberries again and they were really good. White Cap was the highest mountain between Katahdin and the town of Monson, Maine. The view from the top at 3644 feet was awesome. We hiked down the south side and camped at the Carl Newhall Lean To Tent Sites. There was a cold stream nearby and we sat with our feet in the water for a while. We packed six liters of water (3 liters each) with us up and over White Cap Mountain since there was no water for 7 miles and it was hot weather. *During our early hiking career, we got in a situation with lack of water on our first hiking trip at Sal Hollow. We sure didn't want to do that again! Besides, all our food was dehydrated and we had to have water in order to even eat.* We hiked 7.2 miles but they were very hard miles. Roy was still drinking a lot of water and we didn't have any electrolyte powder to add to the water. He finally had agreed to eat some of the salt packets we had on hand. *Apparently, it made him feel a little better since he asked for them several times after I convinced him to try it the first time. I do think lack of sodium may have contributed to him not feeling well.*

August 26, 2021 - Hiking was fairly easy the first part of the day. We stopped and changed from our trail shoes to our Crocs before we crossed the Pleasant River. It was a wide shallow river, even though the water was not very swift we had to be careful not to slip and fall on the rocks. When we got across the river there was a Post-It note tacked on a log with a message about trail magic at the parking lot 0.2 miles away. We dropped our backpacks beside the trail and headed that way. Along the trail to the parking lot every 20 yards or so there was another note, they all had cute little messages on them directing you to the trail magic. Things like, "You won't be disappointed" or "Can you smell them yet?" were written on the notes. When we got to the parking lot there was Herder, an older hiker, and his wife who loved to provide trail magic for the AT hikers. He was grilling hot dogs, and had chips, watermelon, Gatorade and Coors Lite. He asked if we had ever had a Red Snapper. We told him we had the fish Red Snapper, but Maine Red Snappers, were the red hot dogs he was grilling. They were good and the casing on them did snap when you bit into the hot dog. We sat down, ate and talked for a while and really enjoyed their hospitality for about an hour. *This was probably the longest lunch break we had on the entire trail and it was time well spent.* Herder was inviting everyone to a big party at his place near Grafton Notch on Labor Day. We didn't think there was any way we would be anywhere near there by Labor Day. We were just not that fast. To tell them thank you didn't seem like enough to let them know how much we appreciated the trail magic. A few of the hikers we had been seeing off and on also took advantage of the trail magic. Word traveled fast on the trail especially when trail magic like this was involved.

After the trail magic we hiked a big uphill, it was a good thing we fueled up. We camped on the side of a mountain; we made our own stealth campsite in a stand of small pine trees not far off the trail. The day had been very hot and we hiked 8.47 miles. We had two one-liter bottles of water to last until morning.

August 27, 2021 - *Happy Birthday to our daughter Jennifer!* We left camp with one bottle of water to last 3 miles to the next water source, not a problem. *After what we experienced with lack of water on our first hiking trip ever, we would usually carry four liters of water between us and really get concerned when down to one liter. Using the FarOut app, we were able to find water sources, shelters, roads, towns, and other landmarks. The app has more information than I knew how to use, but I became more adept at using it as we went and it became invaluable. I don't know how hikers made it on the trail years ago before cell phones and GPS.*

When we hiked the trail in 2020, we used the Awol Guide, a paperback book with all the same information as the app and there were a lot more hikers on the trail with which to share information. I purchased the app and downloaded it to my phone before we left for Maine. Roy still carried the 2020 paper version in case my phone went dead. The only thing that usually changes in these books is some of the hostels, shuttles or other services and their contact information.

We hiked over all four of the Chair Back mountains, it was a long day with a lot of uphill climbs. We had to put up our trekking poles and get out our climbing gloves twice. We were exhausted and not able to find a place to camp. We finally pitched our tent in the only tiny flat spot we could find which was right beside the trail. The space was barely big enough to set the tent. We can normally climb out either side of the tent but this time one side was set up against a tree so we climbed in and out the one side. This was creative tenting at its finest! *We would later figure out using one side was no big deal and would use one side often.* There was only one hiker that passed us after we set up the tent and I'm sure he thought we were crazy. But when you are tired and can't go any further you do what you have to do. We only hiked 6.3 miles but boy were they tough ones. We have hiked 98.4 miles on this trip so far, it feels like we have hiked 1000 already! Lord, help us get through this 100-mile wilderness.

August 28, 2021 - We only hiked 6 miles, stopped early and set up camp to rest and relax. My right knee, my good knee, has been giving me trouble since Katahdin and was really bad on this day. I had my knee taped with KT tape and also put on a knee sleeve over the tape. Having the knee support helped but it was still hurting pretty badly. I was hoping a shorter hiking day, rest and medication would help. *I would take Vitamin I (Ibuprofen) for several days and continue the regimen of supporting my knee with KT tape and the knee sleeve. Thankfully it gradually got better.* We had hiked most of the day downhill and the downhill seemed to be worse on the knees. The biggest mountains of the 100 Mile Wilderness were behind us even though there were more mountains to come. We crossed over Barren Mountain today and the views were fantastic. Barren made us think of Barren County back home and how it was so far away.

We have been seeing moose poop all over the place, but no moose. *It's funny, the moose always poop at the edge of the trail and not in the middle. I guess they are considerate of hikers, lol! We would like to see a moose in the wild, but much like bears, not too close. Apparently, they can be mean and can charge a person unpredictably. They not only hit a person with their head and antlers, they also rear up and paw them with their front hooves. It sounds like they can actually be as aggressive, if not more so, than bears.* We have heard other hikers talk about seeing moose on the trail. If the poop is any indication, we should run across one sooner or later.

Chipmunks however are thriving in Maine. We hear and see them everywhere. They have become somewhat of an alarm clock for us. Every morning, about the time we are ready to get up we hear a chipmunk call that is loud and nearby. A couple of times we thought one of them had to be sitting on top of our tent. *I guess they are waking their chipmunk buddies and telling them it's time to start their day too.* Beavers are doing well also, we saw a huge area where trees were downed by beavers, the area was completely devastated. Huge trees were gnawed at thigh high; those beavers must have been as big as German Shepherds. *It's amazing what a creature can actually accomplish with their teeth!*

Thankfully the weather was much cooler today which made hiking more pleasant. We were both very hungry and ate double portions of Mountain House meals for supper. *Maybe the hiker-hunger is starting to kick in.*

August 29, 2021 - We hiked 8.3 miles from Long Pond Stream to Little Wilson Falls. Over lots of ledges and cliffs today. We camped only 6.8 miles from Monson and the end of the 100 Mile Wilderness. *It feels as though it has taken forever to get this far. I for one will be glad to complete this section of the trail.*

August 30, 2021 - We made it through the 100 Mile Wilderness and we looked rough! The last 6.8 miles were exhausting, the trail just never gave us a break. We heard road noise for miles and kept thinking the finish was just around the next turn. We were exhausted and ready for some real food, a shower and a real bed. We finally made it to the road after we had just about given up. When we got to the road, we met Cornbread and her dog Boo. She offered us a ride to town and we gladly accepted. Her dog Boo was an old dog who reluctantly shared the car ride with us. We had her drop us in the middle of town, I didn't have any small bills to pay her so I gave her all the change I had which was over three dollars and she was happy to get it, I don't know why I had carried it, I should have gotten rid of the extra weight before hiking through the 100 Mile Wilderness. We walked to the local gas station. they reportedly had good pizza according to the trail grapevine. *The towns in Maine have gas stations that are the general grocery, deli, grill, pizza parlor and they sell beer and wine. They are also frequently the only place to get supplies for the trail.* Our large pizza was made to order while we waited outside with our packs at a picnic table. The pizza was hot and good and we ate the whole thing.

"For hiking is one of those things you can only do when you have the determination in you." - Unknown

Chapter 18 - Back to Civilization (Temporarily)

After filling up on pizza we walked to the Shaw's Hiker Hostel. All places to stay for the night in town were either full or closed due to Covid. We were able to get one of the last tent spots in the yard at Shaw's. This hostel is a popular place with hikers. It was also in the movie, A Walk in the Woods. We had seen the movie starring Robert Redford and Nick Nolte. There were a couple of places we remembered seeing in the movie. Most of the hikers staying at Shaw's are a younger crowd that enjoy partying, we just wanted a shower and someplace to sleep after not showering since we left the Wilderness Edge Campground twelve days ago. We had swum in a lake, a pond and had washed our hair, arms and legs in creeks, and taken baby wipe baths, but it wasn't like taking a shower. *This would be remembered as the longest we went without a shower for the entire trail.* We took showers and in doing so took extra time to enjoy the hot water. Thankfully the water heater in the shower house was huge. I had to shampoo my hair three times to get it clean. We saw several hikers we had seen on the trail, most of them were staying two or three days at Shaw's to enjoy the party atmosphere. There were hikers in the yard who stayed up until 10:00 p.m. talking and having a good time. We just wanted to rest. But as soon as it was quiet time everyone settled and we had a fairly quiet night.

August 31, 2021 - Shaw's was also supposed to have one of the best breakfasts on the trail. We were told we would need to sign up to eat breakfast and we had done so in the main house the night before. As luck would have it, the breakfast was canceled. Apparently one of the workers there tested positive for Covid and they were shutting the breakfast down. *Here we go again, Covid sucking the fun out of everything!*

There were several buildings on the property. The main house, a shower house, bunkhouse and an outfitter building. We went to check out the supply options available at the outfitter building. Shaw's and the gas station were our best options for resupply. We found Shaw's to have everything a hiker might need. *A hiker's diet is limited to what he or she is willing to carry.* Dehydrated meals were expensive and we had eaten them through the 100 Mile Wilderness. We were ready for some different food but options were still limited.

Roy's appetite was not good when we were hiking. He said the tight strap around his middle upset his gastrointestinal system. He is also a picky eater and didn't like a lot of the stuff. I kept encouraging him to eat because he needed the fuel. He ate well when we were in town and when back on the trail would have to drop his pack and head for the woods. I didn't have as much of a problem with that as he did. My appetite was not the best but it was better than his. We both were rapidly losing weight, but at this point we still had plenty to spare.

We saw an antique store in Monson called Lily Cat Antiques and it made us think of our granddaughter Lily. *I was really starting to miss home and this was just a little reminder of what we left behind while hiking.* I took a picture of the sign so we could send it to her.

We stopped at the Monson A.T. Visitor Center. The building was closed due to Covid. There was a table set across the doorway at the entry and we were able to talk to the staff and pick up an AT tag for 2021. Normally we would have been able to tour the center but as usual Covid was continuing to impact things.

We were lucky enough to get a room at the Lakeshore House in the middle of Monson. We couldn't get a room the night before because they were booked. They had just recently re-opened, they had also been closed due to an employee testing positive for Covid. The Lakeshore House was a beautiful old house with a lot of charm. The place was owned and operated by a nice younger couple. The house was located on the shore of a large lake. There were several houses around this particular lake and it was a beautiful site. The Lakeshore House also had a restaurant in the back with tables inside or outside overlooking the lake. We checked into our room then concentrated on preparing to return to the trail the next day. We also made calls and checked on everyone back home.

Between Shaw's and the gas station we were able to find all the supply items we wanted. We purchased tuna packets, pepperoni, nabs, ramen noodles, oatmeal packets, breakfast bars, candy bars, Ritz crackers, fruit chews, Gatorade powder and electrolyte tablets. *We would not be without the electrolyte supplements again. They are very important when hiking in warmer temperatures, but we decided we liked them also for the flavor and we would always carry them in the future.* We only needed supplies for three or four days. Our next town would be Caratunk.

We ate dinner in the Lakeshore House restaurant. *Wait for it . . . I had a cheese burger and fries. It was good, but it had a way to go to measure up to the Kountry Kitchen or the NOC burgers.* We met Annie the dog and her owner Oakley. The dog was a golden retriever mix and was very well behaved. Annie was a little bitty girl.She was having issues with her knee and was taking a couple of days off. We had a room all to ourselves for the first time since Katahdin. It felt good to be able to stretch out in the bed instead of the close quarters of the tent. This was the first time we slept in a bed since we left home two weeks ago.

September 1, 2021 - I took advantage of the shower again before going back to the trail that morning. *Wow a shower three days in a row!* The owner of the Lakeshore House gave us a ride back to the trail. We started hiking about 8:30 a.m. and hiked 10.54 miles before stopping about 4:30 p.m. The trail was much easier than the trail before Monson and we hiked beside a stream for most of the day. The weather was sunny and pleasant. I talked to my brother, Steve, before we left Monson. His birthday is Sept 2 and I was not sure I would have cell service. I also ordered a birthday present for our granddaughter, Autumn, she will be sixteen on Sept 10. *The present would be delivered on Sept 9. I hated that we were missing her birthday party this year. This is an important milestone for a young lady and I can't hardly believe she is already sixteen.* We enjoyed a couple of days in civilization and checked on everyone back home, it was time to go back to the woods.

"A smooth sea never made a smooth sailor."
- Franklin D. Roosevelt

Chapter 19 - Rain, Rain, Go Away

September 2, 2021 - *Happy Birthday to my brother Steve!* We were awakened by the rain about 5:00 a.m. We got out of the tent and were hiking by about 7:30 a.m. It was cooler and there were lots of puddles on the trail. At least the rain didn't continue but the woods were wet and when the trees are wet it seems that water drips for hours after the rain stops. We camped near a stream after hiking about 8 miles. We stopped early so we would have time to dry the tent. There was a fantastic view of Bald Mountain Pond from our campsite.

September 3, 2021 - We were awakened again by rain about 6:00 a.m. After the rain stopped, we hiked most of the morning with it being overcast and cooler. The cooler temperature was a much-welcomed relief from the heat over the past several days. We stopped twice in the afternoon and put on our rain jackets during rain showers. We hiked 9.69 miles up and over Moxie Bald and found a stealth campsite 1.3 miles from Middle Mountain about 4:00 p.m. *A stealth site is a place where you camp, not an official campsite or near a shelter. It's a flat spot near the trail where someone may have camped before. If you are too tired to push on to a shelter or campsite a stealth site is an option. The main thing about stealth camping, or any camping for that matter, is to leave no trace. The shelters on the AT are located approximately a day's hike apart, but sometimes we would get out of sync with making it to the shelters and this was one of those times. We actually seemed to be out of sync a lot with making it to the next shelter and we stealth camped a lot in Maine.* It was cooler and we were glad to crawl into the tent after eating supper. We stayed toasty warm that night. Our tent had served us well thus far.

September 4, 2021 - We hiked 9.1 miles and arrived in Caratunk. Hiking today was mostly downhill and it didn't seem like we would ever cover the last two miles. Caratunk was near the Kennebec River and of course it had to be downhill. Anytime we got near a river it would be at a significantly lower elevation. Caratunk was at 573 feet elevation and in the middle of nowhere. The "town" was nowhere near a town as we know it. There were a few houses along the road and a couple of stop signs. There were no stores, no gas stations, no phone signal, but there was a courtesy phone at a building behind the post office. *Had it not been for the FarOut app we would have never found the phone.* We made a few phone calls and discovered we couldn't get a room for the night, but a tent site was available at the Three Rivers Campground. We did get a reservation for a room at the Sterling Inn the following night.

We were able to get a ride to Three Rivers and set up our tent at what was supposed to be one of their last available tent sites. At least there was a shower house and we took much needed showers before going to eat at the Three Rivers restaurant. I had a Reuben sandwich and Roy had barbecue. *Can you believe I passed on the burger this time?*

Three Rivers was one of the whitewater rafting outfitters in Maine and there was a huge group of rafting folks who were there for a big rafting weekend. *No wonder the campground and lodging there were full.* Outside the restaurant a firepit provided warmth in the cool evening. It was unique to see a fire built with split wood about four feet in length and propped upright. It made a beautiful fire and there was a huge group of people taking advantage of the fire. A live band was playing and everyone seemed to be enjoying themselves.

Normally we would have been happy to listen to the music and have a drink or two but Roy and I didn't quite share their enthusiasm that night. *9:00 p.m. is considered hikers midnight. After a long day of hiking, 9:00 p.m. is about the limit, for us bedtime was usually much sooner.* The band played until midnight and even though we had gone to our tent much earlier, the music was still loud enough to keep us awake. At least we didn't have to hike the next day. We were definitely looking forward to getting a room, and some peace and quiet the next night.

September 5, 2021 - We broke camp this morning at Three Rivers and The Sterling Inn sent someone to pick us up when we called. The inn was a beautiful place, it had a wrap-around porch with several chairs and benches which beckon you to come sit. The furniture inside was mostly antiques and it was decorated beautifully. The inn was an old hotel with private rooms and shared bathrooms. The staff there was on top of things and after each person showered, they cleaned and put out towels for the next person. It was definitely a step up from any place we had slept for the past few weeks. There was a little store within the building and it had plenty of supply items, they would just add your purchase to the bill for the room. We did our shopping to ensure we had enough food to make it to our next stop. This place caters to hikers and the staff was very friendly and helpful. We took a zero day there and just enjoyed the day to slow down and relax.

The inn had a huge common area with games and a TV. There was no cable and apparently no signal for TV, but there was a large video library with all kinds of movies. *We found out later a lot of the places on the trail were off grid and didn't have cable but did have video libraries.* We played a couple of games of rummy and just hung out for a while. We also ate a pint of ice cream that evening and decided to watch a movie. We had not seen "The Client" with Tommy Lee Jones and Susan Sarandon, it was an older movie but it was really good. We also discovered a soft drink called "Moxie". It tastes a bit like a Dr. Pepper and was apparently a regional favorite. *We would enjoy Moxie a couple of more times while we were in Maine.*

September 6, 2021 - *It's Labor Day.* We left Caratunk and crossed the Kennebec River first thing. It is too dangerous to attempt crossing the river by wading. The water was not extremely deep, but it was swift and was reported to rise quickly at times. The ATC (Appalachian Trail Commission), ALDHA (Appalachian Long Distance Hikers Association) and MATC (Maine Appalachian Trail Club) provided a canoe service to take hikers across the river. At this time of year, the canoe was available to ferry hikers across 9:00 a.m.-2:00 p.m. If you miss the window of opportunity you must wait until the next day or call someone and pay $50 for them to take you across. Thankfully we were there in the early part of the day. A guy named Craig and his golden retriever Maggie took us across in the canoe. It was funny to see a golden that didn't like the water, but Maggie didn't like to get her feet wet. She did however enjoy the ride. *We have a special fondness for goldens since we had our golden, also named Maggie, for thirteen years.* We rode in the canoe across the river with Craig and Maggie and picked up the trail on the other side.

The weather was a lot warmer and sunny today. We passed by Harrison's Pierce Pond Camp. It was supposed to have one of the best pancake breakfasts on the trail and they are very friendly to hikers. It was way too early in the morning to stop and eat pancakes and we had already had breakfast so we opted to continue hiking.

We saw a hiker who was holding up in the Pierce Pond Lean-to waiting for his friends to bring him his tent poles. He had accidentally left them at the last place he camped, fortunately he was able to contact them and they found the poles. He apparently didn't do the idiot check. *An older hiker had told us about the idiot check during our first time on the AT. This was the same woman that called the guy a champion snorer. She said you must always look around before walking away from an area when you are on a trail where you have camped or stopped for any reason just to make sure you are not accidentally leaving anything behind. If you leave something behind you will feel like an idiot, therefore she called it the idiot check. It made perfect sense and we adopted the practice.*

In the afternoon around 3:30 p.m. rain started to move in. We tried to make it to East Carry Pond and got within 0.6 miles before the rain started about 4:30 p.m. We had to quickly find a suitable tent site and did the fastest tent set up we have ever done. *We each have our responsibilities when setting up the tent. We had so much practice we could set up the tent in record time if necessary and this time it was necessary.* Backpacks were thrown in the tent and we jumped in with them just in the nick of time. We blew up the air mattresses, got our sleeping bags out and got ready for the night. We were warm, dry and cozy. We hiked 9.3 miles before the rain stopped us for the evening.

September 7, 2021 - We awakened to the weather being sunny but breezy. The tent was wet from the rain the evening before but our gear was fairly dry. This part of the trail was easy compared to some sections we hiked and we covered 9.81 miles. We camped at Flagstaff Tent Sites on the shore of Flagstaff Lake. The wind was strong and waves were white capping on the lake when we arrived. We dried the tent on a big rock near the lake. We had to stay with it to keep the wind from blowing it into the lake. At the campsite we tied a line up and aired our sleeping bags. The wind settled a bit as it got later in the evening and we hoped for a good night's sleep.

September 8, 2021 - We packed up our tent as we were making coffee. The hiking was a lot of up and down and it was some tough hiking. It was 7.5 miles from Flagstaff Lake to Safford Notch campsites where we decided to stay for the night since it looked to be threatening rain, again. It began to rain shortly after we got the tent set up and it rained all night.

September 9, 2021 - It was drizzling rain when we awakened and it lasted most of the day. It was foggy and dismal but there were rays of sunshine at times. The rain clouds with sunshine made for a beautiful contrast of colors. The different shades of blue were amazing. We hiked 5.3 miles from Safford Notch to Horns Pond which was up and over the Bigelow Mountains, elevation over 4000 feet. When we arrived at Horns Pond we set our tent up on a platform, it started raining again before we got the tent totally set up. Once again, we threw the stuff in the tent and finished the set up with us inside. It rained most of the night.

September 10, 2021 - *Happy 16th birthday to our granddaughter Autumn Grace!* We awoke to our tent being soaking wet but thankfully our sleeping bags were alright. After packing our stuff, we headed for Maine Route 27 which was 5.1 miles away. The plan was to get out of the rain and sleep in a real bed for a couple of nights. The weather was cool and breezy. Rain drizzled a couple of times but nothing too heavy.

We saw a very unusual animal in the woods that morning. Roy said he thought a monkey had gotten loose. It was climbing on a tree, it had a long thick tail and body, it had small eyes and a pointed nose. He saw the face but all I saw was its back and tail as it was running away. *When we had internet service, we googled what kind of mammals were native to the area and found the animal was a fisher. It is sometimes called a fisher cat although it is not in the cat family. It is actually in the weasel family and is closely related to the marten but is much larger. Someone also told us they can be quite aggressive when provoked. The picture we found on the internet was definitely the animal we saw. We sure don't have those in Kentucky and I'm glad he ran the other way.*

We made it to a parking lot at Hwy 27 where there were several hikers waiting on rides. There was a guy providing trail magic of ice cream and beers. We got an ice cream and waited for our ride to the Maine Roadhouse Hostel. Before we got to the hostel the driver explained they were having problems with water. The well water was running low due to drought conditions earlier in the year and less than average snow last winter. *Even though she later told us the snow last winter was deep enough that their dogs had walked over the fenced in backyard. And they didn't get enough snow? Wow, we get two inches of snow in Kentucky and it's a big deal. Their fences in their yard were probably five feet tall!*

They had made arrangements with a local motel in town (Stratton). They would take us there to get showers before going to the hostel. We could do a load of laundry at the hostel since it didn't use as much water as the long showers normally taken by hikers. Stopping for a shower first was alright with us, and we were told they would bring us back for a shower or anything else in town anytime we wanted. The hostel was about 5 miles from town.

We got to the hostel and checked in. It was owned and operated by two ladies, both of them named Jen. Jen and Jen were very helpful and attentive to all the hikers. The rooms had wooden plaques on the doors with pictures and names of birds. *Our room was the "Loon" room and I thought it was appropriate we were given that room! We were, after all, as crazy as loons.* This was their first year running the hostel after working hard to get it remodeled and open. From what we could see they were doing a fantastic job.

That evening we went with a group to a restaurant in Stratton, Back Straps. Roy had a fish sandwich and I had . . . a cheeseburger and fries. One of the Jens had taken six or seven of us to the restaurant and told us to call when we needed a ride back. On the way back from town we saw a female moose at the side of the highway. Jen pulled over to make sure we all got to see it and gave us time to get pictures. *This would come to be the only moose we saw during our hiking in Maine, despite all the moose poop.* We went to bed not long after getting back to the hostel and slept fairly well with both of us in our full-sized bed. It was still as big if not bigger than our bed in the tent.

September 11, 2021 - We hung our stuff out back and set the tent up to dry since it wasn't raining. We found some seam sealer in a hiker box at the hostel and decided to use it on the tent to stop the leaks. *Our tent was leaking because we had to pack it up wet so many times it caused the seams to become unsealed. At times you can find some good stuff in the hiker boxes and the seam sealer was an extremely lucky find.* We used the seam sealer on the tent after it dried with hopes it would help. Thank goodness for a zero day, we needed the rest, our tent sealed and the gear dried, again.

Swamp Thing and Sugar Babe came to the hostel later in the day. We had met them in the 100 Mile Wilderness near Rainbow Ledges and we were thrilled to see them again. We had a really nice time talking with them and found we have a lot in common. They had also endured a ride with Cornbread and her dog Boo, although it was a much longer ride. We told them about the Wilderness Edge Campground when we met them before and they had stayed there when they hiked to Mt. Katahdin after they saw us the first time. We talked about tents, campsites, hostels, people we met on the trail, dogs, family and numerous other things. They were from Jackson, Mississippi and had three grown children and eight grandchildren. They have only about 400 miles left to finish the trail. I hoped we could do as well as they have done, they were truly an inspiration. We could have laughed and talked with them longer that evening but hiker's midnight approached and everyone was ready to turn in for the night.

September 12, 2021 - We left the Maine Roadhouse and got a ride from one of the Jens back to the trail. From Route 27 we hiked over the North and South Crocker Mountains, both over 4000 feet elevation. The uphill was not too bad, but the downhill sections of the trail were brutal. I fell flat on my tail once and hoped I wouldn't be sore the next day. We set up the tent at Crocker Cirque Campsites after hiking 7.4 miles.

September 13, 2021 - There were lots of rocks and roots to contend with on the trail again today. *You literally cannot take your eyes off the trail or you will trip over a rock or a root.* We did lots of climbing in the morning but in the afternoon the trail was better. We hiked over three mountains over 4000 feet elevation, Sugarloaf, Spaulding and Mt. Abraham. Hiking was tough and later in the day we couldn't find a site for our tent, the forest was too thick and there was no level ground. We had to hike about 1.5 miles farther than we planned before we found a grassy stealth campsite, a nice level spot near a brook just when we needed it most. After hiking the 9.45 miles on very rough trails, we were really lucky to find the area at Perham Stream and Barnjum Road. Barnjum Road was an old road that had been abandoned long ago and there were remnants of an old bridge over the stream. We had a flat camping spot and water readily available. We were sorely in need of both.

September 14, 2021 - As usual the trail was rough, there was rock climbing in several places. We hiked over Saddleback Junior Mountain and made it 7.23 miles. Five more miles would have been great, but we had to take our time. We keep reminding ourselves, a major injury could end our hiking careers. A platform at Redington Stream Campsites provided a fantastic place to pitch our tent. We were thankful for the tent platform; we had not seen any suitable places to set a tent and the terrain was rough. *Later we discovered the place we camped the night before was about a mile north of where AT hiker Geraldine Largay got lost in the dense forest and died. She stepped off the AT to use the restroom, lost sight of the trail and was unable to find her way back. I couldn't imagine getting lost in this area of Maine or trying to search for someone lost in these woods. We listened to the audio book, When You Find My Body and were impressed with the scale of the search to find her when she went missing in July of 2013. We could also see how a person could get lost if they got too far away from the trail in this area and the importance of hiking with a partner.*

We saw several moose tracks on trails not far from the campsites, they were huge. I took a picture of one of them compared to my foot. Deer tracks are tiny compared to moose tracks; they are probably ten times bigger. Does that mean moose are ten times bigger? Yikes! I may reconsider wanting to see one of them while on the trail.

September 15, 2021 - We broke camp and hiked 0.7 miles uphill to The Horn Mountain. The weather was absolutely horrible. It was cold, foggy, raining and the wind was gusting to the point it was hard to stand up. We couldn't see a thing of what was supposed to be fantastic views. With the backpacks on the wind was even worse because there was more surface area for the wind to push against. The trail went across The Horn Mountains and stayed above tree line for a couple of miles. I didn't feel comfortable trying to cross over the top of the mountain, Roy would have probably gone on across, he could handle the wind pushing against him better than me. After a few minutes of discussion, we made the decision to go back to the campsite and we pitched our tent back on the same platform we camped on the night before. We took a zero day and Roy paced like a caged tiger all day. We were really looking forward to getting to the town of Rangely, but we had to be safe. This was one of the times I had a healthy fear of hiking. When hiking in the mountains a hiker must be prepared to turn back if the weather is bad, otherwise continuing could have dire consequences. You should not gamble with your life when it comes to the weather in the mountains.

September 16, 2021 - It started raining in the middle of the afternoon the day before and it rained off and on most of the evening. It cleared by morning although it was still windy. We packed up the wet tent, again, which didn't leak as much since we used the seam sealer, and again hiked the 0.7 miles up to The Horn Mountain. The views were amazing and we were extremely glad we didn't attempt going across the day before since we would have not seen any of the beautiful views. It was cold but at least the wind had eased up and we could see. The hike up to Saddleback Mountain was another 1.6 miles and also had amazing views. We could see the ski lodge and the slopes at the

Saddleback Ski area. After hiking 6.25 miles, we stopped early to dry the tent. We ate Ramen noodles and instant mashed potatoes, known to hikers as a Rom Bomb. *This was the first time we tried this trail recipe. The Ramen is cooked per package directions and after the noodles are cooked instant potato flakes are added to get the desired consistency. Spam or some other meat is sometimes added. Our portable pantry didn't have any meat suitable to throw in the pot so we ate some pepperoni and crackers with mustard as an appetizer. Not the idea of five-star dining but it was a hot meal.* We were 1.8 miles from the highway that goes to the town of Rangely. Maybe when we got to town the rain would hold off so we could dry our equipment, again. *Rain, rain, go away!*

*"It doesn't matter how slowly you go
as long as you do not stop." - Confucius*

Chapter 20 - Are We in The Twilight Zone?

September 17, 2021 - The weather was very nice, we hiked to where the AT crosses ME Route 4 and from there it was 0.2 miles to The Hiker Hut. It was a nice rustic place that reminded us a lot of Standing Bear Farm in Tennessee. We just had to get an egg sandwich. The Hiker Hut is known by hikers for their $3 egg sandwiches. We got a sandwich each and it was the best egg sandwich ever. Or it could have been hiker hunger that made it taste so good? Two eggs with cheese and seasoned mayo on seeded rye bread. Yum! While we ate our sandwich we watched a couple of chipmunks, they were apparently used to getting a handout and they scampered around waiting for the owner who fed them every day. *I bought some seeded rye bread and made egg sandwiches for us one time after we got home but they were nowhere nearly as good as the sandwiches at the hiker hut.*

The owner of the Hiker Hut agreed to take us to town for ten dollars. We got a room at The Saddleback Inn which was reportedly hiker friendly and one of the less expensive options. Rangely was a ski town and the cost of lodging was steep compared to other smaller towns in the trail. The room cost $180 but we were really looking forward to a hot shower and a bed for the night. It was also convenient as it was near restaurants, laundry and resupply. We walked to town and did a load of laundry at the local laundromat. The IGA, which was in the other direction from the inn, had plenty of options to get our food supplies. We walked back to town again later in the day to eat dinner at Parkside and Main Restaurant. Roy had a fish sandwich and I had . . . a cheeseburger and fries. It was just a shame all that hiking up and down the road didn't count as trail miles.

One thing we found interesting about Rangely, it's reportedly the halfway point between the equator and the North Pole. We saw a sign at the site of the old Doc Grant's Restaurant which indicated 3107 miles to the equator and 3107 miles to the North Pole. *The restaurant opened in 1941 and closed in 2000 but the sign remains. We looked this up on the internet and found it was a marketing ploy by the owner to get tourists into town and although very close to the halfway point is not exactly halfway. It is still one of those things that is unique to think about. It's definitely off the beaten path and we would have never had known about it without being on the trail.*

September 18, 2021 - Neither of us actually slept very well due to noise at the motel. *This was a Friday night and I guess people were out on the town so to speak. The tent was much quieter. If only it had a shower.* We got a ride back to the trail around 9:00 a.m. The hike was fairly easy in comparison to the last couple of days. The weather was warm and windy. After hiking 9.1 miles we camped at Sabbath Day Pond Lean-to, of course in our tent. At least it was quiet, except for hearing an occasional loon on the pond. As usual, after a long day of hiking we were more than ready again for a good night's sleep.

September 19, 2021 - There was a lot of climbing over big rocks and uphill. The leaves were starting to change colors, the reds were stunning. Leaves were already starting to fall and the red leaves on the trail were almost like a trail of rose petals. The colors were amazing. We hiked over Bemis Second Mountain and camped at the Bemis Mountain Lean To. We hiked, or rather climbed, 8.3 miles before we stopped for the evening.

September 20, 2021 - The hiking on this day was difficult. Lots of up and down. The downs were steep and there were several places with rebar or ladders. Rebar is harder to use going down and the ladders are just cumbersome, especially when climbing with a backpack. We held onto anything we could get hold of when going up and down in difficult terrain.

The smaller pine trees at the edge of the trail have branches broken and are worn slick from hands holding on. At times the broken branches can be a hazard. I was holding onto a small tree and my feet slipped, I held onto the tree to prevent falling all the way down. The momentum from the fall and holding the tree caused me to spin around the tree and in doing so I stuck the inside of my right forearm with a broken branch that was sticking out on the tree. It bruised immediately, it was painful and left a mark for a couple of weeks. Another time the same thing happened and a broken branch hit my chest thankfully on my pack strap. I let go when the branch hit my chest because even though it was on the pack strap it hurt like hell. I landed on my back thankfully in a soft bed of pine needles. I had to take my pack off to get up. This fall left a small bruise on my chest and scared me but otherwise I was alright, just thankful the branch hit my strap and I was not skewered. I was also glad there was no one else around to see my acrobatics.

We crossed over Old Blue Mountain and it was definitely a challenge to cover the 8.71 miles. South Arm Road Campsites provided a nice campsite for the night.

September 21, 2021 - Thank goodness for hiking the steeper uphill parts of the trail earlier in the day. We hiked over Moody and Wyman Mountains in the morning. The trail in the afternoon was mostly easier and downhill. We camped at Surplus Pond Road after hiking 8.21 miles. The reflections of the colorful trees and blue sky in the water were amazing. There was a beautiful little pond and it looked like the perfect place to see a moose. We saw plenty of moose poop on the trail that day. I could just see a moose standing in the water and dipping his head down to eat aquatic plants like you see in nature shows on TV, but there was no moose. Our quest to see a moose was to be continued. Andover was the next town and we would be there in the morning.

September 22, 2021 - We called the Pine Ellis Lodge in Andover and reserved a room for the night. We had someone scheduled to meet us at the parking lot at East B Hill Road. We only had to hike about two miles to reach the road. There was misty rain that morning with more rain in the forecast and we were glad to be getting a room. Our driver arrived earlier than our scheduled time, thank goodness. We first thought he was kind of quiet. *We would later find out he had quite the sense of humor.* He gave us the grand tour of Andover, which was about the size of Cub Run, Kentucky back home. He also gave us a tour of the lodge and its amenities. The lodge was an old house with quirky rooms. The folks there were nice and helpful, but the "lodge" had seen better days. We really wanted to stay at a place called The Cabin, which reportedly had wonderful food. But all they had available was bunks and we didn't want to chance the snoring that was bound to be in a bunk room full of hikers. *When bad weather is moving in it can be difficult to find a room because a lot of the hikers want to get out of the weather.* We settled in, took showers and decided to walk to the local gas station for food even though it was still misting rain.

The station was the only place in town and they had most anything anyone would want. It was the local gas station, restaurant, deli, pizzeria, supermarket and beer depot. We got there around 11:00 a.m. and they were just changing from breakfast to the lunch menu. Roy really wanted pancakes and eggs so the lady said she would go ahead and make them for him and he was awfully glad she took pity on a hungry hiker. I ate . . . lasagna. I waited until dinner when we came back and we both had burgers! While we were there, we noted the beer coolers might as well have had a revolving door. Every few minutes the doors to the coolers would pop as they closed. It was apparently the only place to get beer, or anything else in the vicinity. It was foggy and rained on and off much of the day. The weather was supposed to be crappy for the next few days and we were glad to have a room for the night.

We settled down for the evening in our room and were looking forward to a good night's sleep. We had heard church bells in town but assumed they would not continue through the night. Most church bells stop around 8:00 or 9:00 p.m. and resume the next morning. The bells did not stop! They rang every hour, at 10:00 p.m. ten times, 11:00 p.m. eleven times and so on. We couldn't sleep because the church bells rang all night, and they were loud. We decided it was like sleeping in a house near railroad tracks, if you lived there long enough you would probably get used to them. It also rained off and on and we could hear the rain as it pelted the plastic that covered the windows of the old house. *I guess the windows leaked and the plastic was put over them in efforts to keep the house dry. The house was sorely in need of repairs but at least we were out of the rain.* Again, the tent was much quieter.

September 23, 2021 - We got our ride back to the trail from the guy who picked us up the day before. We talked with him several times since we first met him and found he was quite the character.

119

He had a necklace with a piece of moose poop on it hanging from his rearview mirror of the vehicle. He told us a lady once asked him if it was his lucky charm. He said he told her, "No, it's just a piece of shit." This was just one of the times he had us laughing. He also told us moose poop had no smell and if it was slowly burned it was a great natural insect repellent. Fortunately, we had not been bothered by insects so we didn't try it. Although there was no shortage of moose poop if we wanted to give it a try. *We were lucky we missed the black fly season in Maine. We were told the worst is usually May, June and July. But we did bring our head nets just in case.* We hiked 8.1 miles over the Baldpate Mountains. It was sheer rock, uphill and it started to rain at the worst possible time. We were sliding everywhere, unable to stand up and holding on to anything we could grab to climb up. Roy was grabbing at little bushes that kept breaking and he finally crawled on his knees to get where he could stand up. I did have a knee brace on my right knee and it saved me from having both knees skinned, Roy wasn't as lucky. We decided if we ever saw this mountain again it would be too soon. After we got to the top of the mountain, we saw a rainbow in the distance so we at least felt rewarded for our efforts. We hiked, if that's what you want to call it, 8.1 miles and finally made it to the Baldpate Lean To. It was a very welcomed sight. As we were getting our tent set up it started raining again. *Imagine that.*

September 24, 2021 - The wind howled all night and neither of us slept very well. With not sleeping well the past two nights the hike was not going to be any fun. It started to rain again before we got very far on the trail. We had not really planned on going into town this soon again, we didn't need supplies. But the weather was awful. We had no cell service to call ahead for a room in the town of Bethel. So, we hiked on in hopes we would find a ride and a room when we got to the highway. We hiked down the mountain 2.4 miles to Route 26 at Grafton Notch. We call these low places in the mountains, gaps in the south, but up north they are notches.

We met a guy at the parking lot who seemed to be a bit disoriented. He was cold, soaking wet and he had just hiked NOBO over the last mountain before arriving at the parking lot. We were still hiking SOBO. The nurse in me kicked in and I was a bit concerned about this fellow. *Was he hypothermic, dehydrated or something else?* He apparently wanted a ride to Bethel also. He went to the road and attempted to hitch a ride. After a few minutes he came back to the parking lot and stood with us.

There was a restroom at the parking lot where there was also a little roadside park with picnic tables. I went to take advantage of the restroom while we were trying to figure out what to do. When I came out, Roy and this guy were talking to an older lady begging for a ride to town. I walked up to where they were, the lady looked at me and asked if I was with them. *She must have taken pity on me, or felt more comfortable not being with the two men by herself.* She agreed to take us to town for $20. I was afraid that three dirty wet hikers would make a mess in her car but she kept saying it would be ok. We loaded our gear and she drove us to the town of Bethel.

We discovered on the ride to town the guy we were riding with was hiking to bring awareness to TBI (Traumatic Brain Injury). He had experienced an injury that left him aphasic. Aphasia is a condition in which you know what you want to say but have trouble speaking. So, that explained why we thought he was disoriented. He was meeting his wife and she had reserved a room for him at the Mountain Village Motel. He didn't want us to pay the lady, he insisted on paying the $20 for the ride. *I think he was thankful Roy had talked to the lady and convinced her to give all of us a ride to town.*

We arrived at the motel and Roy went in with him to see about getting a room. Turns out Roy also assisted the guy to get checked in at this motel. There was no front desk and the check in was by phone. While they were inside, I looked online to see if I could find a room anywhere in town. No luck on finding anything and the Mountain Village Motel had one room available for that night. I also talked to the lady who had given us a ride and discovered her name was Jean. I told her she was definitely a Trail Angel doing her good deed for the day, maybe even for the year. After all, it was 20 miles from the parking lot at the trail to the town of Bethel and she had saved three drowned hiking rats.

When Roy returned to the car, I told him of my inability to find a room. We decided we would take the room there. Not only did the motel not have a front desk, there was no ice, no vending machines, no laundry, nothing but the room. You had to call or email for check in and the doors all had keypads with codes. They would remotely program the code for your stay to the last four digits of your social security number. *The cost of the room was $180. Bethel is a ski town like Rangely and the cost of lodging is high compared to other towns, $180 must have been the going rate.* After we checked in and looked at the weather report, we decided we would stay two nights if possible. When we called back to reserve the room for the next night, they had no vacancy. We couldn't find a place in town to stay for the next night so we decided we would have to go back to the trail. We spread out our tent and all our gear in hopes of getting things dried before morning, again. Knowing full well it would probably be wet again before the next afternoon.

We showered and turned our attention to getting food. Anytime we could get anything other than trail food we were excited. The nearest restaurants were one to two miles away which wouldn't have been an issue except we really didn't want to get out in the rain after getting warm and dry. The clothes we were wearing when we arrived were drying in the room and we sure didn't need to get more of our clothing wet in the rain at that time. We looked for an Uber, a taxi, or a shuttle to no avail. *So, if we couldn't go get food maybe someone could bring the food to us.* No pizza delivery or delivery from any of the restaurants. Were we in the Twilight Zone or what? Covid was really causing major problems!

The rain slacked for a bit and we decided we would take our chances and walk to a restaurant. We didn't get far until it became apparent the rain was coming again soon. We aborted the mission to hike to a restaurant and opted for the Shell station that was across a bridge nearly in sight of the motel. We settled for hot dogs, chips, snacks and beer and took them back to our room. On the way back to the room it started to rain when we got to the parking lot of the motel.

September 25, 2021 - It rained off and on all through last night. We slept well after having not slept very much the past couple of nights. We were fifteen miles from the Maine/New Hampshire state line. But these miles were reportedly some of the toughest on the AT. We were finally able to find someone last night who agreed to take us back to the trail. As we were waiting for our ride a young man walked up to me and asked if we were hiking the AT and I told him yes. He said he wasn't sure what, but he wanted to give us something and he went to his car and returned with a package of popcorn. I thanked him for the Trail Magic and he wished us well. I hadn't looked closely at the package, when Roy saw it he pointed out that it wasn't just popcorn. It was edible marijuana popcorn. Our ride had arrived and I just threw it in my backpack thinking I would give it to someone else or throw it away somewhere. *We later left it at a neat spot on the trail for some other hiker to find. I had just about forgotten about it because over the course of a few days with unpacking and packing my gear it had gone all the way to the bottom of my backpack. I definitely wanted to get rid of it before we got to the airport.*

Calvin was our shuttle driver and he was definitely a character, he talked the whole way back to the trail. He told us years ago he visited Louisville, Kentucky with his son, they met Muhammad Ali in the elevator at a hotel and he was a really nice guy. He also told us Matt Bevins, the former governor of Kentucky has a house in the area. He talked about a lot of the various hikers he had shuttled to and from the trail and kept us entertained on the ride.

We resumed the trail at Grafton Notch at 1495 feet elevation. Thankfully the forecast for rain didn't materialize. We hiked up Old Speck, a 4000-foot mountain and took a 0.1-mile side trail near the top to go to a fire tower. *We didn't often go off the trail but the view from this tower was supposed to be a good one.* There was a 360-degree view of the mountains and it was gorgeous. *There was no way a picture could capture the beauty of the mountains and the clear blue sky. When we were looking over views like this we could sometimes pinpoint where we had been earlier that day or even the day before. It was unreal to think of the distances we were hiking. It was also unreal to think of all the hiking up and down the mountains.* There were campsites in the area around Specks Pond Shelter and we decided to stay there for the night. We only hiked 4.6 miles, not including the hike to the fire tower.

September 26, 2021 - The infamous Mahoosuc Notch is a 0.8-mile section of the AT and it took us almost four hours to get through it. It was the rock scramble of all rock scrambles. There was a hiker from Alabama who went through the notch with us. We had met him before in the 100 Mile Wilderness, he was going by the trail name 65 at that time. He actually helped us out a lot. We crawled up and over, down and under, over and around or through rocks larger than buses. Several times we had to take off our backpacks in order to get through. We had heard other hikers talking about how bad it was before we got there. However, some of the hikers thought it was a lot of fun. Hiking poles were of no use so we put them away. *I think I was stuck somewhere between being awed by the rocks and feeling overwhelmed. Twice Roy had to physically help me get down off of the rocks so I could continue.* We hiked 5.1 miles and camped at Full Goose Shelter. *Full Goose as opposed to a Half Goose or a Partial Goose? The names of some of these shelters, where do they come up with them?*

September 27, 2021 - We only hiked 4.6 miles; the terrain was horrible. Big ups and downs and bogs. *Alpine bogs occur in alpine areas near or above tree line. It is amazing to me they are located at this elevation. There was vegetation growing over the top of the bog and you would think there would be solid ground where there was nothing but dirty, muddy water. I remember reading somewhere about bodies found in bogs after hundreds or thousands of years and them being fairly well preserved or mummified by the chemicals from the plants and water. I could see how someone could become entangled in the plants and unable to get out. I wouldn't want to be in this area alone. A lot of the AT through the bogs has walkways constructed to allow you to hike through without getting your feet wet. A lot more of the trail was walking on loose planks laid across the bog that may or may not assist you in your quest. I would normally go all day without getting my feet wet and would ultimately slip up and step in water around 3:00 p.m. Too late in the day to dry out before stopping for the night. This came to be known between us as the 3:00 p.m. foot bath. But getting wet at 3:00 p.m. is still better than hiking all day with wet feet.*

There was a threat of rain most of the afternoon, as if the bogs were not wet enough. *There were areas where the logs and planks placed on the trail just sank when you stepped on them and there was no way around. Most of the time hikers just give up and plow through. We were still trying not to get any wetter or more muddy than necessary. If you stepped into the bog, it could be knee deep or deeper.*

It was tough climbing that day, there was lots of rebar anchored in the rocks and ladders. The ladders could be rebar or very heavy wooden ladders built from large trees. It was very slow hiking. *Most of the time on a day like this we had to concentrate on every step we took. We also had to be aware of our balance when climbing with a pack. We really took our time to avoid either of us falling.* We camped at the Carlo Col Shelter, 0.5 miles from the New Hampshire state line, we had been feeling as though we would never get there. We camped on a platform and it was as usual threatening rain. Our newfound friend, 65, had been hiking with us since before the Mahoosuc Notch and he camped on the platform beside ours. Roy found a painted rock beside our platform. I wanted to keep it, but he said it would add extra weight to our loads (every ounce counted). *I decided to leave it, but Roy would reveal to me after we got home that he kept the rock because I liked it so well. We now have it among our mementos from the trail.* We settled in our tent early because of the rain. We looked over the app and studied where the trail would take us over the next few days. This was one of the times we would be in the tent for more than twelve hours. Maine would be behind us in the morning!

September 28, 2021 - We crossed the state line into New Hampshire and crossed Maine off the list of the fourteen states we must hike to complete the AT. The trail in New Hampshire was no better than Maine as far as rock climbing went. We climbed a couple of big uphill with rebar not long after crossing the state line. *It looked to me as though the hills were turning into rock walls to be climbed instead of trails to be hiked. Little did I know at the time*

125

what the remainder of New Hampshire would have in store for us. I never dreamed the ups and downs were so drastic. I now understand the saying, the trails looked so flat on the map. I guess I should have looked closer at a topographical map.

When the trail was not going steeply uphill it still had lots of puddles and ponds, some were completely unavoidable. Hiking was a little easier, but hiking with wet feet was not fun. *We were told about this area when we met some NOBO hikers a couple of days ago. They had just waded through the mud and went on. Their shoes were completely covered in mud and their legs, up to their knees, were just about as muddy. We still just couldn't go plowing through the mud. We were trying to take care of our feet and if it were not for the foot care regimen every night, I fear our feet would have really gotten in really bad shape.* We hiked over Mt. Success and camped at Dream Lake after hiking 7.4 miles. 65 is still with us and is also going to Gorham, NH in the morning.

The past two weeks it was one weird thing after another. Just about like being in the twilight zone, church bells ringing all night, expensive ski towns, no taxis in town, no Ubers, no pizza delivery, alpine bogs, rain, rain, and more rain, Mahoosuc notch and crazy difficult hiking. We were more than glad to be finished with Maine and looking forward to getting to the town of Gorham, NH the next day.

"If you can find a path with no obstacles, it probably doesn't lead anywhere." - Frank A. Clark

Chapter 21 - The Long Trip Home

September 29, 2021 - The terrain was a lot better. Somewhere along the way we lost 65, he was actually a fast hiker and he had waited for us slower folks a lot. He knew we were going to Gorham. *We would never know if he went to town or hiked down the trail. We never saw him again.* We hiked a lot of downhill and had gorgeous views. The blue skies and the colors in the trees were beautiful. We made it to the Rattle River Hostel at Gorham, NH on Hwy 2 which is right on the trail. The place was closed for the season, but one of the guys there offered us a ride to town and we graciously accepted. The next range of big mountains would be the White Mountains and the weather is turning colder. *At 6288 feet elevation Mount Washington is the crown jewel of the Whites and the most dangerous place on the entire AT. Its claim to fame is having the worst weather in the world. There is about 13 miles above the tree line where you are not supposed to camp. The temperatures can drop rapidly, rain or snow can move in quickly, the wind has been measured there at 231 mph. That is hurricane force winds in the mountains. No thank you. Mount Washington holds the record for being the highest measured wind speed not associated with a tornado or tropical cyclone. We decided it would be best to go home and come back to the trail later. It would be too dangerous for us to attempt to hike in those mountains since the weather was going to be deteriorating. This time of year, the weather can be completely unpredictable. Gorham is a good point to either resume or finish the trail at a later date.*

We got a room at the Gorham Motor Inn. It was close to restaurants and the bus station. The motel, although dated, was clean and had very comfortable beds. After we checked in and got showers of course we went looking for food. We ate at J's Corner Restaurant and Pub; the food was excellent. We did a load of laundry so we would at least be traveling in and carrying clean clothes home. We booked flights from Boston to Nashville with a 40-minute layover in Dallas/Fort Worth. $240 each but this was the best we could do on short notice. This was the only flight available to get us back home unless we wanted to hang around Boston for a couple of days. *Nope, we were ready to go home after being gone for six weeks. It was Wednesday, we would spend Thursday traveling and be home for the weekend.* We also had to buy bus tickets for the ride from Gorham to Boston.

We talked to our daughter Christi and found out the Talladega NASCAR Race in Alabama was going to be on Sunday. *We usually go and spend the weekend and just hang out with the gang. It's a fun trip. The race in 2020 was modified due to Covid, no concerts, no vendors, attendance was limited. We were hoping 2021 would be more normal activities. We really wanted to be back for the race even if we were tired.* We stayed up until midnight making sure we had all our travel plans in order.

September 30, 2021 - The Irving gas station next door also served as a bus stop and we walked there from the motel to purchase bus tickets early that morning. We were to be back there at 7:20 a.m. to catch the bus which was scheduled to leave at 7:50 a.m. The bus tickets were $42 each. We caught the bus as planned and were pleasantly surprised when we found the bus route took us through the White Mountains. The windows on the bus were huge and allowed for viewing the landscape even in the mountains. The fall leaves were very colorful and there were awesome views of Mount Washington. Gorham was at 792 feet elevation, Mount Washington at 6288 feet and it looked massive. We got to Boston's Logan International Airport in plenty of time to catch our flight home at 2:50 p.m. We were scheduled to arrive in Nashville at 8:47 p.m. and my sister was going to pick us up. *I would sure be glad to see her.* Our flight was to be routed through the Dallas/Fort Worth airport; this was the best flight we could get on short notice. *It was either that or fly to Miami then back to Nashville which was even a longer flight.*

Before we got to Dallas/Fort Worth the pilot announced the airport was closed due to stormy weather. We would have to fly in big circles around the area until we were cleared to land. We flew in big circles for what seemed like hours. In reality it was about two hours before we were able to land. By the time we got to Nashville it was after 11:00 p.m. My sister picked us up and when we got to her house in Bowling Green, she gave us the keys to her truck and told us to drive it home. *We would bring it back when we passed through on our way to Talladega Saturday morning.* We finally arrived home after 1:00 a.m. We had been traveling for about eighteen hours with only a few hours of sleep. I think we were asleep before our heads hit the pillows. It was a very long day and we were both thoroughly exhausted from the trail and especially from the trip home.

The next day was Friday, we spent the day cleaning up our hiking gear and getting ready to travel south to Talladega, Alabama for the NASCAR race. It was great to be home. I think both of us were more than glad to have the AT in Maine behind us.

We got up early Saturday morning and headed to Talladega. We dropped off my sister's truck as we went through Bowling Green and got there in time for the truck race. The gang couldn't believe how much weight we lost and were eager to hear about our hike and had lots of questions.

We planned on doing some hiking in the fall while the weather was still good. Hopefully the weather and the seasons would be on our side and we could finish the trail within a year from the date we summited Mt. Katahdin. We were still aiming for the thru hiker status.

"The experienced mountain climber is not intimidated by a mountain, he is inspired by it."
- William Authur Ward

Chapter 22 - Here We Go Again

October 12, 2021 - We got our gear together and tied up loose ends in preparation for returning to the trail the next day. The plan was to hike from Allen Gap where we stopped in 2020 and head NOBO to Roan Mountain, Tennessee. We got all our gear packed, we wouldn't need as many supplies as we would need on a longer hike and we wouldn't have to worry about resupplying. This part of the hike would cover about 75 miles and we hoped to complete it in a week or less.

October 13, 2021 - We drove Roy's white truck to Hot Springs, North Carolina and ate lunch at the Smoky Mountain Diner. The food was as good as the first time we ate there in March of 2020. The town appeared to be recovering from the pandemic although I'm sure it was still struggling as were most small towns. We went to Allen Gap to pick up the trail where we left off. We parked the truck at the small parking area and shortly after noon we started hiking the 4.9 miles to Little Laurel Shelter. We decided not to push it too hard and set up our tent there since we wouldn't be able to make it to the next shelter before dark. The hike that day was mostly uphill but a lot easier than Maine. The cheeseburger I had for lunch was fantastic except it was awfully hard to carry it up the hill in my stomach.

The thing I discovered about cheeseburgers and hamburgers, by eating them in several places, was that I liked the southern burgers better. They always try to put the northern burgers on a different bun or roll and have something different than the standard burger. I much prefer a plain white bread bun, toasted and the basic deluxe cheeseburger version with tomato, lettuce, onion, pickles and mayo. Maybe the southern burgers were what I was used to eating all my life. We ate a light supper that evening at our campsite, I was still full from lunch. The tent was comfortable and we slept well.

October 14, 2021 - We hiked through a lot of places with beautiful fall leaves. Hands down, Big Firescald Knob had the best views of leaves we had ever seen. The beauty of the red and golden leaves was indescribable and of course the pictures I took did not capture the beauty of the colors. Nature's colorful canvas was amazing. These colors cannot be found at your local Lowe's or Home Depot. We also climbed over Big Butt Peak today, don't know why it was called that but we thought it was funny. *We would, geriatric delinquents that we are.* A campsite not far from the Shelton Graves was where we stopped for the night. *Two Union soldiers were killed in an ambush by Confederates while visiting family in the area and were buried there. The site was very well maintained and decorated with flowers. You have to wonder who, and why, this site has been maintained this many years since their deaths. This is just one of the many unusual things we would find as we hiked the AT.*

October 15, 2021 - We hiked in pasture fields and woods most of the day. There were wooden steps built up and over barbed wire fences to assist hikers. In other places there were off-set posts and fences placed so a hiker could get through but cattle couldn't.

We met five hikers heading SOBO and they told us they had all been stung multiple times by yellow jackets. They were not able to tell us exactly where the attack occurred, but said there was apparently a nest in the ground that was unseen until it was too late. We had hiked several miles after we met the group of hikers and had just about forgotten about them until Roy was suddenly stung a couple of times on the backs of his calves. He yelped, and with hiking poles in hand ran as quickly as he could to get away. I was well behind him and I stopped and backed up after I realized the flying demons were after him. He ran with his pack up the trail then down a hill to make his escape. He finally stopped, looked up at me and told me he had been stung several times. I was frozen in place, looking for another way to get down the trail without passing the spot where he was stung. The trail where the yellow jackets had built their residence was on a hillside, there was a steep uphill on one side and a steep downhill on the other. I couldn't go any direction except forward or backward. I was standing there contemplating my fate and debating with myself about just running through the spot. *It was not a matter of getting stung or not, but how many times I would be stung.* Suddenly, one of them flew into my arm and stung me. I didn't wait any longer and ran to get through the hazardous area on the trail. I couldn't outrun them all and I was stung once more, poor Roy was stung four or five times. *Thankfully neither of us are allergic to stings. We saw another place on the trail where a huge hornet nest was hanging from a tree over into the trail about six feet high. Someone thankfully had marked the area to bring attention to the nest and traffic was routed around the area. The yellow jackets at this location were aggressive, I don't know of anyone who would get close enough to mark the area and there was no way to route around it. I also wondered how many hikers would be stung. We met several hikers and did tell some others about it, but like us they probably were stung anyway. It occurred to me later that if someone could just put a rock over the hole in the ground that might mitigate the problem, but I don't think there would have been anyone willing to take on the task. If we had this problem at home we would have waited until dark and poured their hole full of gas. We did have this happen once and home, Roy was mowing the yard on a riding mower and went over a nest built into the ground in our front yard. He got off the mower and ran to the back yard and they followed. He was stung several times before he could get away from them. I guess I was extremely lucky to have only been stung twice during this encounter.*

That day we also met Cedar Stick on the trail late that afternoon not long before we set up camp. After talking to him for a few minutes he said we looked familiar. We talked for a few minutes and he mentioned he had been in Maine a few weeks ago. It was then we all realized we had seen each other before. *We saw him at the Maine Roadhouse when we stayed there back in September this year. We were watching TV upstairs in a sitting area near our room when he came through on the way to his room. He stopped and talked with us for a few minutes and asked what we were watching. It was an episode of the show, When Animals Attack. We were there September 11th and 12th, which was about two months ago. He had also flip flopped around on the trail due to weather up north. In addition to NOBO and SOBO, Flip Flop is another way hikers complete the trail. The trail doesn't have to be hiked all in one direction, as long as all the miles are covered. The traditional Flip Flop hiker starts at Harper's Ferry, West Virginia and goes either NOBO or SOBO, then comes back to Harper's Ferry to hike in the other direction. But Flip Flops can begin and end anywhere. There are also YoYo hikers. These hikers hike the trail to completion in one direction then turn around and hike to completion in the other. Yikes! One time, one direction will be enough for me.*

After hiking 10.7 miles we finally found a stealth site at Rice Gap. The camping spot was not perfect but the ground was level enough and it worked. We saw several deer nearby as we were setting up the tent and they were not too concerned with us. We ate our supper and prepared to settle in for the evening. We had turned in for the night and it was getting quiet as we were drifting off to sleep when all of the sudden, we heard the loudest, most shrill, screaming noise I had ever heard. It sounded like a woman screaming a blood curdling scream at the top of her lungs. It was the kind of sound that sends chills up your spine. It took a second before we realized it was a screech owl and not a murder in progress. It made a couple more squawks and flew away from us. We were sure glad it left the area; our hearts couldn't take much more of that noise. *I think we came close to having to clean the tent out after hearing that screech owl!*

Saturday, October 16, 2021 - Thankfully after the screech owl nearly scared me half to death, the rest of the night was uneventful. However, after the shot of adrenalin it took a little while to get back to normal and a lot of laughing before we settled back down for the night. We were awakened by rain on the tent. Luckily, we had cell service so we checked the radar. *Oh great, rain moving through the area off and on.* We broke camp when the rain slacked up for a few minutes. Hogback Ridge Shelter was a couple of miles away and when we got there, we made our coffee and had Pop Tarts. It seemed like a pretty good place to get out of the wind and rain for a few minutes.

Roy had emptied his pack and had stuff all over the shelter, a couple arrived there also looking to take a break for a few minutes. The guy took one look and said, "How many people are in this shelter?" We told him it was just us, and I started laughing because when Roy got his stuff out of his backpack, he had a tendency to have it strewn everywhere. *This became a running joke between us when we set up camp. I would look around at his stuff lying everywhere and say, "How many people are in this shelter?"*

It was cold and windy all day. We hiked 7.2 miles and found a stealth camp site at mile 323.3. *There are no visible mile markers, only white blazes, but all the guides and the FarOut app reference mileage. This is how distances between landmarks on the trail can be calculated.*

October 17, 2021 - The weather was cold and windy but at least there was no rain. We hiked over Big Bald Mountain, 5504 feet elevation. It reminded us of Max Patch. There were beautiful views. We hiked 12.07 miles and camped near Devil's Creek Gap.

The landscape of the trail seems to all run together at times. Rocks, trees, streams, shelters and people. Most of the time our heads were down watching our footing to make sure we didn't fall. I think it would be impossible to describe all the vibrant colors, unique and beautiful sights.

October 18, 2021 - The weather was pleasant. Erwin, Tennessee was the next trail town and we arrived after hiking 8.8 miles. We saw a bridge over the river from high up on the trail and it seemed as though it took forever to get down there. Uncle Johnny's Hostel is located on the Nolichucky River right next to the trail and it's one of the first things we saw when we arrived in Erwin. *Uncle Johnny's is another popular stop for hikers. They have basic supplies for hikers and they sell large Snickers for 49 cents, most candy bars on the trail are at least $2 each. We purchased a couple of them to take advantage of the bargain.*

We called a guy named Paul and hired him to shuttle us back to Allen Gap to get the truck. We found his name and contact info in the FarOut app. The distance back to the truck was about 30 miles by road and it was a curvy little two-lane road where you could just about meet yourself going around some of the hairpin turns. After we got the truck, we drove back to Erwin where we got a room for the night at the Motel 8.

After a shower, food was next on the agenda as usual. We went through the drive through at Bojangles and ordered dinner for four

134

people. They were out of chicken except chicken tenders, they told us the truck had not arrived yet. We went ahead and got the chicken tenders with a couple of sides, bread and a half gallon of lemonade. It was supposed to feed four people but we took it back to the room and ate most of it. I should have known better than to eat too much. I could not go to sleep; I had eaten entirely too much and I was too full. *It was just too much of a good thing and it occurred to me that gluttony is one of the seven deadly sins. At this point I could definitely understand how eating too much could kill you because I was miserable.*

October 19, 2021 - We left the truck at a parking area on the Nolichucky River in Erwin near Uncle Johnny's and hit the trail again. We hiked uphill most of the day, it was not too steep and we hiked 10.6 miles before we arrived at Beauty Spot, a grassy bald at 4436 feet elevation. Beauty Spot was another unique place we came across on the trail. It would be nice to come back to when we had more time. There was a parking lot nearby and it was a very short walk to the top of the mountain with unbelievable views. We pitched our tent at the top of the mountain and waited for the sunset. We talked to several people who had come to watch the sunset and a couple of other campers. They asked lots of questions about hiking the AT and were in awe of what he had accomplished thus far.

We saw a gorgeous fiery red sunset that just kept getting better with each passing minute. *I believe there were some of the best sunsets in fall and winter.* The valley below was filled with darkness and the twinkling lights of nearby towns. There was a full moon that evening and it was almost like daylight outside. Plus, we were met by a gorgeous sunrise the next morning from this location. We experienced a trifecta of beautiful events! We certainly had the timing right, this time. *Of all the places on the AT, Beauty Spot was my favorite.*

October 20, 2021 - It was a cold and windy morning. We broke camp and headed up the trail to find a place out of the wind to fix our breakfast. We found a good sunny spot shielded from the wind so we stopped to make coffee and ate Pop Tarts. *Pop Tarts are a hikers staple for breakfast. They are a little on the heavy side but* packed with calories. Roy could go all day without breakfast, coffee or lunch for that matter, but I really needed my coffee in the mornings to get me going. Also, if I hiked too long without eating, I think my blood sugar dropped, I would get weak, shaky, a little dizzy and nauseated. But the problem was resolved quickly by eating. I had experienced this a few times when we were in Maine and quickly decided it was not smart or safe. After I recognized what was happening, I carried snacks in my pouch for easy access and I would sit down and eat to prevent feeling worse.

Later we hiked through an old apple orchard and there were apples left on the trees. The trees were the tallest apple trees I had ever seen. We picked up several apples, washed, peeled and ate them with our dinner. I carried a few salt packets in my food bag and the apples really tasted good sprinkled with a little salt. Not many calories but a nice treat.

After hiking 10.8 miles we set up the tent and camped on the only flat spot we could find which was in an old roadbed down a small hill from the trail. We were awakened about 10:00 p.m. by deer snorting, we were apparently between them and the orchard. It also made me wonder if bears were feasting on the apples. *That night I dreamed we were being stalked by coyotes and about using my trekking poles to fend them off, I must have heard them in my sleep!*

October 21, 2021 - *Happy 27th Anniversary to us! Can't believe we have put up with each other this long! For that matter I can't believe we have been together 24/7 so much since we retired and are still getting along with each other as well as we do. No one else could probably stand either one of us that much.* We climbed uphill a lot and covered 11.1 miles. Ash Gap, elevation 5329 feet about two-thirds of the way up Roan Mountain was where we pitched our tent for the night. Roan Mountain was at 6270 feet and we would cross over it the next morning. The town of Roan Mountain is about 18 miles away and we should be there in a couple of days. *We usually go out to eat for our anniversary and for many years we would go to Red Lobster because that's where we ate dinner the evening after we got married. This year the best we could do was tuna packets and an I.O.U. for a better dinner at a later date. We did manage to cash in our I.O.U. later had a nice steak dinner at Longhorn's Steakhouse.*

October 22, 2021 - We awakened to drizzle and it was very foggy at Ash Gap, it was also cold and windy. The hike from Ash Gap to Roan Mountain was not as bad as we had anticipated. There were lots of switchbacks that definitely helped with the elevation gain. At the top of Roan Mountain, we stopped at the Roan High Knob Shelter to make coffee and have breakfast. We hoped the enclosed shelter would provide a respite from the wind. There was a thermometer in the shelter and it registered 46 degrees Fahrenheit. We were not really cold until we stopped for a bit and of course saw the thermometer. The coffee helped warm us while we were stopped. Once our hiking resumed, we were plenty warm after a few minutes.

We did slow down long enough to see the very few remains of the old Cloudland Hotel. *It was built atop Roan Mountain in 1885 and had 166 rooms. It was used as a resort for people who had health issues such as hay-fever and also provided relief from the summer heat. Due to numerous issues with maintaining the hotel in such high elevations it was abandoned in 1915.*

We arrived at the Overmountain Shelter in the middle of the afternoon. It was an old barn many hikers had used as a shelter in the past. The barn was considered structurally unsound and there were signs posted to not stay in the barn or camp within so many feet of it. *I really didn't look any worse than most of the old barns I have ever seen.* There was also a huge grassy area for tenting, a huge firepit and absolutely gorgeous views of the mountains. We decided to stay there since we wouldn't be able to make it over the next mountain before time to camp. We hiked 9.2 miles and we were 9.2 miles from town when we stopped for the night. The privy at this camping area was behind the old barn. I went to check it out and found that someone had bedazzled the toilet. The entire toilet was decorated with stick on jewels in multiple colors and patterns. *It would have taken some time to finish this piece of art! I almost felt like royalty using this beautiful throne and of course I had to take a picture, because who would have believed it?*

October 23, 2021 - It was cold, windy and foggy when we hiked over Little Hump Mountain, elevation 5459 feet, a huge grassy bald. The wind was pretty strong and it was really cold, so we didn't waste any time as we hiked across the open areas at the top of the mountain. The large grassy fields on top of the mountains with rocks and few trees allowed for fantastic views of the surrounding countryside.

We hiked the 9.2 miles to Highway 19E at the town of Roan Mountain and the Mountain Harbor Hostel and Bed & Breakfast. We got a private room in the hostel although it had two twin beds. At least it was warm, dry, had a shower and good food readily available. We were unable to get a ride back to our truck until the next morning so we decided to make the best of the evening. We both took long hot showers that felt great as usual after being on the trail for a few days. There was a food truck outside the hostel and they opened at 5 p.m. We put in our orders and sipped on a beer while we waited for our food. We were ready for some real food and it was fantastic. *Roy had chicken tenders and I had . . . a cheeseburger, it was excellent. Lol!*

Mountain Harbor was yet another unique place and a favorite hiker stop. There was a hostel, a general store with hiking supplies and the B&B was in the main house across a footbridge and up on the hill. Many folks who were not hikers stayed at the B&B. The landscaping between the hostel and the main house was gorgeous. There was a stream running between them with the bridge and tiered landscaping on the hill. A covered deck wrapped around the side of the hostel and made an excellent place just to hang out. A mallard duck had made her nest near the bridge and was setting on eggs according to the girl that was in charge of the hostel part of the business. We thought it was a bit late in the year for ducklings but we saw the duck later that evening sitting on the nest. There was a tabby cat that lived in the hostel named Oda Mae, and a friendly dog named Dublin. The owner of the place, who thru hiked the AT in the eighties, was having a birthday party that evening and there was music until 10:00 p.m. *Way past our hiking bedtime but at least it didn't last until midnight. Needless to say, we didn't sleep very well that night since as usual, the tent was much quieter. But at least we were not hiking the next day.*

October 24, 2021 - We packed our stuff so we would be ready to go when our ride left and walked up to the main house for breakfast. The house was big and very deceiving from its outward appearance. The inside of the house was beautiful and very tastefully decorated. The breakfast was $13 per person and supposed to be absolutely the best breakfast on the entire AT. The food was amazing. There was French toast, tomato pie, egg souffle, biscuits, gravy, sausages, breakfast tacos, and more. The owner of the hostel welcomed everyone and described all of the food being served. There were probably twenty people who ate breakfast that morning sitting at various tables throughout the house. The wide-open design allowed for a large gathering of people and didn't feel as though you were confined in smaller spaces. In addition to the house being beautifully decorated with antiques and seasonal decorations the dining tables were decorated with complete place settings in a fall/Halloween theme. A lot of work went decorating the house, not to mention the preparation of the meal. The food was delicious and we of course ate more than we should.

We caught our ride from Roan Mountain back to Erwin not long after breakfast. It was another ride on two lane winding roads to get back to get the truck. This would be the end of this leg of our journey. We had knocked another 105.6 miles off the trail.

After we got to the truck we decided to drive to Mt. Mitchell, the highest point in NC. *We had hiked there a few years ago and when we got to the top you couldn't see six feet because of the fog.* The weather was clear and sunny, we arrived there to find the park service was limiting visitors due to an extraordinary number of people visiting. The park ranger at the entrance waited until so many cars came down the hill before he would allow so many to go up. We got in line and waited for the opportunity to go up to the viewing area. After about an hour we were allowed to drive up to the parking lot near the top. It was a clear sunny day and the view from the top of Mt. Mitchell was fantastic. We were both glad we had the opportunity to come back and see what we missed the first time.

We got home that night at about 9:00 p.m. We would have liked to have made it to Damascus, Virginia on this trip but we wanted to go home to celebrate Halloween and Thanksgiving with our family. Halloween is like a whole different holiday and our kids and grandkids would be terribly disappointed if we didn't all get together for Halloween pizza. Afterall, we have had Halloween pizza with them every year since 1992. We ordered carry out and had it at our house last year due to Covid. Our son Derik had threatened to come find us if we were not home for Halloween this year. If the weather cooperated, we would come back in a few weeks, if not we would wait until next year to resume our hike.

If you are on the right path, it will always be uphill."
– Henry B.Eyring

Chapter 23 – Chipping Away at It

November 30, 2021 - The weather was mild and the forecast for the next week looked good so we decided we could get in another week of hiking. I drove my Kia and Roy drove his white truck to Damascus, Virginia. We parked my Kia at the Damascus Library, instead of getting shuttles we would just have two vehicles this time. It was free for hikers to park at the library, but you had to register. I registered online per the instructions posted at the library and indicated our estimated return date. We then drove Roy's truck to Roan Mountain, Tennessee. We were not able to find lodging other than the hostel in Roan Mountain. Lodging in the surrounding area was very limited, but we finally found a room in nearby Elizabethton, TN.

December 1, 2021 - We parked the truck near the Mountain Harbor Hostel where we stopped back in October and we were on the trail by 8:00 a.m. About a quarter mile from the truck, I was thinking about how good it was going to be to see my car when we got to Damascus. Suddenly I realized I left my car key in my purse in Roy's truck. We dropped our backpacks beside the trail and hiked back to the truck to get the key. *We didn't worry about leaving our packs beside the trail unattended. With Covid still around, no one wanted to touch another person's belongings and usually the hiker was in the woods nearby if their pack was left beside the trail. Thank goodness I thought of the key! It would have been bad if we had hiked all the way to Damascus and had no car key when we got there. Catastrophe averted!* We hiked all day and didn't see anyone on the trail. The weather was good and we hiked 12.2 miles before we set up camp for the night.

December 2, 2021 - It started to rain about 11:00 p.m. the night before but there were only a few sprinkles and the tent was dry when we broke camp. We saw a bow hunter walking to his stand as we were fixing breakfast at our campsite. He said the trail was full of people in November but he was surprised to see us hiking in December. As we were drinking our coffee, I discovered I didn't bring the cable that goes from my battery bank to my phone! I had 41% battery on my phone and Roy had 75% on his. We would have to conserve battery by using the paper AWOL guide and save the phones in case we really need them. *Hikers have hiked this trail for decades without cell phones, I knew we would be ok. But my taking of pictures on this leg of the journey would be sorely limited.*

We stopped for lunch on a rocky outcropping with a great view. As we were getting ready to leave, Roy stood up to fix his pack and we both heard something. I said, "What is that?" and Roy said, "It's a bear!" I thought he was teasing. It was on the trail coming down the hill where we had walked before sitting down for lunch. Roy said he saw the bear a split second before it saw him. As soon as it heard Roy when he spoke to me it hurried back up the hill the way it came. By the time I was able to turn around to see what was happening all I saw was his head, ears, back and his behind as he was leaving the area. Roy said it was a juvenile and it only weighed a couple of hundred pounds. My sister's German Shepard was probably as big as the bear, just not quite as heavy. Roy had gotten a good look at the bear. He said it was walking along with its head down and when it looked up it was about twenty yards from him. As soon as it saw him it whipped around and ran back up the hill. We wondered if he was just a big cub and was his Mama around somewhere? We resumed the trail opposite the direction of the bear, we were going that direction anyway. We didn't hear or see any indication of any other bears in the vicinity. People reportedly often hike the entire AT and never see a bear. Those that see bears say they usually see the tail end of the bear as it is running away. We felt lucky to have actually seen a bear in the wild. It was windy all day and we hiked 10 miles before we stopped for the night.

Later I told Roy I thought he was joking about the bear and he told me he would never tell me there was a bear if there wasn't. Also, he said wouldn't tell me someone was coming when I was peeing in the woods near the trail if there wasn't anyone there. Good to know, he is a joker and these were definitely two situations that were good to know that were off limits of his antics.

December 3, 2021 - The wind was blowing when we crawled in our tent and it finally stopped sometime early in the morning before we got up. The weather was beautiful and the temperature was in the seventies. We saw several hikers, three SOBOs headed for Springer Mountain and a few day hikers out enjoying the weather. We crossed highway 321 near Hampton, Tennessee, and camped at Watauga Lake. Our campsite had a beautiful view and there were geese on the lake.

The fallen leaves on the trail made for a whole new hazard. The leaves could be slick when very dry. I fell once, both feet went out from under me in the dry leaves as I was hiking down a small hill and had let down my guard. *Luckily, I was not injured. Great, this was another way to fall and hurt yourself if you were not careful.* There was a lot of uphill hiking but we hiked 11 miles.

December 4, 2021 - The weather was warm and I hiked in shorts all day. We hiked 12.5 miles and found a good campsite in the woods not far from a water source. I went down the hill to fill our water bottles at the spring while Roy was filtering some of the last of the water, we had to make an electrolyte drink. *We used Propel or Gatorade powder most of the time, it also gave the water flavor. Ever since not having any while hiking in the 100 Mile Wilderness, we carried it religiously.* When I returned, he handed me a peanut butter jar and I drank half of the liquid and handed it back to him. As I handed it back, I thought the jar smelled a little funny and I looked at the lid as he was drinking his half. He had written 14 oz. in black marker on his peanut butter jar, we used it for making drinks or as a cup for collecting water if needed and it was smaller than my peanut butter jar. Both lids were red, but this lid had no writing. I looked at the jar again and realized he had somehow used my peanut butter jar! It was granny's pot, the one I used for peeing in the tent! I don't know why he picked up my jar which was lying on the ground near my pack when he should have gotten his jar. He said he just saw the peanut butter jar and didn't give it a second thought. We decided it wouldn't kill us. *In survival situations you are supposed to be able to drink urine. At least what we had was very diluted, besides I always rinse out Granny's Pot after I used it! We really got a good laugh out of that blunder and I would occasionally ask if he got the right jar when he was filtering*

143

water. Lesson learned, make sure water is filtered into the right peanut butter jar!

December 5, 2021 - The wind started again during the night and it was cold and windy all day. There was no hiking in shorts, it was much too cold. We hiked 10.7 miles to Double Springs Shelter, made a quick dinner and got in the tent early. We checked the weather forecast and found it was supposed to rain the next day. We were hoping the rain would hold off until we could get to Damascus but it didn't look like we would be that lucky.

December 6, 2021 - We knew we had to hike 13.4 miles because the trail through the area was closed to camping due to bear activity. According to the FarOut app, camping between Double Springs Shelter and Backbone Rock had been closed to camping since June 1, 2021. We also knew it was supposed to rain in the afternoon. The weather was tolerable and we hiked as fast as we could. It started raining before noon and drizzled off and on all afternoon. We made it through the no camping zone and set up the tent about 3:00 p.m. We covered the miles quickly because the terrain was not as rugged in this area. There were no huge elevation loss or gains and we made good time. It would get dark early since it was cloudy and would also get colder quickly. If it had not been raining, we may have pushed on. As we were setting the tent up it started to rain harder so we threw our packs in and climbed in to complete the set up inside. *We were pretty good at setting the tent up quickly and also setting everything up with us inside at this point.* The rain stopped about 6:00 p.m. but after the rain it was colder. We ate a little food that didn't have to be cooked and settled in for a long night. We knew we were only 5 miles from Damascus, thankfully it would be a short distance to hike the next day.

December 7, 2021 - *COLD.* The temperature had dropped into the twenties during the night and everything was frozen that morning. We had placed our wet shoes in the vestibule of the tent and they were frozen solid! There was no way to put them on our feet! Everything outside the tent that was wet the evening before was now frozen. Thank goodness our packs and other gear were inside the tent. We had made sure to keep our water filter inside the tent. *If the water filter was frozen it would no longer be effective for filtering water because it would damage the material inside.* We considered just putting on a couple of pairs of our wool socks and hiking in our Crocs. But, we had about five miles to go to get to Damascus and it was mostly downhill. The Crocs didn't have much tread left and would be too slick to hike in, especially downhill. *All hikers carry sandals, Crocs or some type of shoe to wear around camp or when they go to town.* We put on our Crocs and socks when we got out of the tent and decided a fire was more than a must, we had to find a way to build a fire to thaw our shoes. We used every trick in the book to build a fire. The thing that saved us was using the propane cook stove. Roy laid the stove on its side and just kept the fire going on some smaller sticks. It took us about an hour but we eventually managed to get a good fire going and thawed our shoes. I had an extra pair of insoles for my shoes and I changed the insoles and put on dry socks. My feet were damp but not squishy. It would be far better than trying to hike in my Crocs.

While we thawed our shoes, we fixed coffee and ate breakfast. After we got everything packed, we hit the trail by 9:30 a.m. A couple of hours later than normal but we were still doing alright. We crossed the Tennessee/Virginia state line around 10:30 a.m. The library at Damascus was a welcomed sight after hiking 4.8 miles, we were sure happy to see my Kia. I'm really glad the frozen shoes incident didn't happen a couple of days earlier. We had other shoes in the car, so we changed to those shoes and put on another pair of dry socks. *Lessons learned: First, if there is a chance the temperature will drop below freezing, shoes must be placed in the tent. We started carrying big plastic bags and would put our shoes in them before putting them in the tent. Second, an extra pair of insoles for your shoes was very handy. Third, make sure not to leave your charging cables at home. Fifth, you can build a fire when everything is frozen if you are persistent enough.*

We drove my Kia to Roan Mountain to get Roy's truck and made it home with both vehicles by 7:00 p.m. that night. We were sure glad to get home and be sleeping in our bed. Seven hundred and fifty miles down and we had been in six states so far. A little over fourteen hundred more miles to hike before we completed the AT.

We were only about one third finished. It had taken more than a little persistence to get this far. I felt as though the trail was about ninety percent mental and ten percent physical. *If I kept my mind in the right place I was going to finish.* The saying, "No pain, no rain, no Maine", pretty much described it. A hiker had to learn to deal with the pain and the rain, both of which sucked the positivity out of you. We were definitely in the game and I had no doubt if we avoided a major injury, we would complete our thru hike. The plan was to get back on the trail near the end of February 2022, weather permitting. We would enjoy Christmas and New Years with our friends and family. We would also celebrate the birthdays of my brother Perry and of three of our grandchildren, Lily, Isaac and Lyla before returning to the trail. We were chipping away at it, only 1443 miles to the finish.

"I have a restless spirit. The need to roam
and explore this Earth is in my soul." - Unknown

Chapter 24 - Going to See Phil

February 1, 2022 - We had enjoyed the holidays with family and friends and still planned on resuming the AT by the end of the month. But we had a lot of time to kill before we hiked again. While watching TV that morning we saw a segment on the news about Groundhog Day in Punxsutawney, Pennsylvania. Going to see the groundhog had been on our bucket list for several years. Groundhog Day is February 2nd. Roy said, "Let's just go!", and as usual I thought he was crazy. The event started in less than twenty-four hours. We loaded up in Roy's black truck, another Ford F-150 with a crew cab. The truck had not been driven much since he had gotten it so he thought it needed a good road trip. We also thought it would be good to have a different sort of adventure while waiting to return to the trail.

After searching online, we booked a room at the Quality Inn in nearby Indiana, Pennsylvania, the hometown of Jimmy Stewart. It had taken about eight hours to get there and we checked in before going to eat supper at a nearby restaurant. The Groundhog Day festivities were scheduled to start at 3:30 a.m. EST on 2/2/2022. *That would be 2:30 a.m. CST, oh boy, we would be losing an hour due to the time difference not to mention getting up shortly after midnight. At least we would have an easy date to remember our attending the festival.* We were about 30-40 minutes away from the location and had the alarm set for 2:00 a.m. EST. After the park opened, at 3:00 a.m. festivities were scheduled to start at 3:30 a.m. We decided we should arrive at Gobblers Knob around 3:30 a.m., we figured this was a once in a lifetime event for us and we didn't want to miss anything. Needless to say, we didn't sleep much. I think I was awake when the alarm went off, we got up and got ready to go see the groundhog. Both of us were terribly sleep deprived but optimistic when we set out to see the festival and the groundhog's prediction for spring.

Wal Mart and a couple of other larger businesses in Punxsutawney along with the local school system joined in the celebration by providing parking and transportation to and from the park where the festival was held. The school bus ride to the park was five dollars per person and the park entrance was free. We got in line to get our bus tickets and board the bus at Wal Mart. A short time later we arrived at Gobbler's Knob.

There was a carnival type atmosphere. Upbeat music kept everyone bouncing around and dancing. I too found myself dancing to the beat. The temperature was in the upper 20's, we had dressed in coveralls, coats and layered clothing so we were well equipped for the cold. The groundhog was not scheduled to make his prognostication until 7:30 a.m. I couldn't imagine what would be going on until the groundhog arrived. We had a long time to wait in the cold but we were determined to make the best of it. The emcee on the stage said this year was one of the best years as far as the cold was concerned and he commented that it really wasn't all that cold. The temperature was below freezing and it wasn't that cold? Northerners were apparently more conditioned to the cold than southerners. I was just thankful the wind was not blowing in addition to the cold. One of the chants started with the person on stage yelling, "Is it cold out here?" and the crowd would reply by yelling, "Noooo, Lordy, Lordy, it's nearly forty!"

There were actually two couples that got married during the festivities (that we knew of). One wedding was held in downtown Punxsutawney at 2:22 a.m. of course on 2/22/22. Another wedding was conducted on stage at the park while we were there.

Around 6:30 a.m. there was a fireworks display. It was the most spectacular display of fireworks and the closest to the ground either of us had ever seen. We were at the top of Gobbler's Knob and the fireworks were set up at a lower elevation nearby. Not only were the fireworks unbelievable, they went on for probably a full 20 minutes. By this time there were several thousand people on hand and there were lots of oohs and aahs. The fireworks before sunrise were spectacular.

After the fireworks, the Inner Circle as they were called, paraded up on the stage with great fanfare. All these guys were dressed in tuxedos with tails and hats. There was much ceremony to their introductions as each member was presented to the crowd, their standing and title within the group was announced. Finally, the groundhog's handler reached into a large stump on the stage and retrieved him for all to see. The crowd erupted wildly with cheers. I was just at this point thinking I wish they would hurry up so we could get out of the cold. We had been there since about 3:30 a.m., standing the entire time and the temperature was still in the mid-twenties.

The person who interprets the groundhog's prediction was a member of the Inner Circle sworn to secrecy. Not all members of the group knew how the determination was made for spring's arrival. We were told they didn't speak Groundhogese. The groundhog was placed in the designated area and the prediction was made. Six more weeks of winter this year to which the crowd booed and protested loudly.

As soon as the prediction was made the crowd began to quickly disperse. We walked back to the pickup area to catch one of the buses back to Wal Mart. We were happy to mark the attendance of this event off the bucket list. It is an event everyone should see once, but once was enough for us.

When we checked out of our room at 3:00 a.m. EST the staff told us we were welcome to come back and eat breakfast there if we would like. We decided we would take them up on the offer. We came back along with several other festival goers to take advantage of the breakfast. It was a great opportunity to use the restroom, get hot coffee, eat a good breakfast and most importantly get warmed up before we headed home. Believe it or not, neither of us got too sleepy on the way back. However, we were both more than ready for our bed at home that night.

The Punxsutaney groundhog was named Phil. There were signs, banners, songs all dedicated to him and a crowd of several thousand all there to see him. It was unreal to me, the fiasco was dedicated to all things, a rodent named Phil who allegedly predicted the weather.

"When you have a dream, you have to grab it and never let go." - Carol Burnett

Chapter 25 - We Will Stop When We Finish

February 27, 2022 - The day to resume the trail had finally arrived. We drove to Damascus, Virginia. Our daughter Christi, and grandchildren Autumn and Isaac, went with us to drive my car back home. We started back on the trail where we finished in December at the Damascus Library. Saying goodbye to the kids was tough knowing we wouldn't see them for several months. We planned on staying on the trail until we finished this time. Our finish would be in Gorham, New Hampshire where we stopped after hiking SOBO from Katahdin in September 2020. We hiked out of the town of Damascus and the trail ran parallel to US Route 58 for a bit before it crossed the road and veered off up a big hill and into the woods. We hiked 5.7 miles, the trail was fairly easy, but we knew that wouldn't last. There were lots of small streams we crossed repeatedly and uphill climbs but at least there were lots of switchbacks which allowed for an easier climb. We set up our tent near a stream, it was getting dark early and we knew we had to get set up before it got too cold. It was getting cold quickly and we were glad to get in the tent and snuggle down in our sleeping bags for the night after making a quick supper.

February 28, 2022 - *Happy Birthday to Roy! He got what he wanted, getting back on the trail.* The AT joined the Virginia Creeper Bike Trail and crossed a large bridge over Laurel Creek before they separated. We crossed several small streams, most of them had small footbridges. The weather was cold and clear, we hiked 11 miles to the Lost Mountain Shelter 3370 feet elevation and camped there in our tent.

March 1, 2022 - Most of the morning we hiked uphill, tough hiking on sore legs. *It took a couple of days to get into the groove when starting all over. Section hikers hike the entire AT starting over and over. I was glad we were getting back to the trail before too much time passed and we completely lost our trail legs.* It wasn't as cold last night and has been warmer during the day. We met Benny today, the first hiker we have seen since leaving Damascus, he was section hiking. Four ladies were also on the trail later that day, we saw them at Buzzard Rock at 5087 feet elevation, they were day hiking. Roy climbed up on Buzzard Rock and I took his picture. Later I sent the pic to our kids and comments were made regarding a buzzard on Buzzard Rock. *Hey, I thought about it, but they said it.* We hiked 9.3 miles and camped 9 miles from Deep Gap.

March 2, 2022 - The Grayson Highlands were beautiful, the highlands looked like something out of an old western movie. There were open grassy fields and hills with lots of rocks. *Roy later said he could imagine outlaws or Indians hiding in the rocks just like in the movies.* Feral ponies were grazing near the trail and we were pleasantly surprised when one of them walked up and allowed us to pet him. *I later found out it is illegal and you can be fined for petting or feeding the ponies. Oops! I was hoping we would get to see the ponies, I had read about them and thought they would probably be scared of people.* This pony was not scared, he was curious and kept pushing his nose toward me. I quickly quit trying to pet him because he was being too insistent. I think he was hoping to get a treat but I had no intention of giving him one. I finally had to shoo him away before he became too aggressive. It was windy that day and the tall grasses were whipped around as we hiked across the open areas. We stopped at the Thomas Knob Shelter for lunch in hopes of getting out of the wind for a bit.

We saw the ladies we had seen the day before at Buzzard Rock and we stopped and talked with them for a few minutes. They were hiking a short section and they were very interested in our thru hiking the AT. We hiked 9.5 miles and camped at Wise Shelter.

March 3, 2022 - There were more ponies on the trail but they were not as bold as the first one we saw. It was cool, clear and windy all day. Again, we didn't waste much time hiking across the open fields where the wind was blowing. We thought about going to a store near the trail. The app recommended it as a place to stop for a snack or light resupplies. We were not sure it was even open and as it was about a mile off the trail and we really didn't need supplies we hiked on down the trail. We camped in our tent at Hurricane Mountain Shelter that evening after hiking 10.89 miles.

March 4, 2022 - There were lots of up and down hills on the trail. The weather was warm and sunny. Most of the day was spent hiking in the woods with several stream crossings and a couple of roads. We were getting better at rock hopping across the streams. At one point we were in a valley when we heard jets, they were flying close and coming fast. There were two military jets flying low through the valley and they were maneuvering like jets flying through mountains in a movie. The jets were very loud and gone in a few seconds. *I thought about all the unrest in the world and hoped the jets were just practicing and not flying because of a problem, they sure did seem to be in a hurry. We were later told by some of the local folks that it was Friday and there were lots of jets flying because that's reportedly when they practiced at the nearby military base.* We hiked 12.59 miles and camped near mile 527.7 at a stealth campsite, 6.6 miles from Marion, Virginia. We were looking forward to going into town the next day.

March 5, 2022 - We hiked 6.6 miles and arrived at the Mt. Rogers National Recreation Headquarters on Virginia Route 16. The AT went right beside the headquarters building. We used the courtesy phone outside to call for a taxi to take us to the town of Marion, Virginia. There was no cell service there, in fact we had hiked much of the day without cell service. We got a room at the Travel Inn and as usual the first thing on the agenda was getting showers, followed by getting something to eat. We walked into town after our shower and ate at Charley's Philly Steaks before going to the local Wal Mart to purchase supplies. *I'm a people watcher and I know you may see absolutely anything at Wal-Mart. I realized while in the store I shouldn't make fun of people from home at the local Wal-Mart, southern Virginia's Wal Mart's are just as ripe for people watching.* After getting supplies, we spent a quiet afternoon resting, caught up on a bit of TV and did a load of laundry.

March 6, 2022 - *Why did we get so much at Wal-Mart? Lord, help us, these backpacks are too heavy with all the stuff we bought! We know they probably weigh at least 30 pounds without food, we added five or six pounds each. We will definitely eat the heavier food first.* Roy was able to talk the owner at the motel into giving us a ride back to the trail. The guy's English was not great and he was unsure of where we wanted to go, after one or two wrong turns we finally got there.

The trail was mostly uphill, we hiked up and over the last 4000-foot mountain we will have to climb for a while. The AT went through an old homestead at the Settler's Museum in the mountains near Atkins, Virginia. The house was a 19th century white two-story house with a white picket fence and the grounds had all the outbuildings an old farm would have had at the time. It reminded me of my grandparents' farm with the smokehouse, cellar, chicken house, outhouse, the corn crib and the barns. The house was well maintained and we could see through the windows, it was decorated in furniture from that period. We were not able to go in the buildings but we did sit on the porch swing at the house for a spell. *It was nice to think about people living in a simpler time and how they managed to sustain themselves on a farm growing their own food and tending crops. It was hard, but was it any less stressful? There were still worries, uncooperative weather such as drought, hot weather without air conditioning, cold weather with little heat, snow storms, and no weather forecasts on TV. Crops or gardens failing to produce could result in great hardship. Not to mention the lack of modern medicine and shorter lifespans. Haven't you watched Little House on the Prairie? What can I say, I'm spoiled and awfully glad we have running water, central heat and air conditioning but it did remind me of what our ancestors dealt with every day.*

We camped at an old road bed beside the trail. A couple of people rode through on horses as we were setting up our tent and we talked with them for a bit. A NOBO hiker came through using a headlamp after dark. We could hear a train in the distance and not long after that we heard coyotes, they sounded pretty close. I always wanted my trekking poles close to the tent in case we need to fight off something like coyotes during the night and I made sure they were within reach. *Thankfully we never had to use them for anything other than hiking.* Even after all the commotion we settled in and managed to sleep well.

March 7, 2022 - Atkins, Virginia was not a very big place but it had a Sunoco gas station that reportedly was a good place for hikers to stop for a quick bite to eat. It was 9:00 a.m. when we arrived there. They made fresh Hunt Brothers Pizza for us and it was really good! *I know, pizza at 9:00 a.m. but on the trail you take what you can get whenever you can get it and we were grateful.* Rain started in the middle of the afternoon. I got to use my hiking umbrella for the first time and discovered I really like it. *If it is not raining hard there is no need to wear a rain jacket when using the umbrella. A rain jacket is hot and will make you sweat so much you end up as wet from the jacket as you do without a jacket.* We set up our tent about 4:00 p.m. after hiking about 12 miles. We got into the tent early due to rain.

March 8, 2022 - It was a rainy night but we didn't get too wet. *Thankfully we had taken the tent with us on one of our trips to our Florida house and we applied seam sealer in a couple of coats. We hoped our efforts would prevent leakage and get us through the colder winter months. Our tent was a three-season tent and we thought we may have to replace it if we were still hiking in the warmest part of the summer. But for colder weather I don't think our tent could have been beaten. We never were cold at night in the tent. Now, if the tent didn't leak, we would be all set.*

We hiked through pastures that reminded me of the farm where I grew up. There were paths through the pastures made by cows in addition to the path made by the AT. The AT was marked by posts with white blazes. *The entire trail is marked on trees, rocks, posts or on the pavement with white blazes. Sometimes the direction of the trail is not clear, but with the app we used we were able to correct deviations or ensure we were heading in the right direction. I still don't know how people found their way on the trail for the years prior to GPS. In addition to the white blazes there are also blue blazes, these indicate a side trail to a shelter or an alternate route. Hikers called Purists don't take any alternate route or skip*

154

not even one inch of the originally designated trail. Most hikers will take easier alternate routes at times. These count toward completion of the trail so they are okay to hike. There were only a couple of times on the entire AT where we took a blue trail.

We waded Lick Creek, it took a few minutes but we stopped and put on our Crocs. The creek was about a foot deep and very, very cold but wading was the only way across since the old bridge had washed out. *An AT volunteer trail maintainer cautioned us repeatedly a day or two before about the dangers of wading this creek in high water.* There was a rope to hold on to while crossing but, if it rains very much the creek apparently can get deep, swift and dangerous very quickly. *We read comments on the app where several hikers had crossed in knee, thigh or even waist deep water.* We were fortunate the recent rain was not enough for the creek to rise too much. It was only up to our shins, if the creek had been too high and we had to turn back to the detour it would have added another six or seven miles. *Yikes!* Glad we were able to cross in our Crocs. We stealth camped at the 566.0 mile after we finally found a spot level enough to set the tent.

March 9, 2022 - *Happy Birthday to our daughter Christi!* It rained a lot last night but we stayed dry in the tent. Thankfully it was not raining when we broke camp. Chestnut Knob Shelter was 3.8 miles away and he had to hike from 2613 feet elevation to 4407 feet. It started to rain about an hour after we started hiking and we put on our rain gear. There were as usual multiple false summits and I didn't think we would ever get to the shelter. Fog moved in and by the time we got to the shelter and you couldn't see more than a few feet. The shelter was an enclosed rock shelter with bunk space for six or seven people. We decided to hold up until the weather improved although it was only about 11:00 a.m., we stayed there the remainder of the day. We had good phone service and were able to make calls. Phone service was usually better on the mountain tops and we lucked out this time. We put our tent up inside the shelter, we knew we could crawl in and get warm. There was plenty of room and we had not seen many hikers at any of the shelters so far. It was cold and we knew we would stay warmer in the shelter and out of the wind. We were able to set up the tent and not take much more space than two people normally would if they had two sleeping bags placed side by side.

Later that afternoon, a hiker arrived at the shelter and set up his sleeping bag on one of the bunks. He was a section hiker from Florida and he didn't have a trail name. An hour or so later a man with a dog stopped by the shelter to check on things. He was a volunteer and he ensured the shelter was maintained. He offered us chips, gum, a sandwich, fruit and some other stuff he had with him. *Trail magic!* We took chips, gum and fruit and thanked the man for the goodies and his maintaining the shelter. The volunteer went by the trail name Daffy Duck. He was yet another person we met on the trail doing good things for total strangers and expecting nothing in return. Another hiker arrived in the evening, his trail name was Saturn and he was from Switzerland. He was hiking big miles and long days. He talked about hiking 30 miles plus each day. *Wow, how is that even possible?*

March 10, 2022 - The last hiker came into the shelter at 12:30 a.m. and he was also the first to get up and leave that morning. We found out his trail name was Quadzilla. He was hiking up to 40 miles per day and had plans to hike the PCT (Pacific Crest Trail), the CDT (Continental Divide Trail) and the AT all within one year. *Wow, all three trails add up to nearly 8000 miles!* He had hiked over 30 miles the day before and when he crossed Lick Creek last night, in the dark, (we crossed it two days ago) he crossed near the old bridge in waist deep water because he didn't see the rope across the creek where it was shallower. He told us he was on Instagram; he would be documenting his travels and we could follow him. *We would hear of Quadzilla several times as we hiked north; he was something of a legend and we felt lucky to actually meet him. We would later find out through Instagram, he started hiking on February 16, 2022 and he finished hiking all three trails on December 2, 2022. WOW! The calendar year triple crown (CYTC), what an accomplishment! If we could just get through the AT that would be more than enough for me!*

Not surprising, we were the last ones out of the shelter that morning. The weather was cold, windy and there were only a very few minutes of sun late in the day. At one point we accidentally got off the trail and went down an old road, when we realized we were off trail we backtracked and corrected our mistake. However, had we not gotten off trail we would not have seen the huge valley known as God's Thumbprint. A local guy on a day hike told us about the area and we decided it was aptly named. The view of the valley with mountains completely surrounding it was breathtaking. *We sure didn't want to make many of these detours. This error probably cost us about a mile on the trail and every mile counted at least as far as I was concerned.*

We hiked 11 miles mostly downhill over 2000 feet and camped at the Jenkins Shelter. We got our tent set up and ready a bit early because as usual we knew it would get colder quickly. String Bean was a hiker who stayed in the shelter that night and he came in as we were crawling in the tent for the night. He was wearing a very bright puffy jacket the color of frozen green beans, maybe that's where he got that trail name. It was getting colder and we decided maybe we could be more sociable in the morning.

March 11, 2022 - We got up and fixed coffee and ate breakfast. While talking with String Bean, he told us he awakened to a mouse sitting on his chest looking at him. *That would be one more reason to NOT sleep in the shelters for me.*

The moss-covered rocks on the hillsides in the woods reminded us a lot of Mammoth Cave National Park at home. The forest took on a beautiful glow as the sun was coming up that morning and burning through the fog and I had to stop a couple of times for a picture and to admire the view. As usual, pictures didn't do justice to the beauty of the landscape.

At one point a tree had fallen across the trail, it had not been cut away and it was pretty high off the ground. You could stoop over and go under the tree without a problem. Someone had painted a duck on the tree where the trail went under it. *Cute, duck when you go under. We got the message.*

The terrain was better and we covered the 11.3 miles to Bland, Virginia faster than anticipated. The weather was warm, sunny and the wind was cool but it was a much better day. We arrived at highway 52 and called for a shuttle to take us to town. Bobcat picked us up and took us to the Big Walker Motel. The last few hundred feet of the ride Bobcat had trouble with the steering of his vehicle but we made it to the motel. He called someone for a ride and went to an auto parts place in town. He actually did the repair in the parking lot at the motel. It was a good thing he got it fixed because the weather prediction for the next day was not good.

We booked a room in advance since there was supposed to be a big snowstorm heading our way and very cold temperatures the next couple of days. We felt it was best to get off the trail and we were fortunate to be getting to a town and to have gotten a room. It was 65 degrees with sunshine when we checked into our room that afternoon. There was a Circle K station across the road from the motel and it had a DQ. After we got showers, we ate at the DQ, then walked about a half mile to the Dollar General Store to resupply. This was a convenient location, everything we might need was within easy walking distance except a laundry. If we were going to be staying in the motel for a couple of nights, we needed snacks in addition to our usual hiker fare. *Dollar General usually had most anything we needed and we would visit several of them before we completed our AT thru hike.* We stayed up too late watching TV, but knowing we didn't have to hike the next day it really didn't matter. We were apparently in a bit of a TV watching deficit.

March 12, 2022 - This was our first zero day for this leg of our hike. We woke up as usual around 7:00 a.m. Since there was no laundry, we had gotten laundry detergent at the Dollar General and I hand washed all our stuff the night before. Roy hung a line in the room and we had stuff hanging everywhere. We spent the day watching it snow, at times it was like a blizzard. We couldn't see the gas station across the road! The temperature was in the twenties and was supposed to drop to single digits during the night. We were more than thankful our timing was right and we were in the motel during the bad weather. A Jack Hanna's Animal Adventures marathon was on TV and we watched it most of the morning. We called and talked with family and friends back home. We played rummy and were lazy most of the day. Our biggest activity was rotating the laundry in front of the room's heating unit so things would dry. We walked across the road to Circle K when the snow eased up a bit that afternoon. The DQ was closed because of the weather so we got some gas station food. We spent the rest of the afternoon and evening just being lazy. *We later heard about hikers who were stuck in the Smoky Mountains at shelters during the snowstorm, that had to have been a miserable situation. Thankfully we didn't hear of any reports of anyone with major problems due to the snow other than being delayed by having to hunker down and wait for it to pass.*

March 13, 2022 - The snow stopped the evening before and the temperature was on the rise. Bobcat took us back to the trail where he picked us up the day before. He also showed us where to start the trail NOBO, he said a lot of hikers get confused with the trail markings. We were grateful he showed us because it was not clearly marked at all, we would have figured it out with the FarOut app but it would have taken a few minutes. The sun shined all day, the snow was only about an inch deep in most places and was melting quickly. We hiked 11.9 miles and camped that evening at Jenny's Knob Shelter.

March 14, 2022 - Most of the snow was gone and there was abundant sunshine. The temperature was cool, but great for hiking. We crossed over a small river on a suspension footbridge built for the AT. Thankfully we didn't have to wade this one, the water appeared to be much deeper than the ones we had seen before. After hiking 10.2 miles we camped at a stealth site near a different smaller stream. The sound of the water running down the stream lulled us to sleep that evening.

March 15, 2022 - The morning started out really COLD! But we warmed quickly, the trail was awfully rocky and of course there was a lot of uphill climbing. *Nothing like a brisk uphill hike to warm you up.* We hiked 11.7 miles and camped at Doc's Knob Shelter. This was one of the most unusual shelters we had seen thus far. It had a huge deck on the front of the shelter and a piped spring at the steps that ran from under the deck. We were thankful for the easy water source and we set our tent up on the deck. There hadn't been many hikers on the trail that day and it was late enough we didn't think anyone else was coming, we were right, this time. *Anytime we could set up on a deck or platform it was* preferable because it kept the tent out of the dirt and or mud if it rained, which it seemed to do a lot.

"Carry as little as possible, but choose that little with care." - Earl Shaffer

Chapter 26 - Cleanup on Aisle Three

March 16, 2022 - The hike was tough, 2500 feet downhill! There were lots of wonderful views and it seemed we could see forever. It started to rain during the last couple of hours of hiking. We hiked 9.3 miles. Fortunately, right before we got to the road to town, we were offered a ride from a guy and his family from West Virginia who were on a day hike. He said if we didn't mind, we could ride in the back of his truck. I had looked down toward the parking area and saw only one truck and it had a topper on it, at least it was out of the rain. There would not be enough room inside the truck since the man's wife, son and a dog were with him. I was gladly accepting, Roy was a bit reluctant to accept the ride, and I wondered why. Come to find out he had not seen the truck with the topper and he was thinking we would just call for a shuttle. Once he realized there was a topper on the truck, he gladly accepted the ride. We threw our backpacks in and crawled inside. The guy dropped us off at the Angel's Rest Hiker Haven in Pearisburg, VA. It was yet another unique place, there was a bunk house, a bath house, laundry, kitchen and a trailer that was used for private rooms.

Our private room was one of the bedrooms in a single wide house trailer. As soon as we stepped into the trailer we were met by a barking dog. There was a hiker who had injured her foot and she was staying in the only other "private" room. She calmed her dog and we went on to our room. Other than barking when we entered every time, thankfully the dog was quiet.

Our bed was on a platform with the underneath boxed in with woven lattice. The walls were paneled with what appeared to be reclaimed lumber. The bed covering was a patchwork quilt with bears and trees. The room looked nice enough except for the multi-colored lights under the bed made me feel like we were in a brothel instead of a hostel. We asked about turning the lights under the bed off, it took a while for someone to find out how to kill the lights but they finally did it.

We had to go out of the trailer to the shower, use the bathroom or do laundry. *We took our showers in what we would later refer to as the best showers on the entire trail.* There were three bathrooms that were built side by side, the rooms were large, probably 12x12. The building was built into a hillside with shower rooms on the upper level. The lower level, which was entered from the back, had a laundry on one side and a kitchen on the other. There was a large common area outside the lower level with a fire pit and several chairs. It would be a really neat place to hang out if the weather was cooperative but as usual it was raining off and on.

After taking showers we turned our attention to food and resupply. There was a Food Lion, Mexican restaurant and an all you can eat Chinese buffet all within easy walking distance. As we got to the Food Lion it started to drizzle again. We decided to eat at the Chinese buffet, it was in the same shopping center so we could avoid walking in the rain. The food was really good and we both made several trips back to the buffet. It had been a while since we had Chinese food and it really hit the spot. I got a fortune cookie and the fortune inside said something about showing everyone your smile.

We left the Chinese restaurant and went to the Food Lion for supplies. We learned long ago to not go to a grocery on an empty stomach, it definitely was not a problem this time. *Shopping in an unfamiliar grocery store pretty much required going through every aisle and still backtracking a couple of times plus Roy wanted to compare prices on every item. Our grocery trips usually turned into an hour-long venture.*

We were almost finished with our grocery shopping when all of the sudden my belly made a loud noise. It didn't take long for me to figure out I needed to find a bathroom and the sooner the better. I told Roy I had to go to the restroom and took off in a hurry toward the back of the store. There was a young man stocking a cooler and I hurriedly asked him where the ladies' room was located. He quickly pointed to the corner near where we were standing. *He may or may not have heard the urgency in my voice, just saying. Thank goodness it was close.* I proceeded to make my way to the restroom. When I pushed the door open there was a woman picking paper up out of the floor and she said excuse me. I had nearly hit her with the door and I said no problem, you should be excusing me. All I could think was I hope she is on her way out and I had no time for conversation! I went into a stall and she left the restroom. Thankfully there was no one else in there because the door no sooner closed my gastrointestinal system exploded. *I don't think I ever had ever had such an "issue" in my life. If this is what happens to hikers when they eat town food no wonder the privies are a mess. Most of the time we preferred to just go in the woods.* I got finished in the ladies' room, there was nothing lady like about what I had done, and went back to find my husband. *Had there not been a restroom readily available, I would not have wanted to be the person called for cleanup on aisle three and I would have literally died from embarrassment!* We finished with the shopping and went back to the hostel as soon as we could. I feared there might be a round two of the "issue". To my surprise there was not, then again, I don't think there would have been anything remaining for a round two.

I hardly slept at all that night, the bed was not very comfortable, my husband snored like a freight train and my stomach was bloated from eating too much food. I heard the noise as it rained off and, on all night, and getting out of the rain was the only thing that seemed to be a good thing. Thankfully I didn't have to make another emergency run.

"It's not the mountains we conquer, but ourselves."
- Sir Edmund Hillary

Chapter 27 - Virginia's Triple Crown

March 17, 2022 - We got a ride back to the trail after checking out of the hostel. The hike was uphill most of the day and we hiked 11.8 miles from 1601 feet elevation to 3440 feet. Rice's Field had nearly a 360-degree view. *This was a place Roy would reference later as being one of his favorite places on the southern portion of the trail because of the spectacular views.* The weather was warm and breezy. We stopped at the Rice's Field Shelter for a break and to use the restroom. I found a painted rock that said, Love Your Smile. *Strange, especially after getting that fortune at the Chinese restaurant. What a coincidence.*

While at the shelter, Roy found an unopened Mountain House meal, spaghetti and meat sauce. It was lying on top of an area just inside the shelter. Apparently, someone had left it there by mistake. There was a water container there also. We had not seen anyone hiking all day and there was no one at the shelter. We decided to take the meal, no one ever goes back to get things they have left behind. *Hey, it was just like finding a $10 bill. It would make a good hot meal on a cold evening. Yes, we had become opportunistic hikers but we figured we could use all the help we could get on this journey.*

March 18, 2022 - We heard lots of jets while hiking, it was Friday and was supposed to be the day the military base did practice. The hike was not too bad until the last 1.5 miles when we had a 1000 feet elevation gain. Hiking uphill late in the day was difficult on tired legs and it kicked our tails. We were exhausted when we arrived at the Bailey Gap Shelter, after hiking 11.8 miles. The wind was relentless so we set our tent up inside the shelter which helped a lot.

March 19, 2022 - It was really foggy when we awakened. I thought I heard Roy say a camper had backed in beside the shelter last night, I thought he was teasing me. I was thinking of a camper trailer backing in. He said we were going to wake them by talking loudly. In reality, a hiker had come in well after dark and pitched a tent beside the shelter. We later apologized to him for hogging the shelter and told him with the wind we would have understood if he had put his tent in the shelter also. But he said it was about 9:00 p.m. when he arrived and he didn't want to wake us up. *We were concerned with all the wind there could have been trees blown over during the night and the shelter would provide us with extra protection.*

It was foggy until about noon but the afternoon was warm and sunny. In addition to the morning fog the trail was very rocky. The last bit of the hike for the day was 2.5 miles with 1700 feet elevation gain. *Ugh, steep uphill near the end of the day again.* We hiked 12.2 miles and set up our camp at Johns Creek Mountain Trail.

March 20, 2022 - The morning was foggy with a little drizzle but it cleared and the remainder of the day was a little warmer and windy. We passed right by the Keffer Oak, the second largest tree along the AT. *It is white oak tree that is 19 feet in circumference and has stood for more than 300 years.* We stopped and took pictures of us with the tree. It is huge and dwarfs all the other trees in the area. It was really something to see. We hit a new milestone of 15.07 miles, the most we have hiked in one day. There was lots of rock climbing along very high ledges. We crossed over the Eastern Continental Divide while hiking on those high cliffs and rocks. It was cold and windy most of the day but the views on both sides of the trail were fantastic. At one point during the day, we saw a guy who was carrying a bicycle across his shoulders and running along the trail. He quickly passed us and was out of sight in a matter of minutes. *I guess his bike didn't weigh as much as our backpacks. Bicycles are not allowed on the AT, but he was not riding it. We had no clue what he was doing. Maybe training for something? We would never know for sure.*

March 21, 2022 - The weather was warm, sunny, the wind was gently blowing and best of all it was dry. *It's amazing the difference a day can make in the weather. And it is amazing the effect sunshine can have on your outlook.* We hiked to the Audie Murphy Monument and had lunch there. *Audie Murphy was a war hero and a movie star. The things he did in his military and acting careers were amazing. He was one of the most decorated soldiers in World War II and his acting career spanned over 20 years. He died in a*

165

plane crash near the site of the monument on Brushy Mountain in 1971 and he is buried in Arlington National Cemetery. The location of the monument was a few yards off the Appalachian Trail. There were hundreds of items left at the monument to pay tribute. Military toy jeeps, small U.S. flags, military dog tags. military patches, coins, silicone bracelets were just some of the items left at the monument. *It was amazing to me that people continue to pay their respects this many years after his death. It was one of the little side trips off the trail we were glad we went to see.*

We hiked down to Trout Creek where we met a man standing on the bridge overlooking the creek. He was a local, out for a ride on his motorcycle and had stopped for a bit. We offered us a beer and we gladly accepted. *Trail Magic in the most unexpected place.* We talked to him for quite a while, as he was very interested in our AT hike and said he enjoyed talking to hikers. We thanked him for sharing his beer with us and hiked on up the trail. We camped at Pickle Creek Shelter after hiking 10.1 miles. *Our goal early on was to hike 10 miles each day and build up to more if possible. It was getting easier to hike at least 10 miles if not more each day.*

March 22, 2022 - The weather was warm and sunny and we hiked most of the day in shorts. Dragon's Tooth, at 2939 feet elevation, was the landmark for the day. *It is one of the three landmarks included in what is known as Virginia's Triple Crown of hiking. The other sites are McAfee Knob and Tinker Cliffs.* Dragon's Tooth looked like a rock stuck into the ground with the sharp point left sticking up, therefore it looked like a big jagged tooth. *I thought it was appropriately named.*

There was a teacher with a group of twenty-five or so students at the top. The kids looked to be 10-12 years old. I would have been a nervous wreck bringing those kids up there but he was handling it like a pro. The climb up to the Dragon's Tooth was not bad as we were hiking NOBO, but the climb down made up for it. Very steep with high steps, at times I had to sit down and slide off to the next level. The kids went ahead of us until we came to a particularly difficult section. Their teacher was below, talking them through the area one at a time. We were able to pass them and continued on the trail. I was actually glad to get away from them, I don't like seeing kids in this type of terrain. I just knew one of them was going to fall.

We passed through the community of Catawba and ate at the only place near the trail, the Catawba Grocery. The store clerks were very hiker friendly and went out of their way to cook our food just right. We ordered burgers and fries, the burger was big and the large serving of fries were cooked perfectly, it was almost more than we could eat. I did manage to save room for a cup of ice cream, Hershey's Midnight Caramel River. *Oh, my heavens, chocolate ice cream with caramel, what's not to love! I got a new favorite flavor that would prove to be hard to find as we went along the AT.* We left Catawba with full bellies and hiked a little further before camping on top of a mountain for the night at mile 707.4. Earlier in the day we found a marker someone made with sticks at mile 700. *Adding the 300 miles hiked in Maine and New Hampshire, we are nearing the halfway point!*

March 23, 2022 - We had checked the weather forecast the day before and knew rain would be moving in early in the morning. We got up around 4:30 a.m. and packed up our tent. There was a shelter about four miles away and we hoped to beat the rain and hold up there. We of course had to use our headlamps and it started to drizzle not long after we started hiking. I couldn't help but be amazed at the raindrops sparkling in the light from the headlamps, they looked like diamonds in the brown leaves on the ground. *I guessed I would rather be thinking about diamonds than hiking in the dark down the side of a mountain when it was raining.* We crossed over some pretty rocky areas and high cliffs and it certainly seemed a lot longer than four miles to the shelter. It seemed like we just kept climbing up hills. *I don't know if it was better not to see how high we were because of the dark or I was more intimidated by the dark and not being able to see. I just knew I was more than ready to get off the trail and to the shelter.*

I could not figure out how we were ever going to get down off the mountain if we kept going up. I would say this many times while hiking the AT and it finally became the saying, what goes down must go up first. By the same token we also found what goes up, must go down first. Let me explain, if we were at 1500 feet

167

elevation and the shelter was at 500 feet elevation you would automatically think, okay we are going down 1000 feet, but we would climb to 2000 feet before finally going down to 1500 feet This also happened with climbing up, we nearly always had to go down first. Even the elevation map didn't always show the terrain exactly and we finally just quit questioning and knew it didn't matter, either way we had to hike the miles uphill or downhill.

It was drizzling rain and becoming increasingly foggy the whole way to the John Spring Shelter. We finally arrived there about 8:00 a.m., it was slow going on the trail. We had taken our time going over the wet trail in the dark and fog. There were two girls there, they had set their small tent up in the shelter. We set our tent up in the shelter on the other side. The girls were from a local college, they were on spring break and were hiking the Virginia Triple Crown. *That's right, apparently not all college kids go to the beach for spring break.* We changed into dry clothes and made breakfast. *We hadn't taken time for breakfast earlier since we were trying to beat the rain.* Not long after we got to the shelter it started to rain harder. We were glad we made it before the worst of the rain started. We settled in to wait out the rain and it rained off and, on all day, long.

Somehow, I lost my purple and pink buff. I looked everywhere for it and it was not to be found. I knew I didn't leave it when we packed up at 4:30 a.m. because we did the "idiot check" to make sure nothing was left behind. I had looked everywhere. I was sure I just stuck it in some of my gear and would run across it or worst case I had dropped it along the trail and didn't realize it. The longer I searched through my gear the more disgusted I became. I told my husband I was really bummed out about losing it since it was my favorite.

As we were trying to go to sleep after being in the shelter all day Roy's air mattress started making popping noises. It was loud and sounded like firecrackers going off. We discovered one of the baffles was apparently coming loose. It was near the head of his mattress, so we decided to turn it to the bottom, we thought there would be less pressure on it. We made all kinds of noise in our tent getting the mattress moved. but the popping noise stopped after we turned it. The sound sure did make for a few minutes of interesting activity as we tried to stop it from popping. *We would have to replace the mattress sooner than later. It is an essential piece of equipment. Without it our sleeping arrangements would not be tolerable.* Somewhere in all this commotion I found my buff. It was stuck in my bra between my boobs, right where I put it so I wouldn't lose it when I put on my headlamp that morning!

March 24, 2022 - Another hiker came into the shelter last night just before dark, he hiked from Dragon's Tooth and had hiked all day in the rain. He set up his sleeping mat and sleeping bag between our tents in the shelter and apparently slept well after getting settled in, he snored a lot. At one point during the early morning hours Roy and I both were awake because of his snoring. One of the girls in the tent snored also, but it was a subtle tolerable snore. This guy was full-on snoring. He awoke about 5:30 a.m. and stretched as he got up, he was bright eyed and ready to go. At this point all of us got up, made breakfast and got packed to leave the shelter. We had spent entirely too long in the tent and heard more than enough snoring, so we were more than ready to get back on the trail. Thankfully the weather had improved and it was supposed to be a good day.

The girls had a lot of equipment and their packs looked terribly heavy. I knew my pack was heavy but I wouldn't have made it long carrying their packs and they were headed to Dragon's Tooth. *They had a heck of a climb ahead with those heavy packs. I wondered about them carrying all that gear and hoped they made it to finish their hike without problems. One of the girls said she was already having problems with her back.*

McAfee Knob at 3156 feet elevation, is probably the most photographed site on the entire AT. It is a rocky outcropping with absolutely amazing views. I have a healthy respect for heights and this place definitely was high. I was able to walk out on the ledge a little bit, the rock was tilted up away from the edge and it didn't make me feel as uneasy as it would have if it was level or tilted down toward the edge. But I was not able to walk as far out on the rock as my husband. *Places like this usually make my legs shaky and I feel too unstable or unbalanced to go very near the edge of cliffs. I get really nervous if Roy gets too close to the edge of things too. He will go closer than I will and I am always telling him to get away from the edge. I think he finally sees just how much it bothers me.* He walked out to the iconic point to pose for a picture. The sun was not in the best position for pictures, but we did manage to get a few and took a while to admire the views. *I couldn't step out on the rock for a picture like he did, my legs just wouldn't let me do it.* The views from the AT in Virginia seemed to be getting higher up and they were gorgeous.

In addition to McAfee Knob, we saw Tinker Cliffs. Tinker Cliffs is about 3000 feet elevation and is about a quarter mile of cliffs with numerous areas to step out and look into the Catawba Valley below. The AT goes right along the edge of the cliffs in several places. There was also a trail several feet away, running parallel to the AT. I was more than glad to stay on that trail. I named it the Chicken Trail because I was chicken to go on the other trail. *The Chicken Trail was well traveled, I was apparently not the only one who didn't like heights.* I could see into the valley below in several places without getting too close to the edge of the cliffs and that was enough for me. I was glad we got to see this whole area but I was also glad to put it behind us due to the heights.

We made it to the Lambert Meadows Campsites. There were beautiful campsites in green grass beside a running stream. The campsite we chose had a picnic table and bear box nearby also. We also scored a little Trail Magic at the campsites. A couple on a day hike gave us an orange, they were really nice and talked to us for a few minutes about our AT journey. *It continues to be amazing to me that people are so giving to hikers. Of course, we had also heard of hikers who had negative encounters with people who didn't like hikers. Thankfully we didn't meet any of those folks.* The weather was good, it was sunny in the morning and cloudy in the afternoon but at least there was no rain and we hiked 9.5 miles. *We were thrilled to have completed the Virginia Triple Crown of hiking but there was a lot more of Virginia to see.*

"Now I see the secret of making the best person, it is to grow in the open air and to eat and sleep with the earth." - Walt Whitman

Chapter 28 - Will We Ever Get Out of Virginia?

March 25, 2022 - Carvin Cove Reservoir and Tinker Creek Valley presented us with some beautiful views from up high on the trail. The colors of blue in the sky were amazing. This day we were excited to be getting into a town and were ready to get off the trail for a while. We hiked 9.3 miles and arrived at Daleville, Virginia. There was a Motel 8 right on the trail where it crossed over highway 220 and we booked a room there for two nights. We were planning on taking a zero day for some much-needed rest and relaxation. The room was really nice with a king-sized bed, a real step up from the tent. As usual we had a long hot shower then turned our attention toward food. Dinner at the Mexican restaurant near the motel was really good. Thankfully there were no gastrointestinal issues after eating restaurant food this time. Later, we watched NCAA basketball and did a load of laundry. *University of Kentucky was knocked out in the first round, beaten by a Cinderella team. Oh well, better luck next year.* Believe it or not, this was one of the few times we didn't have to dry out all of our gear. There had been no rain in the past few days.

March 26, 2022 - Zero-day number two for this leg of our AT hike. We ate breakfast at the motel and walked to Kroger for resupply. Afterwards we remembered we needed camp fuel, so we had to walk back to the Kroger shopping center a second time to go to the outfitter. Not every place has fuel and we wanted to be sure we got it when we could.

We made our trips to the shopping center in the morning and it was a good thing. It snowed off and on all afternoon. We stayed in the room and watched TV while the snow was coming down. In addition to the normal trail supplies we also got some snacks for the room since we would be there all afternoon. We got chips, cookies, an orange and some other stuff. Later I was doing something when Roy asked if I wanted some of the orange, he was peeling it and getting ready to eat it. I told him I would get some in a minute or two. I turned a little bit later for my piece of orange and Roy had eaten it all. He said he forgot. *I guess it tasted good and he was really enjoying it. Fruit was one thing we didn't get much of on the trail, it was too heavy to carry. We laughed a lot about him eating that orange and it became something I could tease him about. If he was eating something and was going to save a bite for me, I would say don't do it like you did the orange.*

After the snow stopped, we decided to walk to Cracker Barrel. The walk was a death-defying walk along highway 220 with lots of traffic and not much shoulder on the road. When we made it to Highway 11 it was not nearly as bad. We walked almost a mile one way to eat there but the food was great. Roy had a fried chicken dinner and I got chicken fried steak and gravy. *Bet you thought I was going to say cheeseburger! Lol!*

March 27, 2022 - The weather was sunny but cold, it was in the thirties most of the day. We hiked 11.2 miles over fairly easy terrain and stopped early to set up the tent at the Wilson Creek Shelter. We were glad to crawl in our tent and get into our down sleeping bags. *Cold weather usually means good sleep and we were definitely looking forward to it.*

March 28, 2022 - It was cold and windy all day and we hiked 13.8 miles. *It seems we hike faster and get in more miles when it's colder.* We hiked across the Blue Ridge Parkway and along with it for a while. There were several great lookouts along the parkway but it was so cold and windy we didn't take much time to look. We camped at Cove Mountain Shelter and put our tent in the shelter to get out of the wind. There were no other hikers in the shelter that night. The wind was still roaring into the night.

March 29, 2022 - It was warmer with very light winds, much better than the day before. We hiked 11.9 miles up a lot of big hills. We camped at Cornelius Creek Shelter, there was a really good tent site and water nearby. We were starting to see lots of wildflowers and trees starting to bloom. The flowers were beautiful shades of pink, purple, yellow and white. *Bring it on, we are ready for spring!*

March 30, 2022 - The weather was cool and windy. The terrain had lots of big ups and downs. We should be getting to Glasgow, Virginia in the morning. *We thought this was funny since our home is in Glasgow, Kentucky.* Rain is supposed to be moving in the area and we were watching the radar, when we had cell service. We were considering our options and trying to avoid being out in bad weather if at all possible. We hiked up and over Apple Orchard Mountain. Of course, we were at 3167 feet elevation at Cornelius Creek, went down to 2451 feet at Apple Orchard Falls, then up to 4203 feet at Apple Orchard Mountain. *What goes up must go down first.* Apple Orchard Mountain had a huge FAA flight, communications and weather station. It was a huge complex on the top of the mountain and one of the 4000 footers we had to hike over. We were a little bummed because we couldn't see the views because of the fog. It was so cold and windy up there and we were ready to get off the mountain. We stealth camped near Sulphur Springs Trail at mile 780.01 after hiking 12.4 miles.

March 31, 2022 - We broke camp at 5:00 a.m. to try and outrun the rain, again. We had a pickup at the James River Bridge scheduled for 1:00 p.m. and we called and rescheduled for 11:00 a.m. We made it to the Matts Creek Shelter with very little rain. The shelter was 2.2 miles from the bridge and it lightly rained most of the way. The crossing over the James River was on the James River Footbridge, a large pedestrian bridge built especially for the AT. We arrived an hour early but thankfully our shuttle driver was 30 minutes early. Charlie was our driver and he took us to the Stanimals Hostel in Glasgow, Virginia. *Stanimals is one of the more popular hostels on the trail. We didn't stay in the hostels much, but with the heavy rain moving in we took what we could get.*

We got checked in, took showers and then as usual focused on something to eat. Charlie gave us a ride to town and we ate at Scotto's Restaurant. I had a Cowboy Burger and fries, it was fantastic. We resupplied at the Dollar General Store. We had told Charlie we would walk back to the hostel as it was not that far. Before we got back it started to rain and as we got within sight of the hostel we saw Charlie, he was going to come get us since it had started to rain. Charlie was so in tune to what the hikers needed and he also had a wicked sense of humor. He kept everyone laughing.

We spent the afternoon at the hostel, it was a big house with four bedrooms although it had only one large bathroom. There was a pedicure chair in the living room, it wasn't hooked up to water so you couldn't soak your feet, but everyone used it for the massage. I took advantage of the chair for a couple of rounds since there weren't any other hikers there at the time. We did a load of laundry and at one point Charlie left us to go pick up other hikers and told us we were in charge of the place. We met several other hikers there. A couple of women came in a bit after us, they had crossed over Orchard Mountain a few hours behind us and in the pouring rain, they were completely soaked. Seeing them come in made me really happy we got up and hiked early to beat the rain. They both had showers right away to warm up and their clothes went straight to the washer.

We also met another couple who were doing some hiking. I think the man wanted to hike and the woman really didn't. They had logged about 80 miles and had been at the hostel for a week. They had never camped out overnight and had slack packed on the days they hiked. *Slack packing is where you don't carry all your gear and you meet someone at a predetermined place, they bring what you didn't carry or pick you up and take you back to your gear. We talked about slack packing but never did, it was a good thing we didn't as you will see later in our hiking adventure.*

Charlie made dessert for everyone that evening, Congo Bars, and they were delicious served with ice cream and whipped cream. It was his routine to make dessert in the evenings. We had heard he made a killer peach cobbler. Roy was looking forward to the dessert and a little bummed it wasn't the cobbler, but he didn't turn down the Congo Bars with ice cream. Charlie talked with everyone and got their plans for the next day and had everyone settle their bills before morning. This way he didn't get bogged down with everything in the morning when it was busy and the dessert was a real treat for the guests. Getting everything planned the night before also gave him time to make breakfast for us.

Our sleeping arrangements at the hostel were less than desirable. We had twin beds in a semi-private room. We had asked for a private room but there was not one as the couple who had been there for a week had taken the only private room. They had to pass through our room to get to theirs. We settled in for the night about 9:00 p.m. My bed was awful, I couldn't breathe without the bed making a noise. After about an hour of this I got up and got in the bed with Roy. We did manage to get a little sleep. *We had been sleeping in the tent in a confined space and a twin bed for both of us was not that bad. Again, sleeping in the tent was better but at least we were dry.*

The next morning Charlie made blueberry pancakes for breakfast and they were fantastic. We decided that without Charlie the hostel would have been pretty mundane. He really made the hostel and our stay in Glasgow, Virginia.

April 1, 2022 - It was windy and cold all day. We hiked a lot uphill, from 735 feet at Glasgow, Virginia to Bluff Mountain at 3351 feet. The views back toward the James River were awesome and we could see the complex at the top of Apple Orchard Mountain as we hiked up Bluff Mountain. *We learned about the Bluff Mountain Tragedy. In 1890, a little boy nearly five years old got lost from a local school. He didn't return from helping gather wood with the other kids. There were massive efforts to find him but the weather turned bad and it was generally understood there was no way he would be found alive. His body was found several months later on top of Bluff Mountain, about seven miles from the school. No one could believe he had walked that far. There is a small marker up on the mountain where his body was found. We looked up the story on the internet and found it was truly a very sad story. This was the most heart wrenching story we learned about on the entire trail.*

We stopped at Punchbowl Shelter that evening along with seven other hikers. We had hiked 10.6 miles. Four of the hikers stayed to camp there and three hiked on, we set our tent up at the shelter. It was cold and windy all day up on the mountain tops and we were glad the campsite was at a lower elevation. The wind was still howling above us but we were out of the worst of the wind. We met Speedy, he started at Springer Mountain, Georgia on 2/27/2022 which was the same day we left Damascus. *He caught up with us although we had a 470-mile head start! He is Speedy for sure! Of course, he was a whole lot younger than us and not carrying a pack nearly as heavy as ours. I bet he didn't take time to enjoy the views.*

April 2, 2022 - The terrain was good and we hiked 12.2 miles. The weather was sunny and warm, much more pleasant than the day before. We knew there was a lot of uphill coming so we set up camp at a forest service road before Big Bald Mountain. There were several hikers on the trail that day and we met one of them that started at Springer Mountain on 2/22/2022.

Earlier in the day we hiked through the old Brown Mountain Community. There were remains of rock foundations and chimneys of buildings along the Brown Mountain Creek. Wildflowers were blooming in areas near the old foundations. Rock walls along the creek, apparently built in order to keep the creek in its banks, were still standing. There were signs describing the area and what it was like to live there. *Descendants of freed slaves built, worked and lived in the community in the early 1900's. I couldn't help but think of how much work went into building the community and how beautiful it must have been. There is a lot of history like this along the AT. We have hiked a total of 1108.3 miles, this is slightly over half of the AT. There are still 199 miles to go in Virginia.*

April 3, 2022 - We have been in Virginia since February 28th. There is about 550 miles or one fourth of the AT in Virginia. It seemed as though we would never get through this state. It was cold and windy again. The wind was brutal. Our day started with no coffee and no breakfast. It was cold and Roy just wanted to get moving. Having no coffee and no breakfast caused me to be in a foul mood. We hiked over Bald Mountain, there were fantastic views but I was in desperate need of some sort of breakfast. We finally sat down for a while and ate Pop-arts and drank an electrolyte powder with caffeine in a cup of water. *Not coffee but it would do.*

There were lots of day hikers on the trail and nearly all of them had at least one dog. *We saw all sorts of dogs along the AT, most of them belonged to day hikers but we would see several dogs hiking the entire trail with their owners. It would be nice to have a dog but it would come with a whole new set of problems on the* trail. The dog would need to carry his or her own food. Hostels and hotels charge extra for dogs and also sometimes have a size limit on what dogs are allowed. Also, some shuttles might not allow dogs. We were doing good to take care of ourselves.

At one point we were hiking downhill when I tripped and started falling forward. I was close behind Roy and I was stumbling everywhere trying not to fall on my face. I fell into him nearly taking us both down but he managed to somehow stay on his feet. He stopped and I caught onto him and finally gained my balance. *I did hit my face on the back of his pack but it was minor compared to what it would have been if he had not been there. He was forever telling me not to follow him too closely, this was one time we were both glad I was too close. Had I fallen without him to catch me I would have surely gotten hurt.*

There were numerous ways to fall while hiking. A stick could stick through your shoestrings and cause you to trip, somehow you could kick a stick with the end of your toe and it would stick into the ground causing you to unexpectedly misstep left, right or too high, there were slick leaves, rocks or roots that would send you in a direction you were not expecting also. My favorite was when your left foot would slip on a root or something and suddenly slide far right or vice versa. A couple of the worst falls I had was because of this. There was no way to recover from this type of fall with a pack on, you would be on the ground in a heartbeat. These slips and trips were amplified when the trail was wet. I read somewhere later that most falls occur on level ground when you least expect to fall and I believe this to be correct.

Late in the day we were planning where to camp and needed to get water before setting up the tent. The nearest spring was 0.6 miles one way off the trail and we had decided we would just have to hike the extra mileage to it. There were several people camping at a camping area near the trailhead to the spring. We asked if they knew if there was water at the spring, we didn't want to hike all the way there if the spring was dry. A lady at the campsite said they were getting ready to pack up, it was Sunday evening and they had camped there for the weekend. They had plenty of water they would give us. We gladly accepted and she filled all four of our one-liter water bottles from a large jug. *This was Trail Magic at its finest.* We were happy we didn't have to walk the extra mileage that didn't count as trail miles. As it was, we hiked 13.1 miles that day. That night we camped at Seeley-Woodworth Shelter, elevation 3768 feet.

April 4, 2022 - *Happy Birthday to our son in law Jerry!* The weather was better, warmer and not nearly as much wind. We hiked over Priest Mountain. The Priest Mountain Shelter is at 3834 feet. Of course we had to go down nearly 1000 feet before climbing back up to the shelter. We met a guy at the shelter who was at Baxter State Park at Katahdin in Maine on 8/14/2021. *We were at Katahdin on 8/16/2021.* He had flip flopped and was about 15 miles from finishing the entire AT, he would be finished at Maupin Shelter. *It must be a glorious feeling to be that near the finish. He had hiked during a lot of the time we were home for the holidays, but of course he would have still been a lot faster than we were.*

We hiked a lot of downhill in the afternoon coming down from Priest Mountain. The views were unreal. The views were even more amazing since the landscape was starting to get some color. There was a lot of farm land and it looked like a big patchwork quilt. The grass was starting to get greener and it really showed up below. We were glad we chose to hike as early in the year as we did through the mountains in Virginia. The leaves were not out on the trees yet, had they been out we would not have had the privilege of the glorious views into the valleys below. We hiked 11.5 miles before we camped for the night.

April 5, 2022 - Rain was in the forecast. *Imagine that!* We got up and were on the trail by 7:30 a.m. We made it over Three Ridges Mountain. We dropped down to 900 feet after hiking over the Priest then had to climb up and down and finally made it to Three Ridges at 3965 feet. When we arrived at the Maupin Shelter it was kind of early but we decided since rain would be moving in soon, we would just set up in the shelter. We had only hiked 9 miles but it was some really tough hiking. We considered hiking on to Reed's Gap and getting a ride to the Devil's Backbone Brewpub. *We had seen this place on TV at one time and had looked forward to going*

178

there. *Not only did they have food there, but also free tent campsites for thru hikers. It was 5 miles from the gap and we would have to find a ride. We knew it was supposed to rain, would we really gain anything by tent camping vs. staying with our tent in the shelter? We could get some reportedly good food, but we were planning on getting to Waynesboro, Virginia in a day or two.* We decided to stay put for the night.

Not long after we set up our tent in the shelter, a hiker named Burgoo showed up. He was a section hiker and we enjoyed talking with him. He placed his sleeping pad and bag up on the opposite side of the shelter. It was just starting to rain and get foggy when a girl arrived at the shelter. Her name was Carrie and it was her first day on the trail. She was also hiking a section of the AT. She was very talkative to say the least and she set up her sleeping arrangements between us and Burgoo. She did tell us that she snored and she wouldn't be offended if we told her to stop. I thought she was just being polite.

April 6, 2022 - To say Carrie snored was a gross understatement of the fact. We had trouble sleeping because she and Burgoo both snored too. He snored, but not nearly much or as loudly as she did. She had inflated an air mattress, when she climbed onto it, it squeaked loudly and it seemed like it took forever for her to settle down and stop moving. *I had visions of a cat that paws and kneads their bed before bedding down.* It didn't take her long to go to sleep and she started snoring immediately. If you made a little noise she would stop for a breath or two then resume as loud as ever. I don't think either of us slept much. When we broke camp, I was appalled when Carrie informed us, we made a lot of noise turning over on our sleeping mattresses! She apparently didn't realize she made horrible noises on her mattress and snored louder than anyone we had ever heard. *I think she out-snored the "champion snorer" we encountered earlier in our hiking adventures. We would be looking out for her and make sure we didn't get caught sleeping in a shelter or too close to her again.*

We hiked up and over Humpback Mountain. The trail was rough in the earlier part of the day but the afternoon was much easier. We saw lots of hikers on the trail that day. We met Greasy Bacon,

179

while we were getting water at a small stream, he was wearing a Mammoth Cave National Park Cap. He told us he had visited there and really liked the area. *Mammoth Cave is home for us and we told him we knew the park well. It really is a small world sometimes.* We also met ASAP, he and Greasy Bacon were both NOBO's and had started at Springer Mountain in late February. We also met Hippo, he was a section hiker who had hiked some with Burgoo.

We kept seeing rocks piled up like fences through the woods. *All I could think of was how much work it took to pile up all these rocks. As land was cleared early settlers used the rocks to construct fences and establish property boundaries since rocks were plentiful. We would see rocks like this off and on through Virginia and many of the New England states.*

We hiked 14.4 miles and tent camped at Glass Hollow Overlook. There were fantastic views into the valley below. We barely found a level spot to pitch the tent at this location but we were six miles plus from town and knew we would not be able to cover that distance before dark. We would settle in for the night and get to town in the morning.

April 7, 2022 - *Happy Birthday to my sister Patricia!* We were awakened by rain during the night, at least it didn't storm, but it rained off and on until morning. We crawled out of the tent and were met by very thick fog. The place we put the tent was under trees with no grass or leaves on the ground. This made for a horribly nasty tent, black dirt was all over the lower part of the tent. The tent was soaked, when I rolled it up to pack it I could squish water out of it. My hands got really dirty from the black dirt, any attempts to properly clean my hands were futile at this point. Roy carried a large oblong plastic bag to put the wet tent in if needed, this would prevent getting his other gear wet and dirty in his backpack. *The tent probably weighed three or four times its normal weight when it's wet, even though we squeezed out as much water as possible. This was another one of the reasons we would avoid getting the tent wet.*

We had cell service and I was able to check the weather. Based on the radar I thought the rain would hold off until about 10:00 a.m.

We had to get going if we were going to make the 6.7 miles to Rockfish Gap and get a ride into Waynesboro before there was more rain. The rain held off until about 15 minutes before we got to the gap. The rain came in a big downpour and we had to get the rain gear on quickly. We hurried to what was supposed to be a visitor's center. It was long ago closed and the building was dilapidated. There was also supposed to be a food truck, but it of course was closed. There was no place to get out of the rain so we stood beside the old building and tried to get out of the rain as best we could.

Thank goodness for the FarOut app. I found a girl who did shuttle rides for hikers and she said she could be there in a few minutes. We had her take us to Motel 8. It was close to lots of restaurants and Wal Mart. We checked in and proceeded to get hot showers and set our gear out to dry in the room. We threw the wet tent into the bathtub after we got our showers and decided we could deal with it later, we needed food. There was a Golden Corral just up the hill from the motel. We more than enjoyed the food and both of us made several trips to the buffet. We had a quiet evening relaxing and watching TV. It was much needed rest, food and especially respite from the weather.

April 8, 2022 - Zero day #3. We got breakfast at the motel then set our sights on getting supplies and doing something with the tent. We walked to Wal Mart and purchased supplies and got the usual hiker fare. After we returned to the room, we decided to wash the tent in the bathtub. Washing the tent in the tub was sure to make a big mess, but I would clean the tub. I believed the housekeepers would never know a nasty tent was given a bath. I put the tent into the bathroom trash can to transport it outside. We went around the back of the building and found a grassy spot near the garbage dumpsters. We popped the tent up and secured it with stakes. I went back inside and got water in the trashcan and a microfiber towel we packed with us. I proceeded to wipe the tent down inside and out. When I was finished, there was no black dirt remaining. This was essentially our house and I felt much better after it was clean. We also washed our Tyvek ground cloth, spread it out in the grass and weighed it down with rocks from a rocky area near the building. It was a sunny, windy day and the equipment dried fast. While the tent was drying, we went to eat at . . . Golden Corral again! *The food was so good the day before we decided to eat there again. It was good the second time too!* As we returned from eating, we took the tent down and re-packed it and the ground cloth.

We spent another quiet afternoon resting and tying up loose ends in preparation for returning to the trail the next day. We arranged a ride back to the trail and would leave the motel at 9:00 a.m. Roy had not had a haircut since mid-February and his hair was longer than it had been in years. I had a small pair of scissors I used for cutting KT tape. I told him I could try to give him a scissor cut and he was willing to give it a try. We pulled a chair into the bathroom and I proceeded to cut his hair. It took a while, but I finally got it done and it didn't look half bad. I cleaned the hair up as much as I could, hopefully the housekeepers wouldn't know about the haircut either!

We would be entering the Shenandoah National Park at its south entrance when we returned to the trail. One hundred and one miles of the AT goes through the Shenandoahs. We still had to get through the Shenandoahs to get out of Virginia.

April 9, 2022 - Ritzy gave us a ride back to the trail. She had picked us up during the pouring rain and brought us to the motel a couple of days before. We were hoping it would be a little warmer. It was a little cool but sunny at the motel. I started out wearing shorts but when we arrived at Rockfish Gap, which was at a higher elevation than the town, the wind was gusting and it was very cold. It didn't take long before we stopped and had a wardrobe adjustment. Hats, gloves and long pants for me! It was a cold, windy, miserable day for hiking. We saw several trail runners this day, all I could think was I would fall and kill myself if I tried to run the trail. It would have been like an accident looking for a place to happen if I tried to run, I was doing good just to be hiking. Needless to say, most of the runners were much younger than we were and not carrying thirty plus pound backpacks.

We crossed over Little Calf Mountain and met a couple on a day hike, we stopped and talked with them and they gave us lollipops.

A little bit of Trail Magic! We camped at a stealth site about one mile from Turk Mountain at mile 876.2 after hiking 10.9 miles.

As we were resting in the tent, we both drifted off to sleep after eating supper and getting warm. It was probably only 5:00 p.m., but it was cold and windy and the tent was our only respite from the weather. We thought we heard rain on the tent, but we didn't worry about it much. According to the forecast there wouldn't be much rain if any, besides the tent should dry before morning. We awakened again an hour or so later, when we looked up in the tent the roof looked weird. The moon was out, the weather had cleared and the wind settled. We looked outside to discover it had snowed about two inches. It was snow on the roof of the tent making it look strange. We cleared the snow off the roof of the tent by tapping on it from the inside. We went back to sleep and slept well that night.

April 10, 2022 - The snow was already melting when we got up. It was cool, but not as cold as the day before. A couple of hours into hiking the snow was gone. The trail was good and we hiked 13.4 miles. We found a good stealth campsite on top of a hill 0.5 miles from Brown Gap.

April 11, 2022 - The weather was much, much better. It was a little cool in the morning but by the afternoon I was in shorts. We got water today at the Simmons Gap Ranger Station, potable water we didn't have to treat or boil. *Little things mean a lot when you are on the trail*. We hiked a little over 13 miles and finally found a stealth campsite at mile 901.9.

April 12, 2022 - *Happy Birthday to our son Aaron!* Neither of us slept very well, the wind howled all night. We woke up to rain on the tent but it turned out to be only sprinkles, thank goodness. After a cloudy morning it turned out to be a beautiful afternoon. We hiked a lot of uphill, probably more uphill this day in the Shenandoahs than any day thus far. There were fantastic views over Hightop Mountain. We needed water for the evening and there didn't seem to be any nearby. *The FarOut app tells the location of known water sources but we often found sources that were not mapped out. There had been quite a bit of rain off and on, some of the springs dry up during summer but so far, we had been lucky. Thankfully we had no trouble finding water. If you just stop and listen sometimes you can hear water trickling in the woods. This was the case and we just happened to find water downhill a few feet from the trail. When looking for water we tried to make sure it was running and clear, even if it was just a trickle. A green leaf can work well to allow water to run over it and into a bottle if the water is flowing on a small downhill but too shallow to dip. We would use this method many times when collecting water.* I was collecting water with a leaf when a thru hiker named Aussie came along. He was totally out of water and thrilled to know we had found some. The water was slow to collect in Roy's peanut butter jar (not mine), but it was definitely worth the wait. After we filled our water bottles, we left Aussie by the water source and hiked on. *Later we heard about a hiker named Aussie that was hiking from Key West, Florida to Canada. The Eastern Continental Trail is 4400 miles. No thank you, we will do well to finish the AT but we applaud the efforts of those to choose to hike further.* We camped that evening at a stealth site at mile 914.3 after hiking 12.4 miles.

April 13, 2022 - We stopped at the Lewis Camp Store at the Lewis Mountain Campground in the Shenandoahs. Yoo Hoos, breakfast sandwiches, Snickers, chips and a soft drink. It was a strange combination of foods but it was really good. The guy who was minding the camp store was very nice, gave us helpful information about the Shenandoahs and we enjoyed talking with him.

We met the guy who gave us lollipops on Little Calf Mountain at the campground. He and his wife were staying there and he was surprised to see us again. He hollered at the "Kentuckians", as he called us, and said he would recognize my gaiters anywhere. *Gaiters are coverings worn over your shoes. They really help to keep rocks and other trash out of your shoes. They also keep your socks cleaner. My gaiters were purple with bright colors and I got several questions while on the trail as to what they were or what purpose they served. Hikers knew what they were and many of them also wore various versions of gaiters, just not all of them were as colorful as mine. I kept teasing Roy about wearing gators which he chose not to wear. My shoes and socks were a lot cleaner and I never had to stop to get a rock out of my shoes, I sure can't say the same for him. But hey, to each his own. Every time he would get a rock in his shoe I would say, "You know what would fix that don't you?".*

That day we hiked a couple of miles with a guy from Massachusetts, he didn't have a trail name yet. We also met a couple of older hikers on the trail, Momma Cat and Yellow Falcon. *Some of these trail names get a little funny to say the least.*

There are stores in the Shenandoahs called Waysides. The Waysides have camping supplies, some grocery items, ice cream and beer. They are also gift shops and restaurants. Most of the restaurants in the Waysides didn't open until after Memorial Day. We got some snacks and a beer to share at the Big Meadows Wayside.

We camped that night at the Big Meadows Campground after hiking 12.5 miles. The campground had coin operated showers, $2.50 for five minutes. I was so happy to be getting a shower, we got change for the coin operated machines and went to get in the shower. I was completely undressed, had all my stuff staged to reduce time spent tinkering with anything other than being under the running hot water. *I knew my hair would need to be shampooed at least twice. I should have realized something was up when the shower floor in my room was dry.* The shower took my money but wouldn't work! I beat on the box with my fist, turned all the knobs and beat on them too, but the shower would not work. I had to get dressed, put my hair back into a ponytail and go out to find another one that worked. There were probably six showers in a row and all the others were full. I waited and waited for someone to come out but none of the other showers opened up. Roy was still in a shower somewhere there and I thought he would surely be coming out fresh and clean any minute. There were other people waiting for the showers, one of them said there were showers also in the restrooms. I went to check it out and found there were indeed showers in the restroom. I finally told them if they saw a tall white-haired man to tell him his wife had gone to the showers at the women's restroom.

I went into the restroom and started to go into one of the two available stalls. A girl in the other stall told me she had been in the other shower and it wouldn't work, she had to get redressed and switch to the shower she was in. I told her I would wait until she got finished and I had already been through that once. *If I had to go through another shower not working, I would not be responsible for the string of expletives that would come out of my mouth.* She told me she would be quick because she refused to pay more than $2.50 for a shower. When she finished, I got into the shower, staged all my stuff again, put my money in and thankfully it worked. The five minutes was plenty of time to get my hair shampooed twice and wash up. I however forgot my crocs to wear in the shower, so I kept my socks on and washed them with soap while I was at it. I got out of the shower and found Roy outside waiting for me. He took a shower, but the water was cold. He said he was in and out of the shower in two minutes. I don't think I could have managed in cold water as well as he did, thankfully my shower was hot.

We got back to our tent hoping we would sleep better. *Neither of us had slept very well the night before, we kept hearing something walking in the woods near our tent. Roy said it sounded like a deer and we have seen several during the daytime. It was pretty light outside because the moon was really bright, but we didn't see anything. I also thought I heard a mouse in the vestibule of the tent. I was hoping it didn't chew on anything and I tried to scare it away. I fell back to sleep so apparently it moved or it would have kept me awake.* As luck would have it we didn't sleep very well that night either. Quiet time was supposed to be 10:00 p.m. at the campground but there were some people camping near us that didn't get back to their campsite until around 9:00 p.m. and proceeded to laugh and talk until after 11:00 p.m. The wind was blowing and there was a flagpole nearby, the metal clips on the flag clanged against the metal pole all night. *Sleep would evade us for a second night!*

April 14, 2022 - *Happy 4th Birthday to our granddaughter Nettie Lou!* We were still in the Shenandoahs and we ate lunch at the Skyland Lodge Dining Room, Roy had fish and I had . . . a cheeseburger. We drank water and had house chips, fries would have been $2 extra for each of us, the lunch still cost $31.00. We saw several hikers there, NOBO's from Springer Mountain. One guy had a really pretty Siberian Husky dog and a woman and her kids were petting and fawning over the dog. The people in the restaurant even brought the dog a bowl of water and the woman told the guy she wanted to buy his lunch. *Roy said maybe he should get on all fours and start whining like a dog if you could get that much attention and be fed! Lol!* There was an AT detour around the place and it was a cluster, but we finally figured it out.

We passed over an area called Little Stony Man Cliffs high up in the mountains and right on the trail. There was a pool of water about the size of a large bathtub in the rocks. Wow, if it was warm weather, it would be a good place to soak in a tub, the view was unreal. By late that day the wind started to pick up. *It's really weird here, the wind blows worse at night. At home in Kentucky the wind lays at dark and it's usually calmer at night.* After hiking 14.5 miles we got a tent site at Birdsnest #3 Shelter and it was out of the wind. Carrie from back at Maupin Shelter camped there also. Thankfully she was far enough away from our tent and with the wind blowing we didn't hear her snoring. *Roy said she was banned from sleeping closer than 100 yards due to her snoring and I concurred.* The wind was steady and lulled us to sleep that evening.

April 15, 2022 - Thankfully we both slept great the night before after not sleeping well for the past couple of nights. The weather was sunny and warm after a cool morning. It was great hiking weather. We make it to Elkwallow Wayside by 2:30 p.m. We each had a beer and a Blue Bunny ice cream sandwich. It was a weird combination of food and drink but it worked. We bought a package of ham and barbeque chips to eat for supper. We met more NOBO's from Springer Mountain at the wayside, the faster ones were really catching up with us now. We hiked 0.7 miles past the wayside and camped at a stealth site under some pine trees. There was a gorgeous sunset as the sun slipped over the horizon. The wind started to blow as the sun went down and continued through the night. We had hiked 12.6 miles before stopping for the night.

April 16, 2022 - We met a man on the trail today that gave us Trail Magic in the form of Easter candy. He also told us about some bottles of Gatorade hidden behind a rock up the trail. We had hiked quite a way and had about given up when we found the two Gatorade bottles, one was empty, the other unopened one was fruit punch flavored. *Definitely not my favorite but I did make an exception.* We shared the bottle and it was good. This was like having our very own Easter egg hunt on the trail!

The weather was warm and sunny most of the afternoon. I was a little bit hot at one point but overall, it was a good hiking day. There were deer on the trail in the afternoon, they were very tame and didn't seem to be alarmed by us at all. One of them actually followed us down the trail for a few yards, he was probably looking for a handout but we didn't have anything to offer.

We met some hikers from Germany. People come from all over the world to hike the AT. We also saw our first big pile of bear scat and it was full of green grass. *We found out, while in Glacier National Park, bears eat grass when they come out of hibernation because berries are not in season at that time. I guess the Virginia bears are starting to wake up.* We camped at the Tom Floyd Wayside Shelter 2.8 miles from Virginia Route 522 that leads to Front Royal, Virginia. The water source for the shelter was Ginger Spring. It was about 0.2 miles down a steep hill but it was an excellent water source. We made the trip to the spring before we prepared our evening meal. We cooked at the shelter then crawled in our tent for the evening. We were looking forward to getting into town the next day and planned on staying one or two nights depending on the weather.

April 17, 2022 - *Easter Sunday!* We met a couple from Denmark this morning and talked with them for a bit before we started hiking. They had camped in the same vicinity and were hiking south for a section hike. *You literally can meet anyone from anywhere on the trail.*

We hiked to the highway and got a cab ride to Front Royal. We waited for nearly an hour for the ride and were about to give up when it finally arrived. We got to Motel 8 by about 11:00 a.m. and couldn't check in until after 1:00 p.m. so we went to do laundry at a local laundromat. The restroom at the laundry was locked because there was not an attendant on duty. If we could at least change our clothes, we could wash all our clothes then take a shower as soon as we got checked in at the motel. There was no place to change, the shopping center where the laundry was located had several stores but most of them were closed since it was Easter Sunday.

There was a church located in the shopping center and there were people going in and out. We were carrying our clean folded clothes and Roy asked a man who had gone in and out of the church if we could possibly use their restroom and change our clothes. He graciously allowed us to go in, he even offered us food as they had an Easter potluck. We declined the food, I for one felt out of place in my hiking attire with everyone dressed up for Easter, but were happy to be able to use the restroom and change.

We returned to the laundry and put our clothes in to wash. The laundry was different than any one I had ever seen. There was a central station where you paid and programmed the machine you wanted to use, each washer and dryer was numbered. It was an awesome set up although to purchase laundry detergent it cost a $12.50 deposit in a vending machine, plus the $1.25 for the actual detergent. The $12.50 would be refunded to your card in a few business days. After the laundry was finished, we went back to Motel 8 and we were allowed to check in even though it was still a bit early.

We both took showers and then turned our sights toward something to eat. We tried to go to Burger King, but that turned into us getting frustrated and leaving. We thought we were in line for our order to be taken, the workers just kept moving around and no one paid any attention to us standing there. After a few minutes of us being totally ignored, another man came in and walked up beside us. The person behind the register immediately looked up and asked if she could help him. We were apparently standing in the wrong spot at the counter, it didn't appear we were that far out of place to me or maybe we were just holding our mouths wrong. At this point we both looked at each other and just walked out of the place. We apparently needed to be all the way at the other end of the counter, but that was in no way clearly defined. So much for

Burger King. We walked down the road and came to KFC and decided we could surely get good service and good food there. We were helped as soon as we stepped up to the counter and the food was really good. Once we had something to eat, we decided to go ahead and get the supplies we needed.

We went to a local grocery store in the shopping center where we changed clothes. As usual it took a few minutes to find what we needed when shopping in an unfamiliar store. We had only been in the store a few minutes when the announcement came, the store would be closing in fifteen minutes. It was Easter Sunday and the employees were getting off work early. *I was glad they were going to have Easter dinner with their families but it was hard to speed it up in an unfamiliar grocery store.* We hurried as best we could and managed to get our groceries and out the door.

At supper we decided we would try Burger King again. *Maybe a different crew was working.* Sure enough, there was a different crew and they were much more customer service oriented. We ordered our food and it was ready in just a few minutes.

We spent the evening watching the Bristol NASCAR race and relaxing. We had only hiked 2.8 trail miles that day, but we walked up and down the street at least three times back and forth. *I sure wished that counted as trail miles!*

April 18, 2022 - Zero day #4. Snow, snow and more snow! We sure made the right decision to stay in Front Royal. The temperature was in the upper 30s and it snowed most of the day. At times it looked like a blizzard with big feathery snowflakes and it was very wet snow. We ate breakfast at the motel, had snacks in our room at lunch and just spent the day watching TV and reading.

I had plenty of time so I went through my journal and calculated our average miles hiked per day. We had averaged 8.77 miles per day on our first trip from Springer Mountain to Allen Gap. In Maine we only averaged 6.62 miles per day. On this leg of our journey, we had averaged 10.17 miles per day. Hopefully we could increase our average and get finished in plenty of time to meet our August 15th deadline to qualify as thru hikers.

We ordered pizza for supper from a nearby pizza place, Roy walked to the restaurant to pick it up and bring it back to the room.

The pizza was huge, we ate all we could hold and still had a bunch left over. We had a refrigerator in our room and decided to put it in an extra Ziploc bag. We would take it with us for lunch or dinner the next day. It was cool enough outside it would be like the pizza was refrigerated. *It would add to the weight of the pack but it was well worth carrying. I had no problem eating cold pizza.*

April 19, 2022 - We got a taxi ride back to the trail, this time they were quick in picking us up. The temperature was cool and we hiked all day with gloves and hats on. We passed a sign that said, "Ray's Rhino" and looked up at the tree above the sign. Wow, it really looked like a rhino grew out of the tree.

We ate the pizza from Front Royal and it was good even though it was cold. *We needed to get rid of the extra weight.* After 15.4 miles we had stopped at Whiskey Hollow Shelter for the night. We knew it was going to be a cold night and since we hadn't seen anyone on the trail that day, we decided to set our tent up in the loft of the shelter. The wind was howling through the trees and we knew we were in for a cold windy night. We waited for a while before setting up our tent inside the shelter thinking someone else just might roll in at the last minute. Just about the time we were finishing the set up about 6:30 p.m., guess who arrived? Snoring Carrie! We just looked at each other in disbelief. *Surely, we would be safe from the snoring in the loft with the wind howling.* She set up her tent inside the shelter too, on the lower level, there was no way we could tell her to just stay outside the shelter with the wind howling. It was getting really cold so we all settled into our tents for the night. *Our only hope with the snoring Carrie was for us to get warm and fall asleep first and for the wind to keep on howling.*

April 20, 2022 - The snoring had been tolerable, we barely heard Carrie because the wind provided a much-needed distraction. All of us got up to break camp when Roy found his pack had been invaded by a mouse. The mouse chewed a little on his Thermarest bag (his air mattress bag), one of his dry bags, and the tent bag, but it really chewed on his rain suit bags. Thankfully it didn't chew his rain suit. I heard something chewing during the night but it sounded like it was chewing on wood and a lot bigger than a mouse, Carrie said she had heard it too. When she sat down to put her shoes on each shoe had four or five hickory nuts in it. We then thought it must have been chipmunks we heard during the night. *Mice wouldn't store hickory nuts, would they? Do chipmunks gnaw on wood? Could it have been a porcupine? We found out they chew on wood. This was one of those things we would never know for sure.*

Carrie left the shelter before we did but we caught up with her when she stopped to eat breakfast at an area with a fantastic view. We were actually faster hikers and we left her behind quickly. We went through an area at the top of a mountain that still had snow. *It was melting fast but still, who would have thought about snow on April 20th?* The trail was easy most of the day until mid-afternoon when we started on the section called the roller coaster. There was a sign that said, "HIKER WARNING, Entering the Rollercoaster, have a great ride". *The roller coaster is a section of the AT approximately 15 miles that is pretty rocky with constant ups and downs and is considered to be a tough section of the trail. On the elevation map on the FarOut App it looked like a sawtooth of ups and downs. There are only a couple of good views on the section, you are mainly just covering the miles through the forest.* We hiked 15.6 miles and set up camp at the Sam Moore Shelter.

April 21, 2022 - We got to the shelter last night and met a heavy-set woman (no trail name) who set up her hammock really a little too close to us. *I just hoped she wouldn't snore!* She told us she had hiked with her daughter before and used a hammock and really liked it. She told us she was testing her equipment and just doing a weekend trip. We started to cook our supper and she came to the area where we were to cook hers. She had an alcohol stove and we thought she was going to catch the place on fire because she didn't seem to know what she was doing with it. She finally got her food prepared without creating a forest fire or burning the shelter down, but we were really starting to wonder.

It was cold and getting dark soon so we decided we would probably just crawl in our tent early. The "Roller Coaster" had kicked our tails. We still had more of it to hike the next day. *PUDS (Pointless Ups and Downs), this was the Roller Coaster. I was not a fan of the PUDS but they were apparently a necessary evil on the trail.* We did manage to hike 14.4 miles, not counting the 0.25 to get water. It rained off and, on all afternoon, but thankfully stopped by the time we got to camp. We set the tent up not far from a creek, ate supper and got in the tent about 7:45 p.m. *It had been a long day. It was staying light outside longer and we were hiking longer distances.*

We were lying there just about to drift off to sleep when we heard a loud thump followed by someone loudly saying, "shit". Then we heard what sounded like someone struggling and could only assume the woman who was, "testing her equipment" had flipped out of her hammock. I didn't ask if she was ok, I didn't want to embarrass her and reasoned if she needed assistance she would call out. She didn't call out and neither did I. *I tried to contain my amusement at the situation, but failed. Horrible of me to laugh but I couldn't help it, I just did it quietly.*

We went by the Bear's Den Hostel, it's actually a historic stone mansion built in the 1930s and it is just 150 yards off the AT. It is now owned by the ATC and is maintained by the PATC (Potomac Appalachian Trail Club), part of the mansion (in the basement) is the Bear's Den Hostel. We stopped to look at the mansion. We were able to see the grounds and the hostel portion of the property but the main lodge was closed at the time we were there. We drank a soft drink, used the restroom in the hostel and took a break there for a few minutes. I can see why people would want to go there. It was much too early in the day for us to stop so we hiked on.

The wildflowers were really coming out now and there seemed to be more and different ones every day. They were beautiful. I don't remember seeing yellow violets before. They were just like the purple ones, only a little bit smaller. *One more day in Virginia! We will be at Harpers Ferry, West Virginia tomorrow, to finally have Virginia behind us will be an awesome feeling.*

"I see my path, but I do not know where it leads. Not knowing where it's going is what inspires me to travel it." - Rosia de Castro

Chapter 29 - We Ain't Exactly in the South Anymore

April 22, 2022 - We hiked across the bridge on the Shenandoah River and arrived in Harpers Ferry, West Virginia. Harpers Ferry was an old town with a lot of history. It was very warm and sunny and we enjoyed not being in the rain or cold. We found the post office and picked up the package Christi sent to us. *New trail runners will replace the boots. Our boots were sent home along with a few other items we decided not to carry in order to reduce our pack weight as much as possible. Getting rid of our boots will be a big step in the right direction.*

We went by the Appalachian Trail Conservancy to register our AT hike. A lady was at a table outside the building and she gave us some info and took our picture to put in their log book. *They were still taking Covid precautions and we couldn't go in the building. Registering there was another way to document our hike and make it official. You should be able to find us in their Hiker Photo Archive online at some point. As of this writing the archive is only updated thru 2019.*

The Rabbit Hole was one of the restaurants in downtown Harpers Ferry and it was reportedly one of the best places to eat. We ate there and the food was really good. I got a . . . cheeseburger and Roy got a fish sandwich. The old downtown area was where most of the historic stone buildings and plaques were located. There was also a lot of Civil War history there. There was no way we could spend enough time in one afternoon to even scratch the surface of things to see and do.

We left Harpers Ferry and crossed over the bridge on the Potomac River. The bridge was covered in "Love Locks" that had been put on the bridge by couples to signify their love. *I feel this was defacing public property but apparently, it's a thing. The locks were placed on the bridge and the keys tossed into the river. I bet half of the couples who placed these locks aren't even couples anymore!*

This bridge was also the site of a train derailment three or four years ago. Two train cars actually fell into the river and wiped out a huge section of the AT footbridge. For a period of time the AT hikers had to get a shuttle and resume the trail at the other side of the river. I'm sure glad it had been repaired and allowed us to cross into Maryland without a problem. There was a lot of train activity in the area, we often heard trains when we got within earshot of Harpers Ferry and we continued to hear trains as we hiked farther north. The trail was flat and easy hiking for several miles after crossing the river. After hiking a total of 11.1 miles we found a place to camp in the yard at the Cross Trails Hostel in Maryland. *There is only about four miles of the AT that runs through West Virginia so we quickly marked another state off the list.* The guy who ran the hostel came and picked us up from the trail.

April 23, 2022 - Last night we met several people at the hostel. One hiker was documenting hikers who left Springer Mountain, Georgia in 2020. We knew several of the hikers he had documented since they started close to the time we did in February of 2020. The guy's name was Dixie and he played the harmonica that evening, he was really talented. He also offered and we accepted a couple of beers. We met a hiker in the kitchen at the hostel who offered and shared the pasta he cooked and it was really tasty. This was also the guy who abruptly moved his tent twice that evening. He seemed a little uptight at that time but he was much better inside the hostel at dinner time.

There was a group of scouts that had the entire far end of the yard reserved and we had to set up our tent in the yard near the house. It would have been okay except for the fact that the group on the porch talked loudly until 11 p.m. The guy that shared his pasta told them to quieten down once, but his chastisement only served to quieten most of them. A couple of them went on talking, just not quite as loud. There was another flag pole clanging in the wind, at least it was at the other end of the yard but we still heard it loud and clear. *It seemed that anytime we were in campgrounds, hostels or shelters there was always something interrupting our sleep.*

The hostel was nice enough, we had long hot showers, a big kitchen, people who gave us beer and pasta but it was loud and we didn't get our usual twelve hours of sleep. The hike was pretty easy in comparison to most days.

After we left the hostel, we hiked most of the day with a guy from Texas doing long section hikes named Waterbug. The weather was warm and sunny. We all stopped at the Rocky Run Shelter campsites after hiking 12.8 miles. There was a new shelter, old shelter and the campsites all at this location. A group of guys who were military or first responders were on a campout at the newer shelter. They were involved in a program to help these guys by getting them out in nature to decompress. We talked to them for a few minutes and they were very interested in our thru hike and had several questions.

We found the water source in the area to be a piped spring near the old shelter. There was a huge stream of cold clear water coming out of a four-inch pipe. I think we filled our water bottles in record time. We set our tents in the designated sites and settled in for the evening. We were rewarded at day's end with another beautiful red sunset.

April 24, 2022 - I heard a turkey that morning but it sounded weird, I told Roy it sounded like a turkey got strangled. He said it was a jake (juvenile male) turkey. We also saw a black squirrel. *I later googled it and found it is a genetic thing kind of like the white squirrels in Kentucky. Gray squirrels or fox squirrels can be born black or white. I never knew there were black squirrels. But then maybe people in Maryland never heard of white squirrels.*

We crossed over I-70 on a catwalk, there was heavy traffic on the road. It was Sunday and there were a lot of people out on day hikes in the area around I-70. *Come to find out a lot of people go to hike to Annapolis Rocks since it is only about an hour away from Baltimore, Maryland or Washington, D.C.* It was 0.25 miles off the AT but we decided it would probably be worth seeing. The view from the rocks was beautiful and worth the extra time it took from the trail. The history of this whole area was amazing. We arrived at a Washington Monument that was built in 1827. We went up to the top of it for the view and it was amazing. *There has been a lot of civil war stuff on the trail even before we got to Harpers Ferry, but now we are seeing Revolutionary War stuff! Wow!* When I took a picture of the monument the morning sun in the background made the monument look like it was glowing.

We set up our tent for the night at the Ensign Cowall Shelter tent sites. Waterbug also camped at the same location. He was a faster hiker than us, but we usually end up in the same place or see each other in a day or so.

April 25, 2022 - We crossed the Maryland/Pennsylvania border also known as the Mason-Dixon Line. *One more state marked off the list. Seven down and seven to go. We are definitely not in the south anymore. Everywhere we go now people ask where we are from and comment about our accent. Of course, we thought everyone else had accents.*

There was quite a bit of uphill hiking today and we hiked 12.4 miles. The weather was warm and it was sunny off and on. We leapfrogged with Waterbug most of the day. When we got to the highway, we thought Waterbug was ahead of us, but found he was somehow behind us. Waterbug had arranged for a ride into Waynesboro, Pennsylvania and he offered to share the ride with us. We gladly accepted. We got a nice room for the night at the Cobblestone Inn.

After showers as usual we turned our attention to food. There was an Applebees near the inn and we decided to eat there. Of course, the food was delicious, I think a grilled cheese would have tasted like fine dining at that point! The room was also close to Wal Mart and we were able to get plenty of supplies for our next leg of the trail. We did a load of laundry and spent the evening relaxing.

Our weight loss is becoming more than just a little apparent to us. There is no way to carry enough food to not lose weight. We eat well when we are in town. Nutella has become a favorite high calorie food for us and we can eat a jar in about three go rounds. It's heavy but well worth carrying the weight for the calories and the taste. For years I said I didn't like Nutella, but apparently it has changed or my taste buds have changed. It just didn't taste as much like hazelnuts as I remembered. We also liked PB&J in a plastic jar and ate it with crackers. We need more fat and protein than we have been getting. We both feel fine and we have plenty of energy so we will just keep plugging away and put another hole in our belts to keep our pants from falling off.

In addition to the weight-loss we are both suffering from "hikers hobble". This is the feeling you get when you first stand on your feet in the morning and the first few steps you take are extremely painful causing you to walk like your feet are broken. Usually being on your feet for a couple of minutes and moving around will resolve the issue for the day. We would continue to experience the phenomenon each morning throughout the AT hike and for several weeks after we got home. I wondered for a while if my feet could ever feel right again. It took a few months after we completed the AT hike before I could get moving in the mornings without hiker hobble. I reasoned that it took a few months to get that way and it would take a few months for the problem to resolve. Roy didn't seem to have it as long as I did, of course he didn't complain about it either.

April 26, 2022 - We met Tortoise at breakfast and he asked if we wanted to share a ride with him back to the trail, we gladly accepted. Our shuttle driver arrived and announced he was a "Trail Angel" and he was providing rides back to the AT. *He was apparently really proud of his status.* He drove a very nice pickup truck and told us he was retired and just shuttled people back and forth from the trail to have something to do and of course earn a little spending money. He grew up in the area but he had never hiked on the trail at all. He said when he was a kid, hikers used to sneak and sleep in the barn on his father's farm. He always thought they were hobos until he learned later about people hiking on the AT. Although he had never hiked on the trail, he was in awe of those who did. He loved talking to hikers and kept us entertained with his stories all the way back to the trail.

We resumed the trail with Tortoise in the lead and we somehow missed a turn. We later realized we were off the trail and we went cross country (or bushwhacking) to cut over and back to the AT. After a few minutes we were finally back on the trail. Going cross country through the woods was not something we wanted to do again. *During our detour is when I lost the end of the handle on my hiking hands free Z-packs umbrella. The end was a foam piece and it was what allowed for the umbrella to be secured to my pack straps. I later found a piece of wood and duct taped it to the umbrella handle. It worked, just not quite as well, but I still was able to use it. The umbrella had a two-year warranty and after we finished hiking the AT I emailed the company, explained the problem and sent pictures. They replaced the umbrella. Wow, it is still amazing to me they would actually do this because usually there is a problem with warranties: because there is always something in the fine print.*

Trail Magic! "Fresh Ground" was set up in a pavilion at Old Forge Park. He had rice and seafood, drinks, chips and desserts. We had only hiked about five miles and it was a bit early for lunch since we ate a big breakfast at the motel but we ate anyway. The food was awesome, he even had stuff to make sandwiches if you didn't like the seafood or had a food allergy. Waterbug was there when Tortoise, Roy and I arrived. Mingo from China and Cookie Monster from Israel were also there. *We would continue to leapfrog with these folks several more times in the coming days.*

It started to rain in the afternoon and drizzled until about 6:30 p.m. We hiked 12.4 miles even with getting a late start and stopping for a long early lunch with Fresh Ground. *We didn't know it at the time but Fresh Ground and his Leapfrog Cafe are legendary on the trail. The guy sets up at different spots up and down the trail every year and has one of the most elaborate spreads of any of the trail magic. The Leapfrog Cafe and be found anywhere up or down the AT. He wanted to take a picture of us and asked our trail names so he could document meeting us or rather feeding us. We were certainly glad to have met him and hoped we would see him again before we were finished with the trail. The Leapfrog Café is on FaceBook and if you go back far enough, you can find us in the pictures.*

April 27, 2022 - The weather was cloudy, cold and windy all day. There were only a few minutes of sun off and on in the afternoon. We passed by the Quarry Gap Shelters and found these twin shelters to be the best maintained and decorated we had seen on the trail. The volunteers who take care of the shelters had landscaped, built fences, planted flowers and added benches to the area. If there was a prize for the prettiest shelter these one would win the award hands down. It looked so homey and inviting, it was just a shame we passed through too early in the day to stop.

We had lunch with Tortoise at the Milesburn Cabin area and found him to be a very interesting guy. He took a three month leave from his job at a large newspaper in Chicago in order to hike a long section of the trail. We really enjoyed getting to know him. He was a much faster hiker than we were but we would continue to see him off and on over the next few weeks.

We made it to Tom's Run Shelter and met back up with Waterbug. He is from Houston, Texas and is going home after he gets to Boiling Springs, PA. He is a much faster hiker than us also and he went on ahead, he was really looking forward to going home after being on the trail hiking a long section for about a month.

There were several others at the shelter including Tortoise, Mingo and So What. So What was a younger girl hiking the AT, her partner had quit but she was determined to finish. All of these folks were staying in the shelters. There were two shelters side by side and each could accommodate 4 or 5 people. We of course opted for our tent as we didn't want to take the chance of being kept awake all night by someone snoring.

We hiked 19.2 miles trail miles that day and saw a marker indicating 1100 miles. It was made of rocks someone had placed beside the trail and I took a picture. *Wow, we are more than 1400 miles finished at this point when adding the 300 miles we hiked in Maine last summer. We are nearly two-thirds finished! Roy really would like to get a 20-mile day, hopefully we can eventually get there.*

This evening was very cold and for the first time in a long while I put on my puffy jacket. We set our tent in a lower spot down the hill from the shelters to get out of the wind as much as possible. The water source was even further down the hill and we had to make the trip down to fill our water bottles. With the additional distance to and from water we were definitely close to hiking twenty miles that day. Because of the cold we were more than ready to crawl in the tent after eating our supper.

April 28, 2022 - We passed through Pine Grove Furnace State Park. The Pine Grove Furnace State Park was an interesting place, there are remnants of large furnaces built in the 1800's where iron was manufactured. *We would see several of the old iron furnaces along the trail over the next few days.* We also saw The Appalachian Trail Museum, an old grist mill that houses the first museum dedicated to the AT. *The Pine Grove General Store near the museum was where AT hikers try to complete the half-gallon ice cream challenge. If you can eat a half-gallon of ice cream in one hour, you become a member of the Half Gallon Club. But the place was closed, this time of year they were only open on weekends and we were there on Thursday. Just our luck, the timing was all wrong but I don't believe I could have eaten that much ice cream anyway. One of the hikers we met in 2020 at Springer Mountain, Georgia told us he was from a small town near the half-gallon challenge and he was looking forward to a quick visit home when he hiked through the area.*

The hiking was fairly easy until we got to a big rock climb just before we arrived at the Alec Kennedy Shelter for the evening. The available camping spots were not great but we made it work, we had seen worse. We talked with several people who were tent camping and also the ones staying in the shelter. Most of these folks were familiar to us, we may not have known all their names but we did know their faces. Waterbug was there and we told him goodbye again as this was for sure the last time we would see him before he went home. Hiking off and on with him was enjoyable and he was really a nice guy. We would miss his company and seeing him on the trail. We told him to look us up if he was ever in South Central Kentucky. We had hiked another 19.2 miles that day and as usual we were more than happy to stop and rest for the evening.

April 29, 2022 - We went through the town of Boiling Springs, PA. The town had a beautiful lake with a park in town and the trail went right beside it. It was beautiful with the flowers blooming nearby and ducks swimming on the lake. We went by the Appalachian Trail Club Regional Office but it was closed. There was an outfitter in town and it was right on the trail. We stopped and got a replacement for Roy's air mattress. *It was still in questionable shape and we sure didn't need a mattress that could not be used, we felt like we had pushed our luck with it long enough.* He bought a replacement and since the trail also went right beside the post office, we shipped the old one home along with a few other items we thought we wouldn't be needing. *As for the air mattress, it has a lifetime guarantee but we couldn't ship it to the company for a repair or replacement while we were on the trail. We sent it later after we got home and received a new replacement. We had the mattress for several years but the guarantee was still honored.*

The trail went through cleared fields of farmland that looked to be sown in wheat. We stopped at a Mennonite store called Trail View Market. The market was a small building near the road and right on the AT. The store had eggs, raw milk and Gatorade. Paying for your items was on the honor system. There was a book to record your purchase and a drawer in which to leave the money. We bought two bottles of Gatorade, logged it in the book and left the $3.00 in the drawer per instructions. It was cold and really tasted good. *Later Roy would say he wished he had tried the chocolate milk; it did look awfully tempting.*

We hiked 18.4 miles today even with the stops in town. We got a better campsite that night. I got the new mattress and Roy took mine because the new one is about four inches shorter than the other one. *I guess we will see how this works. At least there is more room at the end of it which made it easier to place our backpacks in the tent with us.*

April 30, 2022 - We arrived in Duncannon, PA after hiking 10.9 miles. The trail was covered with a lot of rocks and it was mostly downhill to get to the town. The trail went right on the sidewalks through this town. Luckily, we got a room at the Doyle Hotel which was right in the middle of town. This is another iconic hiker stop on the trail. The old hotel has a colorful history, is hiker friendly and was being remodeled by the new owners. It's a work in progress and they only had a few of the rooms available for lodging. The woodwork on the main stairs, trim work, doors and fireplaces throughout the hotel was unique and we were impressed by the craftsmanship and man hours that must have gone into building the hotel. Our room was available for one night, we would be able to stay a second night but we would have to change rooms. Not a problem, I was looking forward to another zero day. Besides, the weather forecast was calling for rain and it would be nice to be in a nice dry place. As usual the first thing on the agenda was a shower shortly followed by food.

3B's was an ice cream shop that came highly recommended by folks on and off trail. We walked there to get ice cream that afternoon. I got Sinfully Chocolate, and I thought it was sinfully delicious. I got the small waffle cone, but it was two very large scoops of ice cream which was way more than enough. *But who's counting calories on the trail?* Roy got a strawberry shake and he was very happy with it also. *I guess you could say we had ice cream for lunch.* On our way to the ice cream shop, it became apparent there was some sort of festival going on. *We found out it was Sled Fest. There is an old factory in town that made Lightning Guider Sleds between 1904 and 1988. It produced 1600 to 1800 sleds per day, more than any other U.S. factory. The company also made children's wagons, porch swings, porch gates and furniture products. It closed in 1990.* The festival was a big deal for the town. There was an antique car show, music, vendors, food trucks, and a Pin Up Model contest where all the contestants dress up in 1950's or 60's dresses. It was really neat to see them, they made me think of Betty Boop.

Clark's Ferry Tavern was the oldest building in Duncannon built somewhere around 1790. It's a stone building and it sits right on the main street in town. It had been very well preserved. If that place could talk, what would it be able to tell us? The farther north we went the more historical places we found.

There was an outfitter in town called Kind of Outdoorsy and it was just down the street from the hotel. It was also a hostel and provided most anything a hiker might need including being a place to exchange Darn Tough socks. Roy had two pairs of socks that had worn very thin and he wanted to see if the lifetime guarantee would be honored. We asked the lady who was running the place and she said she would take care of any socks we needed to exchange. *As it happened Roy still had the two pairs of socks I found in Maine and those were the ones he had worn thin. He traded those socks for two brand new pairs! I didn't need to trade my socks but I would definitely trade them in later if they became worn.*

While we were out in town, we walked to the historic Pennsylvania Railroad Train Station. The old station was no longer in use. We read the plaques and looked at the old pictures of when it was operational. The station was located right along the beautiful Susquehanna River where trains still run. The river was really wide and we could see huge railroad bridges and traffic bridges up and down the river from the old train station.

We ate pizza that evening at Sorrento's. The restaurant was across the street from the hotel and the food was delicious. We settled in our hotel room for the evening looking forward to taking it easy the next day. There was no TV in our room so we read until we were ready for sleep.

May 1, 2022 - *Zero day #5.* Goodies Restaurant was also across the street from the hotel and was the go-to place for breakfast. Roy's double stack of pancakes was huge and he was in hog heaven. I had eggs, bacon, toast and hashbrowns. The portions were more than generous. We saw another hiker who ordered a triple stack of pancakes and it looked more the size of a triple layer nine-inch cake. We left before we saw if he was able to eat all of it.

We had to have supplies before resuming the trail so we decided to walk to the only grocery in the area. It was ¾ of a mile up a hill from the hotel. There was a very narrow shoulder on the road and we really had to take our time and watch for traffic. After we purchased our supplies for the trail, we were not far from the store heading back to the hotel when a guy in a Jeep stopped and offered us a ride. He told us it was too dangerous to be walking along the road. We accepted the ride from Billy the Kid, he had previously done some hiking on the trail and enjoyed helping hikers. He took us all the way to our hotel. *Trail Magic just when we needed it! We would hear many hikers say, "the trail provides", and I believed it. Sometimes just when you need help it can appear in the most unlikely or most surprising places.*

That afternoon we walked back up to 3B's for more ice cream. *This time I got Chocolate Caramel Heaven and yes, it was heavenly. I felt like I needed to balance out the Sinfully Chocolate from the day before, hey any excuse will work for chocolate ice cream.* It started to rain before we could get back to the hotel. *Lord, thank you again for letting us get out of the bad weather again.*

We had to change rooms at the hotel that afternoon. Come to find out it was Tortoise who had our room reserved for that night. We only saw him for a couple of minutes. He was more than eager for a shower. Our room was a corner room and had windows on two sides so we had an excellent view of the rain. Our first room had a private bathroom, the room we had to move to had a shared bathroom across the hallway. *We didn't see anyone else using that bathroom during our stay.* We were just thankful we were not on the trail and spent the rest of the afternoon watching it rain.

May 2, 2022 - We left Duncannon hiking the remainder of the trail through town. The trail went over the Juniata River bridge and also a huge bridge over the Susquehanna River. There were train tracks beside the river and rail cars sitting on the tracks. We had to figure out how to get around them to follow the trail. After a few minutes of searching out we finally found where the trail went. There was a steep uphill climb on a rocky hillside after getting around the rail cars. *Anytime we were in a town or crossed a river it was at a lower elevation and we paid for going into town again by having a steep uphill climb out of the area.* There were a lot of rocks on the trail that day, but no worse than average. We met Galaxy and Fall Down as they were having lunch at one of the shelters we passed earlier in the day. *We would see them off and on over the next few days.*

We found a campsite at mile 1165.9 after hiking 16.4 miles. Cookie Monster had caught up with us in Duncannon and hiked ahead of us, she was also camping at the same spot. Galaxy camped near us but Fall Down went farther up the trail to the next shelter. We just didn't have enough get up and go to make it any further that day. *For some reason the trail always seemed more difficult the next day if we took a zero day and we were both feeling it. Of course, getting more supplies to carry didn't help either.* Dixie, we met at the hostel in Maryland, arrived as it was getting dark, he set up his tent and after a little while he pulled out his harmonica. We listened as we lay in our tent before going to sleep. He played several tunes and he was really very good. The last song he played was Amazing Grace. I never dreamed of hearing it played on a harmonica. *He played it very softly and it was beautiful. I drifted off to sleep feeling blessed to have heard him play.*

May 3, 2022 - Fort Indian Gap, a military installation was close by and we heard artillery fire off and on most of the day. We met Oh Yeah, Flashlight, No Way and Hound Dog and hiked with them for a while that afternoon. They were slack packing and had been really putting in some big miles each day. There was trail magic in the form of cold drinks and chips provided by a guy called Ice Water on a bicycle. *We would learn more about Ice Water and his trail magic in a day or two.*

We got the trail magic right before we arrived at an area where beavers had dammed up a stream and flooded the trail. A detour was suggested but it would add 1.6 miles to the trail so we decided to take our chances. We changed to our Crocs with no socks and were able to get through the area without a problem. *Thank goodness we didn't have to detour.* The tent site for the evening was at mile 1182.5 and we arrived there after hiking 16.57 miles.

May 4, 2022 - It rained during the night and we awakened to a sopping wet tent. Thankfully we were dry inside. We crossed the Swatara Gap bridge over a small river near Interstate 81 that morning and found out a truck carrying Skittles, Starbursts and other Valentines candies had wrecked on a steep hillside in the woods near the trail. We didn't get any candy, but if we had gotten any we wouldn't have wanted to carry very much.

We didn't see anyone on the trail until the afternoon. We met Greasy and his wife, they had trail magic consisting of cold drinks and candy bars. Since they had chairs set up they invited us to sit and visit with them for a little while. We took our packs off and took a break while enjoying a Mountain Dew and a Snickers. *It felt really good to sit in a chair with a backrest, most of the time we were either hiking or lying down. If we sat it was usually on a rock, log or the ground.* They said they really enjoyed talking to hikers. Greasy was an AT hiker at one time and he wanted to provide a little support to those on the journey. The couple also did some of the work maintaining the 501 Shelter.

We hiked 14.1 miles before stopping at the 501 Shelter. It was an enclosed shelter with large bunks. We didn't want to be kept awake by hikers snoring all night so we opted for our tent at the camping area near the shelter. It was breezy and we set up our tent so it could dry before we settled in for the night. The shelter was near a road that went into town and we could order food delivered to us from a local restaurant. Galaxy took all the orders and called them in for delivery. We just had to meet the delivery guy at the nearby parking lot to get our food. Galaxy, Big B, Fall Down, Tortoise, Maisel, Settler, Stripes plus a couple of other hikers I don't remember all ordered food.

We went to the parking area at the road and as we were getting the food it started to drizzle. *Oh great, more rain.* Everyone took their food to the shelter to eat because it had a huge table. The food was Italian and there were various orders of pizza, calzones, pasta and salads. We got a huge pizza and we ate most of it except for a couple of slices we gave to Fall Down. We had also given him one of our liters of water. *We had carried extra water since we knew there was no water at the shelter. The water sources were 4.1 miles before the shelter or 0.4 miles past the shelter. We decided we had rather carry the water instead of walking nearly an extra mile for water that evening.* He was most grateful since he was completely out of water. He had gotten Skittles, Starbursts and Bubble Gum tape that came from the truck crash and he shared those with us. *He was younger than us and didn't mind carrying them, but he should have carried water too.* We found out how Fall Down got his trail name. He actually fell out of the loft during the night at the Springer Mountain Shelter the first night he was on the trail. It was a rude awakening for him but even more so for the person he fell on who was sleeping below.

Fortunately, neither of them was injured. He said he had to get up during the night and apparently forgot he was in the shelter. *I would say his smoking pot may or may not have had something to do with it. Just Saying.*

Not long after eating, everyone turned in for the night. *Hikers are not night owls, that's for sure and I was more than ready to crawl in the tent.*

May 5, 2022 - We saw Ice Water again and got awesome trail magic for an early lunch. He had sandwich meats, cheeses, potato salad, coleslaw, macaroni salad, Oreo cookies and ice cream. Oh Yeah, Flashlight, No Way and Hound Dog were just finishing eating when we arrived and they graciously gave us their seats. *We learned that Ice Water is providing support for the four of them and he has been with them since Front Royal, Virginia also providing trail magic for other hikers. Wow. We were very appreciative of Ice Water and the group's hospitality.*

All talk while we were eating was of the weather that would be moving through the area in the early morning and it was predicted to rain for two days. *Most folks were looking for a place to get off trail for a couple of days and rooms were getting harder to find.* The crew we met at lunch was going to a town several miles away from the trail to avoid hiking in the rain. We were 3.7 miles from Port Clinton, PA and planned to stay there to see what the weather was going to do.

That afternoon we met Guinea, she was hiking alone and started at Harper's Ferry. We passed her but she caught up to us and camped at the same site as us that night. We talked about hiking and she was struggling with hiking uphill. I told her I count steps and it has worked for me to challenge myself to hike more steps uphill between stopping to catch my breath. *Carrying a heavy pack really weighs you down and it can really be difficult hiking uphill. When I first tried counting steps hiking up a big hill, I thought I was doing good to get to twenty-five. Gradually I was able to increase to fifty, then sixty and now I can do much more. I rarely stop now when hiking up a big hill. I'm definitely not fast but I just keep plodding along, slow and steady.* She said counting steps sounded like a good idea and thought it might work for her also.

Another guy also camped with us that evening, Paul was doing a short three-day hike and it was his first night out. He was hoping to cover a lot of the trail. *Unfortunately, he would likely get caught in the weather that was headed toward us. We later thought about him and wondered if he abandoned his hike due to the rain or if he continued because it did in fact rain for two days.*

It had been a hard day hiking over lots of rocks and we hiked 19.9 miles. *Not quite 20 miles but if you round up it was probably close enough.* I think we made it to the reason Pennsylvania is called Rocksylvania. It seemed we couldn't take a step without touching a rock. The worst part was the rocks had points sticking up that really presented an issue. They might be sticking up an inch or a foot, but they were on edge like primitive blades sticking up out of the ground. It was very difficult hiking conditions and we had to be on guard to avoid a fall. *I don't know how we hiked as many miles as we did in all those rocks.*

> *" Fall down seven times, stand up eight."*
> *- Japanese Proverb*

Chapter 30 - Rain, Rain, Rain & More Rain

May 6, 2022 - *Happy Birthday to our friend Robert!* We got up at 5:30 a.m., packed all our gear and started early to try to beat the rain. It started to sprinkle within a few minutes of us getting up, we quickly got the tent down and packed before it got wet. We had coffee and a little breakfast before we started hiking. The rain gradually got a little heavier as we hiked the 3.7 miles to Port Clinton, PA. The section of trail included a descent of 1000 feet in one mile. *After hiking down that steep section I said, if you make it down without busting your tail, even if it was dry, you deserved a medal. This was one time our hiking poles were priceless. We had come to depend on them and if we didn't have them in hand while hiking it almost felt like we were naked or something.* It was slick because it was muddy, there were lots of rocks and high step downs, the trail was treacherous. Luckily neither of us fell while hiking down the hill but we did have a couple of close calls.

We arrived in Port Clinton to discover there was not much there and the rain was gradually getting heavier. A pavilion in town was maintained for hikers by one of the local churches. We headed for the pavilion and would decide where to go from there. On the way to the pavilion, there were several houses lining the street. One of them had a sign indicating hikers were welcome to use the outside water spigot for fresh water. We did stop and fill our water bottles because we were not sure there was water at the pavilion. *Good thing we got water because there was none. We had learned not to ever pass a good fresh water source.* After discovering the only lodging in the area was either full or closed, we set our tent up in the pavilion and decided to wait out the rain there. We had no phone signal to make calls to check on lodging earlier, but it probably wouldn't have made any difference. All hikers were trying to find a place to hold up until the rain passed through the area.

There was a Cabela's store in nearby Hamburg, Pennsylvania, *it is the largest Cabela's store in the United States.* They provided shuttle service, on a preset schedule, from the pavilion in Port Clinton to and from their store. We caught the shuttle at 10:00 a.m. and rode to Hamburg. The Cabela's was also near several places to eat, Aldi and Wal Mart. We ate at McDonalds and went to Aldi, then Wal Mart to get supplies. We walked in the rain with our raincoats from the Cabela's and back. Hopefully we would not be completely soaked by the time we got back to the pavilion. We got a ride back at 1:00 p.m. per the schedule. It was still raining non-stop. Light drizzle at times but still raining. Our shuttle driver would not accept tips he said the service was compliments of Cabela's. *Wow, thank you Cabela's.*

A lady came by the pavilion and said she was with the local church that provided the pavilion for the hikers and she would very much appreciate it if we would log onto the website per the posting in the pavilion and pay the suggested donation for staying there overnight. She said it took a lot of money to mow the grass, provide the port a potty and keep the grounds clean and the church could use the money. *We had already read the signs and made our payment online. I could see where a lot of hikers may have not been willing to pay to stay there but she did have a point.*

Later that afternoon we went to Frank's Barber Shop, yet another hiker friendly place that must be seen. We found out Frank is a retired marine and he caters to hikers. The place was part barber shop, music store, antique store and a gathering place for locals and hikers. *Frank provided coffee, pastries, will fill your water bottles with fresh water, allow you to charge your phone, use the restroom and he provided entertainment for the many hikers that come into his shop. All of this is done while providing haircuts for his loyal customers, and hikers that want a cut.* He allowed me to leave my battery pack there to charge overnight as we planned to come back to see him the next day.

We got back to the pavilion and settled in to watch the rain. At 7:30 p.m. there were five of us staying there. Green Light, Grasshopper and a guy with a dog. One of the guys had pitched a tent outside the shelter in a grassy area, we couldn't believe it. He swore he was dry but we couldn't see how because it was raining nonstop. Oh, it would slow for a bit but then it would rain really hard, it never completely stopped. We figured the tent had to be like raincoats, it would eventually leak.

As we were lying in our tent drifting off to sleep, I remembered seeing painted rocks on the trail early that day. The rocks were inspirational with words like Determination, You Can, Strong and Adventure. I wondered who placed them there and if they knew how much encouragement it gave to hikers like me.

May 7, 2022 - Zero day #6. Derby Day (the Kentucky Derby). We sure did miss the derby party at the marina at home. We found out later a horse with 80-1 odds, Rich Strike, won the race. Wow, and we missed it! I wished I could have bet at least $1000 on that horse.

Rain, rain, rain. We were staying at the pavilion another night because of the rain. The rain was supposed to move out the next day. We walked in the rain to the 3 C's Restaurant for breakfast that morning. I had patriotic pancakes, not my usual but I made an exception. Blueberries, strawberries and whipped cream on pancakes and they were delicious.

We decided to catch the shuttle again and make another trip to Cabela's to pass the day. This time we went through the entire store and found the area dedicated to the display of trophy deer to be more than amazing. They also had an African section that contained a full-sized elephant. The displays of the animals throughout the store were unreal. It was worth the trip just to see them. We also thought this might be a good opportunity to put some more waterproofing on our tent since we were staying at the pavilion.

When we returned from Cabela's we sprayed the tent with waterproofing, it smelled really strong so we decided to go back to Frank's Barber Shop while it dried so Roy could get a haircut. It was much needed because my scissor cut was not the best. We also decided we needed to clean up a bit so we heated some water and with our soap and microfiber cloth we were able to hit the high points, change clothes and put on fresh deodorant. There was a port-a-potty across the road from the pavilion and we also took advantage of it as a bathing and changing station. It was large enough, really clean and had apparently just been serviced, otherwise we would have had to try to bathe and change in the tent which is not an easy task.

Roy really wanted to wait for Frank to cut his hair but there were several customers waiting and he took his time cutting hair as he was talking to everyone. Good things come to those who wait but there was also a woman working there too and Roy decided it would be okay if she cut his hair. *Beggars couldn't be choosers; his hair was so long and thick it was long overdue for a cut. I hadn't seen him with his hair this long since before we married.* He got his haircut, we filled our water bottles, I picked up my battery and we said our goodbyes and thank you to Frank. His kindness was more than appreciated.

Back at the pavilion we found out Green Light and Grasshopper were also going to spend another night at the shelter as was the young man with a cute little dog named Clifford. The guy had a couple of things to do and needed to go to the post office so he asked if we would keep an eye on his dog. We told him we would and we were dog sitters for a couple of hours that afternoon. I petted the little dog two or three different times; he had a friendly disposition and such a sweet little face you couldn't help but like him. After his owner returned Clifford jumped for joy, he had looked up every time anyone came into the pavilion and it was obvious, he adored his owner and couldn't wait for his return. *He may have had a little separation anxiety. I believe this went both ways as the guy later told me Clifford was three years old and he got him when he was a puppy. He had worked at home through the early part of the pandemic and the dog had really gotten spoiled to him being around.* It was evident they were the best of friends.

We walked to the Port Clinton Hotel to eat supper. It was apparently a local hot spot and the restaurant was really very busy. There were no rooms to rent because the hotel was being remodeled, according to the FarOut app. The restaurant was very busy and the food was excellent. Roy had fish and I had chicken parmesan. *Can you believe I didn't order a cheeseburger?* We went back to the pavilion and it was still drizzling rain. We all settled in for another long night of rain, rain and more rain.

May 8, 2022 - We were awakened last night around 9:00 p.m. by fireworks a couple of houses down from the pavilion. We were both sound asleep and thought it was much later in the night and we first thought it was gunfire. We went back to sleep and were awakened at 3:30 a.m. by loud music. Around 4:45 a.m. we heard a gunshot and called the police. The music finally stopped at 5:10 a.m. and the police never came. We were extremely glad to be leaving the pavilion that morning. We had about all of the rain, commotion and not covering miles we could stand. At least the rain had stopped.

That morning Clifford's owner, Mash, discovered that he had what appeared to be an abscess and he needed to get him to the vet. He stayed behind to care for his dog while the rest of us returned to the trail. We said goodbye to them and hoped Clifford would be okay.

Sprig was a girl we met on the trail that day, she had problems with blisters on both her feet and had actually had to take a few days off trail because of them. I talked to her about foot care and gave her a couple of strips of KT tape for her feet. She was really appreciative. *Thankfully I never had but one teeny tiny little blister for the entire hike. Roy got a blister a couple of times, but it was early on in our hiking and they healed quickly. I couldn't imagine hiking with blistered feet. Not to mention the discomfort, blisters can get infected and we had heard horror stories about hikers and their foot problems having to leave the trail.*

We met Catch Me and Where Are You, an older couple, as we were looking for a place to set up our tent for the evening. Catch Me was working on his seventh time hiking the AT. *I still don't know what would make someone hike the trail that many times, but apparently, he was in good health and enjoyed hiking.* He was a thin guy with long gray hair and a beard to his chest. He told us they were hiking sections and would get a shuttle from Port Clinton to go back to their car since they were hiking southbound. They had left their car a few days north of where we were. We camped that night at a stream near Catch Me and Where Are You after hiking 15.5 miles. We were sorely in need of a good night's sleep after staying the previous night at the pavilion in Port Clinton.

"You're off to great places, today is your day. Your mountain is waiting, so get on your way." - Dr. Seuss

Chapter 31 - Pennsylvania a.k.a. Rocksylvania

May 9, 2022 - Lots of rocks, we had to be in the thick of Rocksylvania! We hiked over the much talked about Knife's Edge. It really was not that bad, not when compared to Knife's Edge on Mt. Katahdin in Maine. It was along the steep top of the mountain ridge with drop offs on either side, but we made it through without a problem. My fear of heights didn't kick in too bad, but I did carefully navigate the trail through the area. The trees now have leaves on them and I guess I really don't see how high up we were at times.

We got off the trail by accident. We were following what looked like an old road bed through the woods when we realized we had not seen any white blazes for a while. I checked the app and found we were clearly off the trail about half a mile. We backtracked and found the trail took a hard right turn at a spot where there were several branches lying across the trail. It appeared to be a place where you were not supposed to go. *This situation reminded me of a quote attributed to Daniel Boone, "I can't say I was ever lost, but I was bewildered once for three days". Thankfully we were not lost and only bewildered for a few minutes.* We finally got back on the trail after about a half hour spent backtracking. Even without our unplanned venture off the trail we hiked 14.61 trail miles!

May 10, 2022 - The trail was again over lots and lots of rocks. *Rocksylvania! Ugh!* We climbed up rocks about 1000 feet in elevation after crossing the Lehigh River. We had to put up our hiking poles and rock climb up. We saw a young couple after we got over the worst part of the climb. The girl was apparently scared to death of climbing on the rocks. She was shaky and holding on to anything she could reach. I really felt sorry for her because she was so scared. We tried to encourage her and told her to take her time. *We later found out there was a bad weather bypass around the big climb we had done. Knowing Roy, he would have wanted to stay on the main trail. There is no way the couple we saw had come up the way we did. They had to have gone on the bypass but from what I understood by reading in the FarOut app later, the bypass was not exactly a piece of cake. It really reminded us of the climbing in Maine.* We camped at tent sites at mile 1265.4 after hiking 15.17 miles. Two other hikers who were at the Eckville Shelter we passed a couple of days ago stayed there as well as three younger hikers who came in later. Our tent sites were under pine trees and the pine needles made a great place to set the tent. Everyone was talking about the big climb up the rocks. *Just wait until they get to Maine and they will find out all about rock climbing! We should be in New Jersey in about two days, we will be really glad to put Pennsylvania, I mean Rocksylvania, behind us.*

May 11, 2022 - The weather was sunny and hot. We saw our first snake on the trail, he was not easily scared. He stood his ground for a little bit before he finally decided to move out of the trail. We also had been seeing lots of colorful wild flowers. I was in awe of the different varieties and colors. We hiked 16 miles and made it to Wind Gap, PA. We got a room at the Gateway Motel. *We had read reviews about the motel in the app and talked to a couple of hikers on the trail who had stayed there and there were mixed reviews of the place.* The man who ran the place was very kind, he gave us a bottle of water each and a package of cookies while we waited for our room. There were no other lodging options in this area anywhere near the trail, we really needed supplies and we were really looking forward to a shower but we probably should have hiked on instead of staying there.

The linens on the bed were stained, had burn holes in them, etc. I refused to sleep on the sheets so we pulled out our sleeping bags and used them on the bed. At least the bathroom was clean and had an endless supply of hot water. We found out the clothes dryer on the premises was on the fritz and the owner was hanging the sheets out to dry on the rails of the deck out front which may have accounted for some of the sheets not looking clean. The guy did a load of laundry for us and we also had to hang our stuff outside to dry.

Going into town required a ride since it was about three miles away. *I know in the grand scheme of things three miles is nothing for us to hike but since we had already hiked 16 and didn't want to hike 6 more and carry our supplies back, a ride was in order.* The owner agreed to arrange a ride to town for us but said we would have to get a ride back or walk. Our ride was with him and a friend who was going to a nearby casino and they agreed to drop us off on the way. *He had changed his clothes and spiffed up to go gambling, no wonder he gave us a discount for paying in cash. Maybe he would win enough money to fix the dryer. Lol!*

They dropped us off at a shopping center where there were several restaurants and a grocery store. We went to Anthony's Italian Restaurant and discovered they didn't serve beer but allowed you to bring it in to drink with your meal. We ordered our pizza and Roy went to the Giant Grocery next door to get a couple of beers while I waited for our pizza. The food was excellent and the staff was very kind and helpful. After we ate, we went grocery shopping for supplies. As usual we probably bought more than we needed to carry. Luckily, we were able to get a Uber ride back to the motel and didn't have to carry the groceries. *The fact we got an Uber was almost a miracle in itself, we had asked the waitress at the restaurant about getting a ride and she told us there were no taxis or shuttles but we might be able to get an Uber, but not always. Luck was on our side, this time.*

Back at the motel we brought our laundry in to finish drying in the room next to the heater. We would have to just hope it all would get dry by morning. Roy strung up a clothesline with the rope he used to hang our food to keep it from bears while we were camping. We watched a little TV and tried to sleep. *If it was not for needing a shower, I wouldn't have bothered with staying at the motel.*

May 12, 2022 - As we were leaving the motel that morning it occurred to me to think why the motel was called the Gateway Motel. *Gateway to what? Not sure I wanted to find out.*

The day was sunny and hot. We saw three snakes at Wolf Rocks. *According to the app there were lots of snakes in that area. I wondered how many we didn't see!* We crossed the Delaware River and into New Jersey. *Eight states finished!* The bridge across the river was huge, it was probably over a mile long. There was supposed to be an ice cream shop in the town of Delaware Water Gap that was a must see. When we got there, we found the shop was closed. *Lots of small businesses in this town apparently had closed, more than likely victims of Covid.* The visitor center at Kittatinny Point was closed also, we were looking forward to at least a vending machine for a cold drink or snack but it was not meant to be.

We hiked 20.3 miles. *Our first twenty-mile day!* We didn't intend to hike that far but had to find a place to camp. There were no suitable places to stealth camp along the way in this area as it was mostly uphill from the town and the river as usual. At least the trail went alongside a stream and I was entertained by watching the water cascading down the hill.

We passed the Lehigh Valley Amateur Astronomical Society area, according to the signage the society was founded in 1957. There were several very well-maintained buildings and a cleared area at the top of a mountain apparently maintained for viewing the skies. It was definitely another unique thing we saw while on the trail.

We both were getting very tired but there was no place to stop until we arrived at the Backpacker Campsites. All of the bear boxes had bugs or water in them. When we went to hang our food bag, we discovered we had left Roy's rope at the motel when we used it for hanging clothes to dry in the room. We would have to find another one when we got to the next town. We pitched our tent and cleaned out a spot in the bear box to store our food bags for the night. We hoped the next day would be a better day.

"Mountains are not stadiums where I satisfy my ambition to achieve, they are the cathedrals where I practice my religion" - *Anatoli Boukreev*

Chapter 32 - There's Bears in Them Woods

May 13, 2022 - The Mohican Outdoor Center was open and we got really good sandwiches for lunch. We were told about an aggressive bear in the area up on the hill from the center. *Rumor had it that someone had to hit at it with their hiking poles! That would be entirely too close for me!*

We saw a bear trap on the trail a few miles away. We had seen those on TV before but seeing one in real life and up close was an experience. *We wondered what they were using for bait in the trap and thought they should have been using Krispy Kreme donuts and PBR beer.* Our campsite for the night was about seven miles from the bear trap. Thankfully we did get a new rope at the outdoor center so we were able to secure our food for the night. I fell earlier in the day, thank goodness nothing hurt but my pride. My right foot quickly slid to the left unexpectedly as I stepped on a rock and, down I went onto my right side. I had my hiking poles in my hands but fell so fast they just went down with me. I had to take my pack off to get up. T*his was the first fall for either of us on this leg of the journey but it wouldn't be the last. I was just surprised I made it without falling as long as I did, considering all the potential hazards.* We set up camp near Buttermilk Trail at mile 1317.8.

May 14, 2022 - We stopped for lunch at Gyp's Tavern. We both had burgers and fries this time. It was a really neat place on a lake with tables and chairs out back and the food was good. The waitress was really nice and she filled our water bottles for us with fresh water. It was nice to have water that we didn't have to filter. It started drizzling rain in the afternoon, there was one downpour for a few minutes. We did manage to get the tent set up when it slacked for a bit but it was still raining at 7:00 p.m. *This was the third day we carried a wet tent. The waterproofing we put on it at Port Clinton was getting a workout.* We camped at Mashipacong Shelter, mile 1334.3 after hiking 16.5 miles. The snake count at this point was at nine, including one copperhead. *Yes, we were keeping ourselves entertained even by accounting snakes.*

May 15, 2022 - We hiked 12.4 miles and went over High Point, New Jersey. It's the highest point in New Jersey at 1685 feet elevation. Not the highpoints we were accustomed to seeing but it was much higher than anything around. We stopped at the visitor center before hiking up to the War Memorial Monument at the highpoint which was about a half mile off the trail. The visitor center had drinks, candy, snacks, etc. for sale and the prices were reasonable so we got several things there to add to our portable pantry. They also had a hiker box with several dehydrated meals and other items. We picked up a couple of the meals since they were free and lightweight. *These were meals that cost ten to twelve dollars each.* We left plenty of more meals for other hikers. The staff at the visitor center were very nice and one of the ladies filled our water bottles with fresh water. *Wow, we felt really lucky to have our bottles filled with fresh water two days in a row. Yes, little things mean a lot on the trail.*

We met some hikers from Kentucky while we were at the visitor center. A man hiking with his wife and daughter was taking a break. They talked about hiking the AT over the past year or so. We thought they must have been hiking in sections. They surely were not thru hikers because they hadn't lost weight like both of us.

We hiked up to the monument, we couldn't go in it as it was not open but there were good views from all around. *It was one of the few side trails we would take to see something that was not right on the trail. We didn't want to spend much time or energy hiking off the trail for miles that didn't get us any closer to our goal of completing the AT.*

That afternoon at about 2:30 p.m. we were hiking at the edge of a large field behind an overgrown fence row. Roy suddenly stopped and walked back to me saying there was a bear in the field. *I thought he was joking, but he had told me he wouldn't joke about bears. He wanted me to see it before it moved.* We quietly walked to the gap in the fence row where we could see into the adjoining field. There was a huge male black bear, we knew he had to be a male because of his size and he was about 25-30 yards away. I was going to try to get a picture but as soon as Roy made a noise by hitting his hiking poles together the bear turned and looked at us, in a split second he jumped up and ran away. His feet pounded the ground and it sounded like a horse galloping. We were amazed to see a huge bear that close, and we were also glad he quickly ran away from us. We had been walking the trail behind the fence row, not talking, the wind was blowing which was making a lot of noise and we were downwind from him. The bear apparently didn't hear or smell us. We continued on down the trail but kept an eye out for him. We kept talking to each other and making louder noises, if he was anywhere nearby, he would know we were there.

We decided to go to the Secret Shelter and check it out. It was a little early to stop, but rain was moving in that evening and we decided to stay there. We pitched our tent and it had time to dry out before we took it down and decided to sleep in the shelter since there was no one else there. We could hear thunder in the distance and the rain moved through quickly, we were just on the edge of the storm and only got a few sprinkles. After the rain moved through there was a rainbow. The colors of pink and purple in the evening sky with the rainbow were gorgeous.

This shelter area was unique. A gravel road leads to an old farm privately owned by a former AT hiker who is now in his 80's. His goal was to make a place where hikers were welcome to stay and he wanted to provide everything they might need free of charge. There is a well with an endless supply of fresh drinking water, no need to boil or filter. The shelter has electricity for charging cell phones, it also has a fan or a heater if needed. The floor of the shelter is black and white checkered tile. No need to worry about nails or splinters poking a hole in your air mattress. There is a caretaker who we talked to for quite a while, he cuts the grass, checks on the buildings and takes care of the donkey. The donkey's name is Jake and he is 26 years old. He keeps the bears away according to the caretaker. Jake is like a big puppy and he reportedly likes Gummy Bears. Before the caretaker arrived, we didn't pet him or feed him because we thought if we ignored him, he would give up and go away. He would just stand by you and nearly put his face nearly on you, it took a while but he finally wandered off to pick grass. As of 9:00 p.m. we were the only people staying that night. *I don't think we could have tolerated the snoring from other hikers that evening, we were really needing a good night's sleep. I'm sure they may have had the same to say about us at times. We settled in glad to have found the Secret Shelter that is not so much of a secret any more all to ourselves.*

May 16, 2022 - *Happy Birthday to our friend Pam!* We went to Unionville, NY this morning and stopped at the General Store. There were signs posted in the store, cash payments only. But they had an ATM if you needed to get cash. *We saw several businesses accepting cash only or offering discounts for paying in cash while we were in New York. Businesses in most every other state had wanted card payments only.* We both got huge honey buns and shared a quart of milk. When we got back on the trail it routed us back into New Jersey. It started to rain in the early afternoon and it rained hard at times but we kept on going. Roy took a hard fall, banged his knee pretty hard but he said he's okay, thank goodness. We are camping in the tent at the Wawayanda Shelter, 4 miles from the New Jersey/New York border. The snake count is at 13 including what we saw today and I also counted 30 orange salamanders. *We did some of the silliest things to keep ourselves entertained at times.*

We hiked up a big rocky hill this afternoon, 1000 feet up called Stairway to Heaven. *I told Roy that was not exactly what I had in mind to call it when we were climbing up it! I still think we hike much more uphill than down or maybe I just take the uphill harder. The uphill climbs can deplete your energy, that's for sure.* Despite the stairway, we hiked 18.59 miles.

May 17, 2022 - The morning was cloudy but at least it wasn't raining. We had coffee and ate a little breakfast as we broke camp. After a few minutes of hiking, I felt something in my right shoe that didn't feel right and it hit me all of the sudden that something moved under my foot. I yanked my shoe off forgetting I had my gaiters on, they were around my ankle and attached to my shoestring on top of my shoe. I nearly fell trying to get my shoe off as quickly as I could. Of course, I was also carrying my pack and I stumbled all over the place. Fortunately, and by some miracle, I didn't fall. A giant worm fell out of my shoe when I turned it up and shook it. It had curled up under my toes. We had been seeing these worms, they were huge. They were a lot like nightcrawlers but they had lots of legs, I guess they were technically some sort of centipede. *All I know for sure is you don't want one of them moving about in your shoe. Note to self: Shoes must be placed inside the tent at night even if the weather is not freezing.*

We hiked through a swampy area with reeds and aquatic plants. There were also several beautiful wildflowers. Thankfully a boardwalk constructed through the area provided easy hiking for about two miles. *I was amazed at the work that went into the construction of this walkway. It was yet another unbelievable example of how the AT is maintained through areas that are not hiker friendly. There would be no way to hike through this area, it was apparently easier to build the walkway through the area than reroute the trail. Most often the work to build and maintain the trail is accomplished by an army of dedicated volunteers and their work is truly amazing. We saw teams of volunteers several times while hiking the AT. They used chainsaws to cut trees that were blocking the trail, placed rocks on hillsides to build steps, and even used hoes to dig trenches to drain flooded sections of trail after heavy rains with plans to go back later and add rock to those areas. Without the work of these volunteers the trail would not be possible. We would always tell the volunteers thank you when we saw them working, I hope they knew how much we truly appreciated them.*

We crossed over the New Jersey/New York border. *One more state marked off the list, five more to go.* We took a picture of our feet with Roy in New York and me in New Jersey. I sure hope all of New York is not like the first few miles. There was lots of rock climbing and rebar in one place, a very tough 10 miles this morning. We got a nice room at Lake Lodging in Greenwood Lake, NY. It is a cute little motel/hostel, the owner Jim was awesome! He picked us up on the trail, took us to two stores to help us get supplies and did a load of laundry for us. *I think I am getting a little spoiled not having to clean the house or do laundry!*

We ordered huge pulled pork sandwiches at Beer Pockets BBQ, and we waited out back down by the lake while our food was prepared. The lady told us she would yell when our food was ready. Apparently, she was accustomed to yelling out orders. We waited by the lake and enjoyed the gorgeous view of the lake and the surrounding houses and docks. We took our food back to our room. The sandwiches were very good. We walked back toward town a little bit later and got ice cream at the Ice Cream Shack. I got a Salted Caramel Truffle waffle cone. *Yum!* Both places wanted payment in cash.

That evening we found out about a hiker that had gotten lost. Jim was going to pick him up and bring him to Lake Lodging. According to the people he spoke with, the hiker had gotten lost and couldn't find his way back to the Wildcat Shelter. This was the next shelter we would pass and it was about two miles from where we would resume the trail at NY Route 17 A. The hiker's gear, including his cell phone, was found late in the evening by some hikers who knew him. Jim said they didn't know if he had a medical issue that contributed to him getting lost but he was asked to keep an eye on the guy. He was going to put the hiker in room #1 nearest the office.

"The best way to be kind to bears is not to be very close to them."- Margaret Atwood

Chapter 33 - Where Did Mingo Go?

May 18, 2022 - We found out this morning the lost hiker was Mingo. We had seen him several times at different places and camped at the same location a few times. Roy talked to him a little bit, from what he understood Mingo got turned around after dark and he was not able to find his way back. He also told Roy he was lost for two nights and at one point he saw a bear and was very afraid. Mingo was from China and spoke very little English so it was difficult to get a clear idea of what had happened. He also didn't know at that time if he would be returning to the trail.

Jim took us back to the trail. The terrain was rough and hiking was tough that day. As we were getting ready to find a place to camp, we met a hiker named Syrup and he mentioned a hiker being lost a night or two before. He said he and a couple of other hikers came into the Wildcat Shelter about 10:00 p.m. and found Mingo's belongings including his cell phone and his shoes. Mingo was nowhere to be found. They called out for him and looked around but didn't find him. He said Mingo stayed lost in the woods for two nights, barefooted. Everyone thought he must have had a medical issue or an accident. They finally figured out he had gotten lost when he went to put his food in the bear box after dark and was not able to find his way back to the shelter. Two days later he finally found his way to a road and flagged someone down, he was about 10 miles from the shelter. Syrup and two other hikers called the police but they were initially not much help. They made several calls to authorities and also spoke with Mingo's wife at one point, they didn't sleep much knowing Mingo was out there lost somewhere or worse. It had even crossed their minds he may have been attacked by a bear but thankfully they didn't see any signs to indicate a bear attack. We told him we saw Mingo at Lake Lodging and he appeared to be okay. Jim had taken him to get food and said Mingo had acted fine, just exhausted.

We had been off trail a couple of times but used the FarOut App and got back on track. We knew Mingo also had the app, but he had left his phone at the shelter. We had camped at the same shelter as him a couple of times and he always seemed alright, just a little hard to talk with because of the language barrier. The hikers who discovered he was missing thought he may have had a medical issue and were still concerned about him. Guess we will never know.

Lots of uphill hiking and rock climbing again today. Roy fell once today going downhill on slick black dirt. I was right behind him and all I could do was watch he was down almost before I could blink. *Thankfully he was not hurt.* Despite the rough terrain we hiked 14.72 miles.

May 19, 2022 - Lots more rock climbing today, through the Lemon Squeezer! We had to take off our packs to get through this part of the trail because it was too narrow, it was also uphill. Even without the packs we had to walk through sideways. There were lots of steeper uphill climbs today. It was cool all day, no sunshine until very late in the day.

Last night just before we crawled in our tent for the night we met two more hikers, Right On and Storm Trooper who were there when Mingo went missing. They also told us he was gone for two nights. Right On said it was the most terrifying thirty-six hours of her life. She said they called 911 three different times before they finally convinced someone there was a problem. With bears in the area, they thought he could have been attacked, had a medical issue or accident. None of them had slept much those two nights due to worrying about Mingo and they were exhausted. The whole event had left them shaken and they were still very concerned about him. We told them we had seen him at Lake Lodging, Roy had talked with him and he appeared to be okay but he wasn't sure if he would be back on the trail.

We camped 0.2 miles from Palisades Interstate Parkway after hiking 11.4 miles. The hiking had been tough, there were lots of rocks in New York and most of them were huge. We had hiked over, around and through large rocks most of the day. We saw blueberry bushes everywhere but they were loaded with little green berries, it was much too early to enjoy them. We also saw a little buck deer that was not the least bit concerned with us and we passed within 10 yards of him as he was eating grass. We got our tent set up as it was starting to drizzle rain. Thankfully the rain didn't last long. We settled in for the night and slept well after a tiring day of hiking.

May 20, 2022 - We crossed the Palisades Interstate parkway early in the morning at a time when the traffic was light. In the FarOut app hikers were cautioned about this road crossing due to heavy traffic and an alternate route was suggested. It would mean adding miles to the hike and we had decided we would take our time to wait on traffic and cross the road early. We were able to cross the parkway without a problem, no waiting for traffic.

We crossed over Bear Mountain about 10:30 a.m., the fog was so thick you couldn't see anything from the top. Reportedly the NYC skyline could be seen from Bear Mountain and we had really been looking forward to seeing it, we would have to see it sometime later from another vantage point. The edge of the mountain just disappeared into the fog, there were no views. The observation tower was closed due to fog. The fog was beginning to clear a little bit, but we didn't want to wait around and lose precious hiking time so we decided to move on. We got a couple of cokes to have with our lunch from a vending machine near the observation tower.

We saw Mingo at Bear Mountain! He is apparently doing well and decided to continue. He is a fast hiker and he left us behind quickly as he had done before. We were very glad to see him, know that he was okay, and also know that he made it back to the trail.

We hiked down the mountain to the Bear Mountain Recreation Area which was on a beautiful lake. We saw Spic & Span near the lake, we first met him in Duncannon, PA but didn't get his name at that time. He remembered seeing us also and we talked with him for a little bit.

The Trailside Zoo was near the lake and admission was free to hikers, the trail went right through the zoo for about a quarter mile. The animals at the zoo were supposed to be mostly local wildlife brought in due to injury and were being rehabilitated. There was also a history museum where hikers could enter without cost. We thought it would be neat to see the zoo, but it was closed at the time. We took the blue-blazed bypass trail around it and continued to hike. The zoo was at the lowest elevation on the entire AT, at 129 feet above sea level. *All I could think of was how steep the climb would be when we left the zoo area.*

We crossed the Bear Mountain Bridge over the Hudson River, the bridge over the river was one of the bigger bridges we crossed. We were thinking about Captain Sully and wondered if we were anywhere near where he landed the plane in the Hudson River. We saw several ferry boats as we were crossing the bridge. But we were still too far away from New York City to see anything. We were bound to pay for the lower elevations and of course had a big uphill climb after crossing the river.

That afternoon we met some women taking a break at the edge of the trail. We stopped and talked to them for a few minutes and they told us they were looking for Lady Slippers, a flower in the orchid family, and it only grows in certain areas. After being told what they were and having them described to us, we looked for them too. *We saw several of them over the coming days. Most of them were pink but we also saw a few white ones. We also saw lots of blueberry bushes in this area and wished they had been in season but we were much too early to enjoy them this time.*

We made it to the Appalachian Market by about 4:00 p.m. We got a few supply items, some much needed insect repellant, cheeseburgers and onion rings. We sat at tables inside and enjoyed our food. After we left the market, we barely beat the rain and got our tent set up at Graymore ball field. The church allowed camping for hikers at the field 0.4 miles off the trail. It was a nice grassy area with a porta potty, a pavilion and a water hydrant. The church has provided this area for camping to hikers since the early 1970's. We filled our bottles with fresh water and settled in early to get out of the drizzling rain after hiking 14.9 miles.

May 21, 2022 - The weather was HOT! We made it through the morning pretty good but the afternoon was brutally hot. *I much prefer the cooler weather for hiking. We are drinking more water in the heat and we have to make sure we have enough. Thank goodness for the FarOut app, it helps so much with planning not only for water but almost everything. I don't know how hikers made it before without the technological advances we are spoiled with today.*

The interesting point for the day was the Hempstead Huts. *In 1779 and 1780 the Continental Army camped there. There were also remnants of an inoculation station. George Washington ordered the Continental Army inoculated for smallpox and this location was where a large number of inoculations had taken place. The inoculation process was conducted when a physician lanced the infected patient's lesions with a knife or scalpel then inserted the same blade under the skin of a healthy person. The "inoculated" person contracted the disease, but in a much milder form. Early disease prevention, Washington was credited with accomplishing an impossible victory over an invisible enemy. Chalk this up to another interesting piece of history I would not have learned about if not for the trail.*

We camped at Canopus Lake Beach Shelter. Mingo came into the campsite after us. He talked to Roy and asked about water. We walked up to the concession/restroom area, of course it was not open for the summer yet, but we did get to use the restroom and got cold water from the drinking fountains outside. We set our tent in a grassy area not far from the shelter. At 7:30 p.m. it was still 85 degrees! We hiked 13.5 miles in the heat. *I sure hoped tomorrow would be cooler.*

We found out through the trail grapevine, the Brink Road Shelter in New Jersey was closed by the AT due to a bear sticking its nose into a tent! *Per the website it said the shelter was temporarily closed due to bear activity. There was no camping or access to drinking water in that area. We were glad to have New Jersey behind us and even more glad we didn't have to detour off the trail or worry about the bears there.*

May 22, 2022 - We hiked 13.94 miles today. It was very hot again, 90 degrees plus. It was not that hot at home in Kentucky or in Panama City Beach today! We hiked to Mountain Top Deli for lunch. On the way there we met Mingo on his way back to the trail, he had stopped for lunch too. We had ham sandwiches, chips and a pint of ice cream each. Moose Tracks, it was nice to have something cold and delicious. A guy at the store offered us a ride back to the trail and since the deli was a half mile from the trail we gladly accepted. The ride was greatly appreciated. This was one half mile addition to the trail that was well worth the trip.

On top of a mountain, we saw a huge United States flag painted on the rocks and the words, "In memory of Sept. 11th". *We would see many places as we went through some of the Northern states where rocks had been spray-painted. There was signage posted about fines for defacing the rocks with paint but of course the people painting the rocks would just spray the sign too. I really wished people wouldn't paint the rocks because it did detract from the natural beauty of the landscape.*

We camped at Morgan Stewart Shelter. Mingo camped there also. He seemed to be doing well. He is a much faster hiker, but he has been taking his time a bit more. I think his being lost for two nights had made him more aware of the hazards of hiking the trail. We washed up a bit to get the sweat off of us and got everything into the tent due to the impending rain. A fierce sounding storm moved through about 7:00 p.m. The next few days were supposed to be cooler with temps in the 70s. *Only seventeen more miles and we will be finished with New York.*

May 23, 2022 - Today we stopped in at Native Landscaping, the lady there was very nice. She was hiker friendly and enjoyed meeting people. *There are some people along the trail who think hikers are dirty freeloaders and look down upon them. But thankfully there are far more people who are helpful and generous.* We got ice cream and Pepsi and talked with her for a little while. The plants at the place were beautiful and I wished we could have plants like some of these at home. We hiked through beautiful grassy fields and farmland. There were several cows, they seemed to be a bit interested in us and were walking toward us. We hurried along through their territory; we sure didn't want to be chased by cows. The trail crossed a fence and into the woods, there were no more cows thank goodness. *I grew up as a farm kid. This would not have been the first time I crossed a fence and went through the woods, or climbed a tree to get away from a bovine creature.* We hiked through a lot of fields and farmland in New York. *There were also sections of trail of that went past houses and at the edges of people's yards. These people mowed the trail with their lawn mowers thereby becoming trail maintainers. A couple of times the person on the mower would stop mowing to allow us to pass.*

We hiked 16.69 miles and set up camp at Wiley Shelter. Mingo came in after us. He told us he had resupplied at some point and he couldn't get a ride, he had to walk an extra five or six miles which put him behind us this evening. We found trail magic a little while before we got to the shelter, Gatorade, Propel powder, Oreos, etc. It was awesome to find it, just when we needed a boost. There was a large cooler with cold drinks sitting beside the trail with a note taped to the top and a smaller cooler containing dry items. The person's contact info was also available if you needed a shuttle in addition to the goodies. The Gatorade was still ice cold, apparently the cooler had been stocked recently. We drank it right away because we didn't want to carry it with us and we sure didn't want it to get warm. After being so hot all day the cold Gatorade was fantastic and more than appreciated. We took a pack of Oreos and a couple of Propel powders for later and left the rest of the trail magic for other hikers.

May 24, 2022 - We crossed into Connecticut and camped at the Algo Shelter after hiking 12.78 miles. We saw a mother bear with two cubs this afternoon. As usual, Roy saw the bear first and alerted me. We stopped and watched as the mother walked quickly away from the trail. She didn't run, it was apparent she was making sure her cubs could keep up. The trio of bears climbed up on a rock and looked down where we were. It was some distance away and even with the camera being zoomed all the way it was too far away to get a very good picture. Seeing the mother bear solidified our opinion about the first large bear we saw being a male. The size difference between the two was significant.

We decided to camp at the shelter and in the morning, we would go into Kent, Connecticut for supplies, showers and laundry. Mingo was at the shelter with us again. He told us he was a teacher in China and he taught children with special needs but he is now retired. I told him my daughter also teaches children with special needs and we knew it was a very demanding job. We told him about seeing the bear with cubs, he said in China bears are very dangerous and his wife told him not to try to take pictures of any bears. He said he saw a rattlesnake and he was not afraid. I told him I'd rather see the bear than a rattlesnake and he laughed. *This would be the last time we saw Mingo. He was a very determined man and I'm sure he made it all the way to Mt. Katahdin to finish the AT.*

"Courage is going from failure to failure
without losing enthusiasm." - Winston Churchill

Chapter 34 - I Would Really Like a Shower That Works

May 25, 2022 - We made it to Kent, Connecticut. New York has been crossed off the list. There was a visitor center in town where hikers can go to shower and get fresh water but camping is not allowed. The shower located around the back of the visitor center didn't work. I was already undressed and ready as it was a coin operated shower, Deja vu. I got redressed and we went to the laundry, there was no bathroom there for the public so we couldn't change our clothes or anything there. The lady at the laundry called the town hall and reported the shower problem at the visitor center. We went back to the visitor center and did sink baths in the restroom, washed hair and changed our clothes. Thankfully there were large restroom stalls and larger than average sinks. We went back to the laundry to wash our clothes and sleeping bags. A man from the town hall found us at the laundry and gave me $2.00 back that was lost in the shower. We decided our sink baths were good enough and we didn't go back to try the shower again.

The lady at the laundry was insistent a mask had to be worn inside because she was still scared of Covid, she was also more than ready to tell you exactly what you needed to do from which washing machine to use, how much detergent to use to how many of which coins to put in the machines. The machines used $1.00 coins, so they were a bit different. She also gave directions for the dryers. *I had read reviews on the app about this laundry and they all said the lady was a bit crazy. She was definitely a micro manager. I decided to just go with it and let her tell me what to do if it made her feel better.* We got the laundry going and headed to the IGA for supplies. While we were getting supplies in the grocery, we decided to get a whole roasted chicken for lunch! There were not any fast-food options or restaurants nearby and roasted chicken sounded good to me. We sat outside the laundry and ate our chicken. After we polished off the chicken, Roy went back to the store and got ice cream. He came back with a box of ice cream; it was one of the ones that used to be half a gallon but are smaller now. We ate all of the ice cream except a couple of bites and just couldn't eat anymore. At about 1:15 p.m. we headed to the trail. Our sleeping bags didn't dry nearly enough and we had no time to hang them up to dry them before bedtime. Roy saw Spic and Span again when he went to get water from a nearby stream. We were surprised to see him again because he is a much faster hiker. He apparently had spent some time off the trail somewhere. I said he was surprised to see us too, the last time we had seen each other was at Bear Mountain in New York. We left my sleeping bag hanging in the Stewart Hollow Brook Shelter, slept on the mattress in our tent and covered up with Roy's bag. Roy didn't seem to mind the damp sleeping bag but I was really bummed about it.

I was about at my wits end with all the hoopla of trying to get a shower and laundry done and the sleeping bags being still damp. Despite all of this I slept well. Because of the time spent in town we only hiked 7.3 miles.

May 26, 2022 - We hiked beside the Housatonic River for what seemed to be miles. This river from what we could see was not very deep but it was fairly wide. Rocks of different sizes could be seen in the river bed as the water flowed over them and the trees on either side had limbs hanging out over the water. The scenery was different and often unique each day and this day was no exception.

The trail was really tough for some reason. We resupplied the day before so I guess it must have been that the packs were heavier. *Adding six or seven pounds to packs that were already too heavy was not fun.* We stopped for lunch and hung our sleeping bags up for a while. They were still damp and we hung them again when we got to camp. They were getting better. *Note to self: sleeping bags must be bone dry after washing and before you pack them.* We heard turkeys gobbling this evening where we pitched our tent at the Sharon Mountain Campsite. We hiked 13.2 miles before we set up camp.

May 27, 2022 - We stopped at Falls Village, CT and had brunch this morning at the Falls Village Cafe. We left our packs outside at the side of the building and went inside. The cafe was beautifully decorated. We placed our order at the counter and sat down at a table to wait. The girl had told us she would bring our food when it was ready. Roy had French toast & bacon; I had a . . . BLT. The food was delicious. We were still hiking along the Housatonic River when we left town. An old dam and Great Falls were visible through the trees. Not the biggest or most spectacular waterfalls we have ever seen but they were unique and beautiful.

Later in the day we contemplated going to Salisbury, CT about a half mile off the trail for ice cream or other treats but decided we had better push on to the Riga Shelter before it rained. We arrived at the shelter before the rain started. At least we didn't have to pull out the rain gear. We hiked 15.46 miles and I counted 36 orange salamanders, a new record for the most in one day. I was still keeping myself entertained.

May 28, 2022 - We hiked most of the day in the rain, 10.2 miles up and over Mt. Race and Mt. Everett. There were supposed to be great views but we couldn't see anything because of the rain and fog. The trail was over lots of rocks, with all the rain I don't know how we kept from falling. We had to keep our eyes on the trail to safely ensure each and every step. The downhill sections were more treacherous than the uphill. After trekking through the rain all day, thankfully it was not raining when we arrived at the Glen Brook Shelter. The shelter was small and didn't look very inviting so we opted for the campsites near the shelter. This shelter is where we found porcupine quills lying in the shelter and on the ground in front of it. Porcupines had chewed on the wood a lot at the shelter. *We had seen privies that had the bottom wrapped in chicken wire all the way around to prevent porcupines from destroying the buildings. We saw privies, shelters and walkways that had been chewed along the trail. I wanted to see a porcupine, but like moose or bears, just not too close.*

The tent was still wet from last night's rain but we were able to get everything set up. We got wet today while hiking so we changed into dry clothes and crawled in the tent to warm up. The rain finally stopped and it showed no rain in the forecast for the next few days. We crossed into Massachusetts; we were 378 miles from our finish of the trail. We couldn't cover those miles soon enough for me. Hiking in the rain all day was definitely bad for morale.

May 29, 2022 - *Happy 9th Birthday to our granddaughter Ella!* We tried to book a room for the night in Great Barrington, MA and there was no vacancy at the Monument Motel which came highly recommended. I was feeling overwhelmed and had an absolute meltdown. We had not stayed in a room since Greenwood Lake, NY, twelve days ago. I wanted a real shower, we only washed up in Kent, CT after the shower took my money. I was really looking forward to a room with a hot shower and a warm, soft bed. There have been numerous times we didn't get to do something or see something because of Covid. The rain had been relentless the past few days. When it wasn't raining the weather was hot. I had been bathed in insect spray which if I didn't wipe off at night made me itch. We had dealt with our sleeping bags being wet after washing them in Kent, CT which was a fiasco. We were missing Memorial Day Weekend at home with our friends on the lake and I was missing Ella's birthday party. I was at the end of my rope. For the first time on the trail I cried, not just a little cry, I had an ugly cry/meltdown. I was tired of pretending to be happy in the face of multiple disappointments and the prospect of not getting a room was just the icing on the cake. We had both maintained positive attitudes despite the weather conditions and disappointments along the way, but I guess I had finally just had enough of being hot, wet and dirty, plus I was really missing home. After a little while Roy asked if I was going to be okay. I told him I would be fine, I just had to get it out of my system. We did get a room booked for the next night. We hiked on not knowing for sure where we would stay the night when we got to Great Barrington which also added to my frustration. I finally finished my pity party after about an hour, I knew I needed to get myself pulled together before we got into town. I just had to get my head back in the game and push on.

The last obstacle before we got to the town was a forested area where the ground was very damp and the mosquitos were as big as birds. We had seen on the app where people were saying the only way to get through the area without being eaten alive was to just run. We had insect repellant and sprayed ourselves with it a couple of times. *Our insect repellent had 100% DEET and even with us being bathed in the insect repellant we still got a few bites. We used so much of it, it's a wonder we didn't overdose on it.* We got through the mosquito infested area and came out of the woods in a grassy field full of purple and white wildflowers, they were so pretty. I felt like the flowers were our reward for getting through the mosquitos.

We hiked 8 miles that morning and finally made it to US 7 and Roy called the motel to see if we could get a room there for the night. While he was on the phone, I met a man named Harry Sand. He had his car parked at the edge of the road and was collecting wood to make hiking sticks. He asked if we needed a ride, bless his heart, I could have hugged his neck. I told him my husband was on the phone trying to get a room and we very well might need a ride. He said he wasn't in a hurry and he would wait to make sure. Roy got finished on the phone and thankfully he reserved a room for two nights! He knew I really needed a break after my melt down that morning.

Harry agreed to take us to the Monument Mountain Motel. He was really excited to see AT hikers and he said we were the first ones he had seen this year. He wanted us to sign his hikers log and we were the first to sign the book for 2022. He asked if he could take us by his house on the way and we told him it would be okay. He showed us where he made his "tiger tail" hiking sticks. He used a propane torch and burned the sticks as they were turned making a dark burned swirling pattern on the sticks. He also had two canoes hanging in the building where he made stuff, they were made of Cedar and Ash and were absolutely beautiful. The craftsmanship was amazing and there was no telling how many hours went into making them. He was really proud of the things he made and with good reason. Harry went into the house to tell his wife he was giving a ride to a couple of hikers and I heard her tell him to make sure we signed the log book. Harry was full of information about Great Barrington. He moved from Montana to Great Barrington in the 1960s and has been there ever since. He also agreed to give us a ride back to the trail on Tuesday. I had six one-dollar coins left from the laundry at Kent, CT and we gave them to him to at least pay him something for our ride, plus it would lighten my load.

All of the stuff we had been through while being on the trail didn't seem to faze my husband. If he had been hiking by himself, he would have not stopped half of the places we did. He was programmed to hike and he was not stopping until we finished. He was a hiking machine. I, for the most part, felt like a very reluctant participant for the last few days. I guess I was just really tired, needed to rest and was really missing home.

At the Monument Motel and were assigned to a very clean room with a wonderfully comfortable bed and a shower with endless hot water. This would definitely work for a couple of nights, just what I needed when I needed it most. I was really excited to get a room with a hot shower and a warm bed and I got in the shower within a few minutes after we got in the room.

After we showered, we walked to a nearby shopping center for food and supplies. There was a McDonald's close by and we ate there before going to buy food for the trail. Dollar Tree had several items we could use for the trail along with snacks to keep in the room. *We watched TV that night and settled into the most comfortable quiet room we had on the entire trail.*

May 30, 2022 - *Memorial Day, Zero Day #7.* We had a nice quiet day. The Monument Mountain Motel and the Fairfield Inn were owned by the same people. Fairfield Inn had a washer and dryer for customers' use and we were allowed to do our laundry there. The Fairfield Inn was right behind the Monument Motel and was a little fancier. I walked there with all our dirty laundry in a bag. The guy at the desk called the office at our motel to make sure it was okay for me to do laundry. I felt very out of place there. I went to the laundry room and stayed there until the laundry was finished. I didn't want to be going back and forth checking on it and being under the scrutiny of the staff. I called home and talked with friends and family. I was really still having a hard time because of it being the holiday. Normally we would be on the lake with friends, eating too much, drinking too much and having too much fun. And going to our granddaughter, Ella's birthday party. All of this really made me miss home. But after talking to everyone I did feel somewhat better. We just have to get through a few more weeks. I calculated our average miles per day since leaving Damascus, Virginia and determined if we could continue at our current pace, it would be possible to be finished by the first week in July. Our average miles per day had increased to 11.33. I was excited at the possibility of getting finished well before our deadline of August 15th. *This gave me more incentive to buckle down and get the hike completed. Wow, if we pushed hard enough maybe we could make it home by July 4th!*

We walked to TSC and got more insect repellant since we were running low and we sure didn't want to run out. We also went to Dollar Tree for the 4th or 5th time in two days. They had several things we could use for resupply, plus they had ice cream. We saw some other hikers that came into the motel today. Click and Clack got a room near ours, they started at Springer Mountain on February 21st. They said the hiker's bubble is about one and a half weeks behind us. I hope we can stay ahead. I called Harry to schedule him to take us back to the trail in the morning, he would pick us up at 9:00 a.m. We got all our gear cleaned/washed/dried and we got plenty to eat. We also had an excellent bed! The motel was very clean, comfortable, plenty of hot water in the shower, quiet and much appreciated. I was recharged and ready to resume the trail the next morning.

We read on Facebook that night about a 23-year-old hiker from the Netherlands that fell about fifty feet off a cliff near McAfee Knob in Virginia. Grandmaster was his trail name. He was rescued but died later at the hospital. According to other hikers he was sitting at the edge of the cliffs, not right on the edge, not posing for a picture, he just slumped forward and fell over. They said he had not been ill but they thought he may have passed out. We were at McAfee Knob about two months ago and I remembered the tall cliffs there and my fear of getting anywhere near the edge. I felt so sorry for his family and his tramily members who were witness to his fall, I can't begin to imagine being there when something like that happened. It really made us think, it only takes a split second for your life to be gone.

We were rested, refueled and ready. I enjoyed the much-needed shower at least three times before we left the motel. The break from the trail also gave me a much-needed opportunity to talk with friends and family and get myself centered. I was ready to return to the trail and finish our hike.

*"Walking: the most ancient form of exercise
and still the best modern exercise." - Carrie Latet*

Chapter 35 - We Met a Hermit

May 31, 2022 - Harry picked us up at 9 a.m. and took us back to the trail as planned. We found out he leaves his "tiger tail" walking sticks (as he calls them) at the trail for anyone to take one. He agreed to allow me to take his picture with the sticks. He is really an interesting guy. I would have loved to have one of his sticks but I sure didn't need to try to get home with it from Massachusetts.

We saw a mother bear with two cubs about 3:30 p.m. The mother moved on slowly and waited for her babies to catch up just like the other one we saw. Our AT bear count is now at eight! One in Tennessee, one in New Jersey, three in Connecticut and three in Massachusetts.

We camped in the tent at North Mt. Wilcox Shelter, we hiked 13.6 miles before arriving at the shelter. We met Guppy and had a nice conversation with him before and during supper. He started in Damascus, Virginia on March 15th. We are definitely a bit slower than a lot of the younger hikers but we are making progress. Guppy didn't carry a stove and he said he always built fires to cook his meals or ate his food cold. I think we wouldn't do as well without our pocket rocket stove; I need my coffee in the morning and didn't want to wait long enough to build a fire for it.

June 1, 2022 - Around 10:00 a.m. we came across the AT Trail Stand. It was a small wooden building about the size of an outhouse but it had several things a hiker might want. A refrigerator inside had soft drinks, candy, and ice cream. There were chips, Oreos, a few personal items and a jar with buttons, needle and thread to use. There was a price list on the door to the fridge. Another place on the honor system and the person who put it together had thought of several things a hiker might need in the middle of nowhere. A money bag was there to leave your payment or you could scan the code for Venmo. We took advantage of the available goodies and spent $9.00 for Mt. Dew, Oreos and chips and we both enjoyed the snacks. The extra calories were definitely needed. That afternoon we hiked at the edge of cleared fields of farmland and the AT went along a paved road for a bit before going back into the forest. *It's funny how much different it feels to your feet when hiking on asphalt. It's actually somewhat uncomfortable, the bare ground is much better.* The rain had started about 12:30 p.m., just a slow drizzle and we pushed harder to try to get to the campsite before it started raining harder, thankfully we made it! The terrain was not too bad, we covered the miles before stopping at 3:30 p.m. We hiked 14.2 miles and made it to the Upper Goose Pond Cabin. We pitched our tent on a wooden tent platform. *If we found an available tent platform, we always used it. The platforms were definitely preferable if it was raining.* The cabin was an old house with a caretaker. The caretaker welcomed us to the cabin and made coffee for us that evening. The cabin was closed due to Covid but we could walk around and look in from outside. *We probably wouldn't have stayed inside anyway; we much preferred our tent. Covid was still impacting a lot of stuff on the trail and we kept coming across things that are different or closed completely. I guess we were lucky the caretaker was even there.* We met English from Iowa, he was a SOBO section hiker. We all had a nice conversation around the picnic table that evening. The coffee the caretaker made for all of us was much appreciated.

June 2, 2022 - We were surprised to be called to breakfast by the caretaker at Goose Pond Cabin. She made pancakes and coffee for everyone. It really hit the spot. We were really glad we stayed at the cabin. It was definitely a hidden jewel.

We hiked 17.6 miles before tenting at the Kay Wood Shelter. We caught up with Fall Down and he told us Galaxy had to get off the trail due to plantar fasciitis. Fall Down was smoking pot as he was most every time we saw him. I wondered if he would even remember being on the trail. *At one point a few days before this we had stopped at a shelter to have lunch and use the privy when we encountered a group of five hikers who were taking a break and sitting on each side of the trail sharing a joint. We actually had to walk between them to get to the shelter. I was wearing a knee support and favoring my left knee. One of the hikers noticed I had a knee problem and one of the hikers asked if I wanted a joint because it "sure would help with that inflammation". I politely declined the offer. Thankfully my knee didn't bother me the entire time we hiked but the pain and swelling did flare up occasionally. Ibuprofen (Vitamin I) and wearing the knee support for a couple of days usually took care of the problem.*

We counted 89 Red Spotted Newts, a new record. *We had called them salamanders but saw them in the Awol Guide, they are newts often seen by hikers on the AT through several of the northern states. After hiking the AT, we were on an overnight hike at Cumberland Gap in June of 2023 and saw a couple of these newts, their range must be further south than we realized or maybe we just overlooked them before. We sure couldn't overlook them due to their abundance when we were hiking up north.*

The mosquitos have been relentless. We are both covered in bites despite using the insect repellant several times each day. *I keep thinking we will poison ourselves with the stuff, but so far, the only ill effects have been that we continue to be bitten and I have to wipe off my arms and legs with a baby wipe before settling in the tent at night. If I don't wipe it off it causes me itch. It didn't seem to have that effect on Roy. I have come to the conclusion that nothing bothers him, and that bothers me too!*

June 3, 2022 - We hiked through Dalton, Massachusetts where we stopped for pizza at 10:00 a.m., it was hot, fresh and very good. The trail went through town on roads and sidewalks for a couple of miles. There was a house up on a hill where the trail went right beside their driveway and there was a water spigot with a note saying hikers were welcome to use the water. It was yet another small kindness, greatly appreciated by hikers.

We arrived in Cheshire, MA after hiking 11.79 miles. We tent camped at the Father Tom Campsite. It is a nice grassy area, plenty of space for tents, a porta potty, fresh water and bicycles. There was a place to charge phones, an area where hammocks could be used and the campsite was close enough to several resupply locations and restaurants to walk or ride a bike. We rode bikes to the Berkshire Outfitters to get camp fuel and to Dollar General to get supplies. The nearest restaurant was about four miles away and we decided we didn't want to ride that far. So we got chips, ham and tortillas for supper when we got our supplies. We had the pizza earlier plus we had ice cream from Diane's Twist ice cream shop when we arrived in Cheshire. We didn't want a big meal and were just ready to relax.

When we got back to the campsite Fall Down was just outside the fence smoking a joint. There was a sign at the entrance that said no alcohol or drugs allowed on the grounds. We laughed because he was at least being respectful and following the rules.

We had baby wipe baths before we went to bed. *We would be ready for a new application of insect repellant the next day.* Mt Greylock, 3489 feet elevation would be the next big mountain and it was 8.3 miles from Cheshire.

June 4, 2022 - Last night at about 9:00 p.m., we were visited by the Polish Hermit at the Father Tom Campsite. *We had read about him in the hiker comments in the FarOut app. and we felt fortunate to meet him!* There were several hikers there at the time and he brought enough goodie bags for each hiker to have one. The bag was a one-gallon Ziploc bag and it contained a small Gatorade, a package of oatmeal, a package of peanut butter and crackers, Oreos, raisins, a Kind bar, trail mix and a large Band-aid. He came back this morning with a basket full of coffee, mugs, sugar, creamer and breakfast goodies. *The guy is a very unique person, so loving and so giving. He is so kind and supportive of the hikers. He is full of jokes and keeps everyone entertained during his daily visits to Father Tom Campsite. He is on Facebook and he allowed me to send him a friend request. I continue to follow his visits to the campsite and his posts about his Polish family and working on the family farm. He is a very caring individual and the world would be a better place with more people like him.* The goodies we received were much appreciated and we felt lucky to have met the Polish Hermit

We have 302.3 miles to get to Gorham, NH and the finish of the hike. We are counting down the miles and the days. We hiked up and over Mt. Greylock, the highest point in Massachusetts, elevation 3489 feet. The view from Greylock was fantastic! The weather cooperated and we were treated to sunshine, blue skies and white puffy clouds floating by. We got a beer at the Bascom Lodge near the top of Mt. Greylock and found a place at the top near the memorial tower to sit and have lunch. Looking out over the landscape you could see for miles; we were definitely rewarded for our hike up Mt. Greylock. The memorial building at the top of the mountain was another veteran's war memorial. This one was open so we left our backpacks outside the stone structure and entered. I was amazed, the floor inside was sparkling clean and made of polished tiles. The tiles were laid in a way to accentuate the circular room and there was a wreath of red and white flowers on a stand in the center. The walls were white about ten feet up, then there was a section of granite, about two feet tall, inscribed with capital letters that went all the way around the room. The inscription said in part, "dead who live again in the minds made better". But my pictures didn't capture it all. Above the letters was a blue band with white stars that also encircled the room. The ceiling was dome-shaped and painted gold and white with a design of overlapping half circles giving it the appearance of feathers. In the center of the ceiling there was a large circle painted with an intricate design of dark red, teal, gold and black. A large lantern type light was hanging from that area. The entryway was beautiful. To get to the top of the monument there was a very narrow stone stairway, too narrow to pass other people. It reminded me of something you might see in a castle although it was much smaller. Thankfully there were places where the stairs turned and there was a landing where you could wait and/or pass people when you were going up or down. At the top there were four plaques for north, south, east and west and a list of what could be viewed in each direction. A large light at the top operates at night as a beacon. The view from the top of the tower was even more spectacular than being on the ground at the bottom. The landscape dotted with green fields, numerous towns, the clear sky with the various colors of blue and the big puffy clouds made for a wonderful view.

We left the top of Mt. Greylock, thankful for the beautiful views. A short distance down from the top of Mt. Greylock we hiked along the Thunderbolt Ski Trail. Per the signage, the ski trail was cleared by the Civilian Conservation Corps and a stone warming hut was built in the 1930's. The Thunderbolt Shelter remains standing and is in good shape. Hikers are only allowed to stay in the shelter in case of emergency. It was too early in the day to stop and we of course had no emergency so we hiked on down the Thunderbolt Trail. We camped later that evening at the Wilbur Clearing Shelter on a platform.

Roy always had to have a little snack of some sort after we ate our supper and before we went to sleep for the night. *The snack usually consisted of a couple of snack sized Snickers, raisins, peanuts or some other sweet. He would put the wrappers in his peanut butter jar. I kept telling him a bear could smell it anyway and he was going to get us eaten. But I'm not sure a bear even wanted to get between him and his sweets.* We had our snacks that night compliments of the Polish Hermit. "

"If there's one thing I've learned from hiking it's that the early bird gets a face full of spider webs." - Unknown

Chapter 36 - The Trail Has Gone to the Dogs

June 5, 2022 - We crossed into Vermont at 12:35 p.m. and crossed another state off the list. We didn't get to set up camp until 6:30 p.m. We hiked 17.06 miles and camped at Congdon Shelter. We met the hiker named Hound Dog at the shelter as we were eating our supper. We had seen him before and he recognized us but neither of us could remember his name or how we knew him at the time. Not long after we got to camp, we saw Clifford the dog we met in Port Clinton, PA. His owner, Mash, said they were off trail for three days after taking him to the vet for the abscess he discovered. They resumed the trail at a slower pace to allow time for the dog to finish his round of antibiotics and heal. Clifford recovered without further problems and they had hiked 23 miles that day and actually jogged the second half of the trail. *Where in the world do they get the energy to jog?* His pack was definitely not as heavy as ours. We were really glad to see them again and know Clifford was okay.

We saw a deer, a turkey and a snake this morning. Some days we saw lots of animals and other days we didn't see any. We just couldn't see the ones we would like to see like moose or porcupines, although we did see porcupine needles and moose poop. *I took several pictures of small lakes because I am obsessed with reflections of the clouds and trees in the crystal-clear water. We don't get reflections like this on the lake at home.*

June 6, 2022 - We only hiked 4.3 miles this morning and then got a ride into Bennington, Vermont. Catamount Motel was an older but very clean motel/hostel that caters to hikers. A nice hot shower, a comfortable bed and a quiet room. Our room included a ride from and back to the trail and they did a load of laundry for us for $5.00. Hound Dog has the room next to us and we shared a ride to Wal Mart with him. We both ate entirely too much junk today, then we walked downtown and ate supper at the Madison Pub. Roy got a fish sandwich and I got a cheeseburger! *We don't need to lose more weight, both of us are really starting to look scary. I don't know how much weight we have lost but it's a lot.*

June 7, 2022 - We left the Catamount Motel and were shuttled back to the trail about 8:30 a.m. The folks there really know what hikers need and we sure appreciated their attention. Lots of uphill as usual but we managed to hike 14.44 miles and hiked up Glastonbury Mountain, elevation 3750 feet. A fire tower on the mountain had some great views but it was too windy and cold to stay up there very long. *We did climb several of the fire towers because there were usually awesome views from the top but always dropped our packs at the bottom before climbing up.* Rain was in the forecast but we made it to the Kid Gore Shelter. We set our tent up before it started to rain. 266.5 miles to the finish line. *I had been counting down and calculating miles and estimated we should be finished with the hike by the first week in July and we were still on target for that. I was getting more and more excited at the prospect of getting finished and going home.*

June 8, 2022 - Lots of uphill again, Stratton Mountain was at 3940 feet elevation. Another fire tower there had fantastic views. We camped on the shore of Stratton Pond. We didn't get everything set up and supper done until 9:00 p.m. We had a long day hiking even though we got a late start due to rain. It is at least staying light later in the day and we are not spending 12 hours plus in the tent, we are hiking more hours. *I'm good with hiking as much as possible, let's get this hike finished!* We saw moose droppings today, so there are moose in Vermont. We counted 26 Red Spotted Newts today and saw one garter snake. We ran into some hikers today who were hiking the Vermont Long Trail. It runs with the AT for 100 plus miles, when it breaks from the AT it goes all the way to the Canadian border. We hiked 15 miles and now we have 251.5 miles to our finish at Gorham, New Hampshire.

June 9, 2022 - Rain, rain, rain! We were awakened by rain and waited for it to pass through before we broke camp. We again had a sloppy wet tent. After it stopped raining the trees were dripping so I felt like it rained all day. We met a guy on the trail with a Jack Russell Terrier named Timba. He spoke with an accent and we thought he must have been Australian. He was hiking the Vermont Long Trail.

We arrived at the Spruce Peak Shelter and were welcomed by two small yapping dogs. They ran at us and barked like they were going to eat us up. One of them looked like a Boston Terrier cross and the other must have been a Chihuahua of some sort. *Roy calls a little dog, "five bark a second dog". In this case he was spot on, I think these dogs could do more than five barks a second.* There was a guy at the shelter who was doing a section hike and the dogs were his. He had set his gear in the shelter and would be sleeping there. The shelter was neat, it had a sliding door and could be completely closed. It would have been a great shelter from the rain or wind. The guy was constantly telling the dogs to shut up and they were just barking anyway. Every time you stepped away from the shelter and walked back, they would run at you and bark again like it was the first time they had seen you. We walked down the path to the water source, and they barked when we returned. We walked away to look for a tent site, and they barked when we returned. They were like two bratty little kids that didn't pay any attention to a parent who was nattering at them the whole time. *There was no way we could stay in that shelter with those dogs, they probably snored too!* We found a tent platform nearby and got our tent set up. Even at that the dogs came down and barked at us a couple of times. *I wished they would have come down with a case of laryngitis, at least that would have temporarily shut them up.*

We strung up a line so we could dry some of our stuff since it had truly stopped raining. It stopped raining long enough for us to eat supper, semi dry the tent then it started again. We did half of the inside set up with us in the tent. At least the trail was not as much elevation up and down that day. But there was lots of water, slick rocks and roots which made up for the lack of going up and down hills. It would have been easy to fall in these conditions but luckily, we stayed upright. We saw lots of boards on the trail today that had apparently been chewed by porcupines. I would still like to see one, we were apparently in their territory. We had hiked 8 miles before stopping for the evening.

June 10, 2022 - There were a couple of big uphill climbs early in the day. The trail went right through a ski resort at Bromley

Mountain. We ate lunch at the Ski Patrol Lodge since it was unlocked. It was nice to get out of the wind for a bit. The ski resort is of course closed for the season but it still was a really neat place to see. We walked to the ski lift area and was amazed how much the building at the top looked like some sort of spaceship. There were several ski slopes, the green grass was now growing on them instead of being covered with snow. There were great views from the summit of Bromley Mountain at 3263 feet elevation. Vermont has not had as many views as other states and it was nice to finally be able to see over the landscape from higher up. The top of the mountain had been cleared for the ski lifts and slopes and allowed for amazing views. We have been in the Green Mountains and all we had been seeing was thick green leaves of trees and bushes throughout the forest, sometimes the trail was nearly taken over by the foliage.

Vermont was the area on the AT where we saw the most warnings posted regarding ticks and tickborne diseases. It was even mentioned to us by a couple of the locals. With the thick foliage and the abundant wildlife, I guess it must have been an excellent habitat for ticks. *We had used a lot of insect repellant as we hiked the AT but we were using it for mosquitos. Neither of us got a tick the entire time we hiked the AT. I guess we were lucky or maybe enough insect repellant soaked in us from previous use. If a tick had been anywhere around it would have found Roy, he often gets one on him when I don't. He says it's because he is so sweet. Maybe his blood is sweet, he sure eats enough sugar.*

We camped that evening on a tent platform at Griffith Lake. We saw a couple of people here we camped near last night. We dried the tent and some of our gear down by the lake since it was still wet from the past couple of days. The day was cold and cloudy with only a little bit of afternoon sun and we both wore long sleeves all day. I also wore my buff to cover my ears and Roy wore his toboggan most of the day. It was cooler but good weather for hiking. We hiked 13.34 miles and are now 230.3 miles from the finish.

June 11, 2022 - The weather was a little warmer but it was a good day for hiking. After climbing the rocks at Baxter Peak there were some really good views. We were going to camp at Greenwall Shelter 0.2 miles off the AT but were met by the two barking dogs from two days ago when we arrived! They again ran out barking like they were going to attack with their owner yelling at them. *Roy named them Poco and Loco. Loco because they act crazy and Poco because it rhymes and Roy thought he remembered a puppet show or something from when he was a kid where there was a character called Poco.* We had to go down a big hill to get to the shelter and we considered staying there but there were no good tent sites. If the dogs hadn't been there, we would have worked with what was there but we just couldn't handle the commotion. *I guess we had been in the woods too long and we really liked the quiet.* We left the shelter area, climbed the steep hill back to the trail. We finally found a stealth site 0.3 miles from VT Route 140. We hope to get a light resupply tomorrow since we are starting to run a little low on food. The next big mountain will be Killington Peak.

June 12, 2022 - We hiked 5.9 miles this morning to VT Route 103 and we only saw three Red Spotted Newts along the way. We ate lunch at Goucheberg Farms Market and Deli. We got a really good sub sandwich and sat outside at the picnic tables while we ate our food. There were a couple other hikers there also taking advantage of the picnic table. The girl had actually stowed her hiking poles and was carrying two hiking sticks made by Harry Sand back in Great Barrington, Massachusetts. I really don't know how well those will hold up to the slick rocks and such on the trail but I agreed with her, they were unique and I would have liked to have had at least one of them.

The guy with the Jack Russell caught up with us at the deli and we found out he is from South Africia; his name was Danny. After a bit of discussion and scrambling we were able to get a ride to Rutland, Vermont, it was about 10 miles off the trail. Danny and Timba rode with us and the driver took us to the Day's Inn where Danny had a room reserved, we got a room there also. Timba is a pleasant and well-behaved dog and if he were to bark there would be a reason, unlike Poco and Loco. We resupplied at a local grocery after we got much needed showers. I was also able to get my medication refilled there so I didn't have to worry about it running out before we got home.

We ate supper at Denny's next door to the Day's Inn. Roy ate four pancakes, four eggs and two orders of hash browns. I had . . . a cheeseburger and fries. We got refueled, resupplied, bathed and rested in preparation for returning to the trail the next day.

June 13, 2022 - We left Rutland this morning. Danny and Timba rode with us again. Tom, the same shuttle driver from the day before, gave us a ride back to the trail. *He drove like a maniac but I guess if you don't step on the gas, you don't get anywhere here.* We climbed uphill all day to get to Killington Peak 4235 feet elevation; we were at around 865 feet that morning. To get to the top of Killington peak we had to climb approximately another 450 feet up a steep rocky mountain side from where we would set our tent. Of course, we had to go to the top. The trail up required hand over hand climbing, the hiking poles were of no use. The views from the top were spectacular! There was an area with chairs where you could see for miles. Luck was on our side, this time, we had awesome views. We also walked around the ski resort looking at the lifts and the slopes. It was amazing but of course it was closed because it is not skiing season. Killington Peaks is the largest ski resort in Vermont and it was definitely something to see. *One of the funniest signs we saw the entire time we were on the trail was near Killington Ski Resort. It said, and I quote," WARNING KEEP AWAY FROM BEARS, do not feed, pet, or pose for a photo with a bear. Do not approach bears. If encountered, back away slowly and act confident by speaking loudly and clapping." People really have to be told not to pet or pose for a photo with a bear? I guess they were just covering all the bases or perhaps the world is a lot crazier than I thought.*

After admiring the views from the top of Killington we carefully descended the steep trail back down to where we had set our tent on a platform near the Cooper Lodge. The old stone shelter building had been vandalized and the windows were all broken, it was not a good place to stay. *I guess those who had been feeding and posing for photos with the bears had been vandalizing shelters too.* If it had been raining it may have provided some shelter but as usual, we preferred our tent anyway. I went down to look at the shelter, since it had been reportedly a nice shelter at one time. I was looking around thinking it was a shame it was in such a state when I looked up and saw two dehydrated meal packs tied on a small rope up near the ceiling. There was only one other tent there when we set ours up and we hadn't seen anyone else around until Danny came in not far behind us and also pitched his tent on the platform. *I think someone put the dehydrated meals up there to keep the mice out of them and accidently left them, it happens all the time.* I took them and went back to our tent. I showed them to Roy and he was as amazed as I was. We decided we would keep them for a day or so and if no one said anything about losing them we would eat them. One of them was three cheese mac & cheese and the other was chicken alfredo.

We found out the guy who was in a tent when we first got there had arrived a couple of hours before us and crawled straight into his tent. He had been sick with Norovirus and had just returned to the trail after taking two weeks off to recuperate. Wow, his first day back on the trail and he climbed Killington. He said he was exhausted and when he arrived at the campsite, he put up his tent, crawled in and immediately went to sleep. *Giardia or Norovirus are two illnesses you don't want to have on the trail. Consistent water filtration, even when the water looked good and good hand hygiene (we carried hand sanitizer) were musts. There were no handshakes, usually a fist bump or an elbow bump if anything. On the trail you are too far away from medical care to deal with severe illness. We were fortunate, neither of us ever got truly sick while we were hiking the AT. There were a few days with minor aches and pains but nothing that prevented us from hiking. The problem Roy had experienced with foot pain on our first leg of this journey in 2020 had thankfully not plagued him this time. We were thankful for our good health.*

We hiked 11.44 miles and only saw two Red Spotted Newts. I thought we were almost out of the Red Spotted Newt territory. But we were definitely in wildflower territory. I can't believe how many we saw. The wildflowers were in full bloom and we continued to see more of white, purple, orange and yellow flowers growing all along the trail.

June14, 2022 - The trail was pretty tough and mostly downhill, I slipped on a root with my left foot that slid far right that morning. I fell to the left and caught myself with my left hand. My pack of course was pushing me down too fast and to keep my face from hitting the dirt I threw out my left hand to catch myself and fall over on it with my fingers bent back. I had on gloves and didn't see it but by the way my pinky popped I'm sure it was dislocated. It popped again when I grabbed my left hand with my right and held it tightly because it hurt so badly. It all happened in a split second. I sat up and held my injured hand with the other. Roy asked if I was okay and I told him to give me a minute. I was in severe pain and I was almost afraid to take off my gloves and look at my hand. I finally looked at my finger and decided it was okay, hurting like hell even up the side of my hand, already starting to bruise, but okay. Roy helped me to my feet that time and dusted me off. Later in the day my hand was swollen, bruised more and really hurting. I took some Tylenol and put away one of my hiking poles. *I would only use the one in my right hand for now. I had taken off my wedding ring and put it on my right hand just in case my left hand swelled. I buddy-tapped my fourth and fifth fingers together and hiked with my hand up to my chest. When I let it hang down or tried to use the hiking poles it throbbed, it felt much better not using it and keeping it above my heart. I knew it was still a minor injury and in the grand scheme of things and it would be alright. I suppose if something had to be hurt, besides my pride, my left pinky would be the least of the evils and as the old saying goes, it was too far away from my heart to kill me. At least I am right-handed.*

We had to say goodbye to Danny and Timba at the AT/Long Trail split. We had been with them a couple of days and would definitely miss their company. We took a break at the split and talked to Danny for a while. He had some really difficult hiking coming up on the Long Trail, as bad or worse than what we would encounter as we continued on the AT and into New Hampshire. We parted ways at the split, having enjoyed getting to know each other for the past few days.

Before we went to the shelter, we wanted to get water so we wouldn't have to walk further. We could have waited and hiked 0.2 miles or so past the shelter but this water was within sight and going to get water and back to the shelter was adding almost another half mile. I set my pack on the edge of the trail up on a hill and went to get water from a small stream below. As I was getting water I heard Roy hollering, "look out". My pack was rolling down the hill toward the water, it started falling and he hadn't been able to catch it, thankfully it stopped before it got there. Good thing because all either of us could do was watch. I was too far away to run and catch it. *Note to self: don't set your pack on the edge of the trail at the top of a hill. Thankfully this hill was not too big and my pack stopped. Some things you just have to learn from trial and error as you go.*

We camped at Stoney Brook Shelter, elevation 1774 feet after hiking 13.34 miles. When we got there, we ran into Hound Dog again. We hadn't seen him since Bennington and it was nice to catch up with him, he was actually a much faster hiker but he had spent an extra day somewhere along the way. The three other folks he had been hiking with had to part ways with him a few weeks ago. Oh Yeah was a very fast hiker who went on ahead. Flashlight and No Way was a married couple who had to return home to Missouri for a few weeks to plant crops. Therefore, he was hiking alone again and really missing his tramily. *That's how we knew him, we met him and is tramily while enjoying trail magic the day before we got to Port Clinton, PA. We also ran into them a day or two later when we had accidently gotten turned around and were hiking SOBO. I was starting to question the direction we were going and looking at the FarOut app when we met the group. They asked why we were heading SOBO and we told them we thought they were heading SOBO. We all laughed a bunch about the mix up and we turned around and hiked with them for a little bit. They were all slack packing and not carrying heavy packs. We didn't hike with them for very long, they were much faster.*

There were a lot of people camping at the shelter and we had to get creative to find a spot to set the tent. But we were accustomed to making a tent setup work almost anywhere. At least the ground was flat enough for the tent, we just had to have enough room to get in and out. We set the tent where we both had to crawl in and out one side, we had set up like this before so it was not a problem. *This would also be where we met Prancer and Double B and would hike with them and Hound Dog leapfrogging off and on throughout most of the remainder of our hike.*

"Find a group of people who challenge and inspire you; spend a lot of time with them, and it will change your life- Amy Poehler

Chapter 37 - We Are Becoming a Tramily

June 15, 2022 - The trail was a bit easier and the weather was warmer than the day before. We ate our lunch at The Lookout, a privately owned cabin that allows hikers to stay. There were awesome 360-degree views from the crow's nest on top of the cabin. There were stairs leading to a small deck with places to sit on top of the cabin. We enjoyed staying up there for a few minutes and taking in the views, no wonder it's called The Lookout. It would be a perfect place for a hiker to hold up if the weather was bad as it was fully enclosed and had a fireplace. We did have to go off trail to see The Lookout but it was only 0.1 mile and we had heard it was a neat place. We were really glad we went to see it.

No newts counted on the trail. We were most likely out of newt territory but we did see seven bunches of moose poop. I still wished we could see a moose in the wild but our time to see one is growing short. We hiked 10 miles before stopping to camp at Winturri Shelter. There was a wonderful piped water source there and we took advantage of the cold clear water. Lots of people were camping there and we saw several of the same hikers from the night before. Hound Dog, Prancer, Double B and Thunderhead were there plus a few more. Thunderhead talked non-stop, most of us could only take him in small doses. *You know, there is always that one kid . . .*

June 16, 2022 - We hiked all day with Hound Dog and we really enjoyed the company. We all stopped at On the Edge Farm Market on VT Route 12 that morning. We got there just as it was opening and patiently waited outside at the picnic tables until the lady was ready for business. It was a couple of tenths off the trail but more than worth the trip. We got ice Cream, Mt. Dew, and pastries. The extra food would give us energy and was much needed since Roy and I both had lost too much weight. Hound Dog told us he had lost about 40 pounds since starting his AT hike so he was glad to get extra calories too.

We met a man on the trail we would refer to as the Wizard. He had long gray hair and a beard down on his chest. He was very animated in his actions and he talked and talked and talked some more. We were in the middle of the Green Mountains somewhere when we met him and he looked like a wizard standing on the hillside in the forest. He gave us lots of advice about hiking the tougher parts of the upcoming trail through the White Mountains and places to stay. We decided he was just a lonesome older guy and he was very excited to talk with us. We let him ramble on and listened as he talked and talked, we thanked him for his advice when we left him. *Hound Dog, Roy and I would later recall some of the things he told us and he was correct. Sometimes you can learn a lot if you just listen.*

For some reason the trail was tough, a lot of uphill. Everyone complained about the trail being tough on this day. I was busy admiring the wildflowers again and that helped distract me from the difficulty of the trail for a little while. *I told myself things to stay positive like, at least I was not sitting in an office and we were not hiking in rain or mud. We were lucky when we hiked through Vermont that we didn't have to contend with the much touted "Vermud". There were a few muddy spots that we were able to go around but we had seen that much mud in other states. Vermont a.k.a. Vermud is much like Pennsylvania being called Rocksylvania. However, Pennsylvania did have more than its fair share of rocks. We had seen hikers in Maine going NOBO when we were hiking SOBO and they all talked about the mud in Vermont. Maybe they were in Vermont when the weather was rainy and we just lucked out.*

We crossed the White River and were hiking toward the small town of West Hartford, VT when a woman on the porch of her house motioned for us to come. We headed that way and were pleasantly surprised when she offered us coffee, soft drinks and snacks. She also had boiled eggs left where she had made them for hikers for breakfast. We each had a boiled egg and a soft drink. Linda told us her parents and other family members had always provided Trail Magic to hikers and it was just something she felt compelled to do. Her porch was set up with a small refrigerator, seating, a log book and several other things to make it hiker friendly. The only time there had been a problem for her and providing help to hikers was when hurricane Sandy moved through the area in October 2012 causing major flood damage to the area. She actually lost her house as had many in the community. The flood also damaged bridges and roads. Her family had to build a new house. We talked with her and visited for about a half hour. *Any time we had trail magic it lifted our spirits and this was no exception. If everyone was as caring and giving as Linda and her family, the world would be a much better place.*

We camped at Thistle Hill Shelter after hiking 12.6 miles. We caught up with Prancer and Double B. There were lots of the same hikers at camp again and several different ones too. I think the hiker bubble headed to Katahdin may have caught us because we seem to be camping with more hikers than usual the past few nights.

There was one guy camping near the shelter who was not an AT hiker, he was just camping out for a few days. We did talk to him for a few minutes. He had a black dog that looked like he was part lab or some mix thereof. The dog barked as we walked up and continued to bark so the conversation was short. In fact, it barked its head off every time anyone passed by his tent. The tent was set right beside the side trail to the shelter area so everyone coming in or out of the area received the same welcome from the dog. Of course, the guy would yell at the dog and of course the dog paid no attention. *Oh wonderful, just what we needed, another barking dog.* The dog thankfully quietened down after everyone settled in for the night.

June 17, 2022 - During the previous night, sometime after midnight, the hikers in the shelter started screaming, yelling, beating on the shelter with the broom and causing a horrible commotion. We would find out the next morning someone thought they heard a bear. Another guy who had pitched his tent in front of the shelter was also camping there with a dog. He said had there been a bear his dog would have alerted him and it did not. He thought someone had heard a noise, had an overactive imagination or was paranoid from smoking too much pot. We were not sure what happened, but those who made all the noise were up and gone early that morning. We saw no signs of a bear but

259

pieces of a broom were laying on the ground beside the shelter, it had apparently been broken during the uproar.

We both had a little trouble going back to sleep after the fiasco at the shelter when we heard a loud cracking, popping noise followed by hearing what was apparently a large tree as it hit the ground. The sound echoed in the night. It sounded fairly close by but thankfully it was down in the woods away from the shelter and the campsites.

Prancer, Roy and I needed to go to the Post Office in Norwich, VT. We had to pick up our new shoes we had sent to us before crossing into New Hampshire. Prancer had to pick up a battery bank she ordered because hers had stopped holding a charge. *We had 725 trail miles on our shoes to the best of my calculation and that's a lot. Rule of thumb says you get about 500 miles per pair on the trail.* We didn't think we could make it to the post office before it closed at 5:00 p.m. and we had no reservations in town. We could get there before noon tomorrow so we all reserved rooms at Hanover Adventure Tours Hostel (The Wizard told us about it).

We hiked with Hound Dog, Prancer and Double B most of the day and the hiking was much easier than the day before. Of course, we had camp set up by 1:30 p.m., but we could use a little break or two before we got to the White Mountains. We hiked 9 miles before we arrived at Happy Hill Shelter.

Prancer told us about falling in New Jersey. She sustained a laceration to her forehead requiring eight stitches. Luckily there were people nearby who helped her get off trail and to a medical clinic. One of the people who helped her was actually an off-duty rescue squad member. *Talk about luck!* The woman called the rescue squad, coordinated the nearest place for Prancer to be picked up, and hiked with her to meet EMS. After the fall was when she and Double B started hiking together. Double B was 57 years old; her partner had quit the trail and her family didn't want her hiking alone. Prancer's family also encouraged her to get a hiking partner if she was going to continue on the trail. So, they decided they could help each other and they planned on finishing the trail together.

260

We carried extra water to the shelter since there was reportedly not a water source nearby. We had seen comments in the FarOut app about the nearby creek being dry. I took a short walk up the creek and found a small pool of water that appeared to be flowing. Sometimes there is water, you just have to know where to look. I let the rest of the hikers in the area know I had found water. Since we had stopped so early in the day it would be great to have an extra liter of water and the others were happy about having water there as well.

We saw a large maple sap collection operation set up in the woods that morning. There were literally miles of blue plastic tubing set up in an intricate system from tree to tree and routed toward larger piping downhill. At first, we didn't understand what it was but when we discovered the trees were tapped, we knew it had to be a maple syrup operation. *We were told by a local a bit later about the set ups. Apparently when the sap is running the large operations cook sap twenty-four seven to make maple syrup. They run around the clock to process the sap. There is only a small window of four to six weeks when the sap runs. These sap farms apparently have thousands of trees tapped. Wow!* Admiral Butterflies were also a unique sight that day. Double B told us what they were called. They were bright black and white and very pretty. I don't remember ever seeing them at home.

We were 149.7 miles from the finish! We were counting down the miles every day and getting really excited at the prospect of being finished in a couple of weeks.

June 18, 2022 - We hiked 4.3 miles and picked up our shoes at the post office in Norwich, VT. *It was nice to be able to put on new shoes with no worry about breaking them in. These shoes would get us through the end of the trail and we will still get plenty of use out of them when we get back home.* Prancer and Double B hiked on into the town of Hanover to go to a grocery and would get a ride to the hostel from there. Hound Dog, Roy and I decided to shop at Dan and Whit's General Store in Norwich for supplies. Afterwards we got a ride from Norwich to the hostel. We were still in Vermont but would cross over the bridge and into New Hampshire the next morning. *The last state on the trail for us, woo hoo!*

After taking a long hot shower we decided to get some good food. We got a ride from the hostel to a restaurant across the bridge in the town of Hanover, NH. Hound Dog went with us and we all had a nice dinner of burgers and fries at Molly's Restaurant. We had a bit of trouble getting a ride back and we finally called the hostel and begged them to come get us. Prancer and Double B had brought food from the grocery to prepare for their supper so they didn't go with us. They were going to be about four miles ahead of us when we all returned to the trail but maybe we could catch up. We also got our laundry done while at the hostel that evening. The hostel was a lot like a bed and breakfast, it was quiet and at least we did have a private room.

June 19, 2022 - We left the hostel after a good breakfast of pancakes and eggs. The food was included with our room but we had to cook our own food and clean up the kitchen. *I didn't mind, it made me feel almost normal.* The food was good and we needed the calories. Prancer was anxious to get going, she and Double B called for a shuttle and left about 30 minutes before the rest of us. We told them goodbye and hoped we would catch up with them later.

Hound Dog, Roy and I crossed the bridge over the Connecticut River that runs between Vermont and New Hampshire and stopped to take pictures of each other. New Hampshire was the last state for us and we were more than glad to check Vermont off the list. Hound Dog had to go through New Hampshire and Maine all the way to Katahdin to finish. We hiked through the town of Hanover and saw Dartmouth College. *It's a private Ivy League college that was chartered in 1769 before the American Revolution. Walking through the area and realizing the history of the area was amazing. The trail went right beside the campus and we were in awe of the old buildings.* The three of us also stopped at a local grocery, Hanover Co-op Market. We got a few supplies and a sandwich to pack with us for lunch.

We met some local folks on top of Moose Mountain, not far from where we stopped for lunch. They showed us some airplane wreckage on the mountain from a plane crash 50 plus years ago. *I later looked it up and found the plane was a small commercial*

262

airliner that crashed on its way to Lebanon, New Hampshire. Northeast Airlines Flight 946 crashed in bad weather in October of 1968. Of the 42 passengers and crew onboard, there were 10 survivors who were rescued. Emergency personnel arrived at the crash scene 90 minutes after the crash which in itself is amazing considering the remoteness of the area, the terrain and the weather that evening. It was also probably a miracle that anyone survived.

We hiked 13.5 miles and camped at Moose Mountain Shelter. We caught up with Double B and Prancer, they had stopped to camp there earlier in the day. We had a great opportunity to talk and get to know each other better over the past few days and during our stay at the hostel since we were the only ones there the night before.

Prancer was 71 years old, lives in Franklin, TN and is retired. She is very fit and I just wish I had her motivation and self-discipline. She also has a son who is a musician with a well-known country group and he is a member of the Grand Ole Opry. She started her flip flop hike at Harper's Ferry.

Double B was 57 years old and hiking with Prancer since they both needed a hiking partner. She was from New Hampshire and she started her hike at Rockfish Gap at the south end of Shenandoah National Park. Her previous partner had left the trail and her family encouraged her to find a hiking partner.

Hound Dog was the same age as Roy. He was born and raised in South Carolina and retired to Georgia. He was hiking because he was challenged by his niece who hiked the trail a few years ago. She will be meeting him to hike with him through the White Mountains. He has been taking it easy the past couple of weeks because he will be too far ahead of her plan to meet him if he keeps pushing ahead. We told him he needed to conserve his energy and rest up for Maine and the climb up Mt. Katahdin. He is a retired Navy Seal, now we know where his drive comes from. Thanks to him for his service, he has our admiration and respect. You sure meet a lot of interesting people on the trail hiking for different reasons. We kept traveling at about the same rate as these folks. Even though we didn't hike right along together we

263

would usually end the day and camp in the same place each night. *We were becoming a tramily.*

June 20, 2022 - The trail was tough, brutal uphill. We camped at the Smart Mountain tenting area at 3211 feet elevation after hiking 12.3 miles. We climbed the fire tower and there were breathtaking views. *One guy was camping up in the tower that night. It seemed to be cooler and windy in the tower, not sure I would want to be up there, although you probably wouldn't have to worry about a bear getting up there.* I was afraid the uphill climbs we hiked earlier in the day was a preview of what's to come.

Prancer is a beast; she is more than ten years older than me and hikes like her tail is on fire. No way I can keep up with her. She and Double B were well ahead of us most of the day, but Hound Dog beat all of us! Roy could keep up with them if he really wanted to, but he usually hangs back with me. The end result was the same, we could get there, it would always just be a little later.

June 21, 2022 - Hound Dog, Prancer, Double B, Ryan, Roy and I all hiked from Smart Mountain this morning. We met Ryan, a high school science teacher hiking a section hike and he camped near us the night before. As usual the race was on, between Hound Dog and Prancer. The retired Navy Seal vs. a very determined older lady. *It's funny to watch them. She is so determined to out hike everyone and he is determined not to be out hiked! He always wins the race but she really pushes him to stay ahead of her. He told us she just about caught up with him a couple of times. We got more entertainment from those two that we probably should have but it was all in good fun.* We all camped at the same place again.

Oh, it was Hike Naked Day! None of us participated and we didn't see any participants. We had heard stories of those who hiked in their birthday suits and were amazed at some of the things people do to gain attention. We decided our suits were too old and wrinkled anyway.

June 22, 2022 - We all made it to Hikers Welcome Hostel after hiking 7.4 miles. Prancer and Double B decided not to stay at the hostel and got a shuttle to Lincoln, NH. They planned to hike Mt. Moosilauke SOBO the next day. The rest of our crew stayed at the hostel. Roy and I pitched our tent in the yard. *There was no way I would have slept inside the bunk room or upstairs at the hostel, I was fine with our tent.* We did get a hot shower and shared a load of laundry with Ryan and Hound Dog. *Yes, shared. We figured laundry detergent and hot water would resolve any issue with the shared laundry, besides there were several other hikers there who wanted to do laundry and it would expedite the process.*

The set up for showers and laundry was interesting to say the least. Everything was outside. The shower, laundry and toilet were built on composite decking. There were PVC frames with dividing walls made by tarps and divided into three sections. There were also tarps overhead so I felt comfortable taking a shower without putting on a show for someone. I was afraid it was going to be a bit cold outside but the water was hot and it was wonderful.

We all ordered pizza from Apple Knockers, only six people could ride in the van to pick up pizza, there were seven of us so I volunteered to stay behind. Roy went with the crew to pick up the pizza and got a couple of things for us at a store near the pizza place. *I played a few rounds of solitaire and watched a short documentary video about marine life. As usual the hostel didn't have cable but they did have a big library of videos.* The gang soon returned and we all thoroughly enjoyed the food. We were also able to get some supply items at the hostel since they had the usual hiker fare available. No problem, what you picked out would be added to your bill. It was set up like a little store and the guy took us back to it one or two at a time to make our selections. We felt like we had sufficient supplies to make it to the next town.

Ryan, Mess and the Tennessee Crew were all at the hostel. This was our first exposure to the group of five we called the Tennessee Crew, and they were a source of constant entertainment for us. Mess was also a very talkative person and kept all of us laughing. After eating there was a lot of discussion about hiking Mt. Moosilauke the next day, whether it was best to hike NOBO or SOBO over the mountain and there were differing opinions. *Hound Dog, Roy and I would be hiking NOBO, the others were all hiking SOBO. I guess we would see how it works out. We settled into our tent for the night looking forward to the next day and crossing over the dreaded Mt. Moosilauke.*

June 23, 2022 - We slept pretty well in our tent, Hound Dog however told us didn't sleep so well in the bunkhouse. He said someone in there snored like a freight train all night. He told us who it was and we committed it to memory so we could avoid any future encounters with him. We hiked up and over Mount Moosilauke, the first 4000-footer in the White Mountains (if you are hiking NOBO). It was cold and windy at the top and fogged in, we couldn't see a thing! Hound Dog was ahead of us and waiting at the top, he was nestled down in a bunch of rocks, he popped up and said he was hiding in his bat cave. It was amazing how much warmer it was in there as it blocked most of the wind. We only took enough time for a picture with the sign and got off the top of that mountain! There was no view from the top of the mountain so there was no reason to stay any longer. We met Prancer, Double B and several from the hostel on our way down. They had been told the mountain was easier to hike going SOBO and that's what they were doing. We went down the trail they hiked up and I didn't see that it would have been any easier one direction or the other. It was a big uphill climb or a big downhill descent hiking either direction.

There was a very long waterfall that went for miles down the mountain side. It was not very wide but it was long. I took several pictures and videos of the water. *I love waterfalls and this one was the mother of all waterfalls. I had to stop several times just to admire it.* The trail was also damp due to the fog. Hound Dog fell twice going down Mount Moosilauke, the second time he tweaked his back pretty badly. The last 3.6 miles today was on some treacherous trail to say the least. The 40% chance of rain turned into full on rain by afternoon and we were glad we had already hiked over Mount Moosilauke. The weather for the next few days was supposed to be warmer with no rain, thank goodness.

We camped near Kinsman Notch after hiking 9.3 miles. Hound Dog was really favoring his back although he didn't complain I could tell by watching him move that he was in pain. We helped him find a spot to put his tent and I cleared branches and stuff off the ground so he could put his tent up. We offered to help more and even hang his food bag after supper but he said he could do it,

266

I'm sure he has endured worse in his military career. Hopefully his back will be better by morning. Hiking and hurting is no fun.

June 24, 2022 - We hiked 7.63 miles from Kinsman Notch to Eliza Brook Shelter. 1870 feet to 3464 feet elevation at the top of Wolf Mountain, then down to 2401 feet at the shelter. *What goes up must go down first and vice versa.* The trail was slow going again. Hound Dog's back was a little better today, it didn't seem to slow him down. There were lots of ups and downs, rocks and sippy holes from rain the day before.

Moose poop was all over the place, I stopped counting at 30 bunches on the trail. You would think we would have surely seen a moose by now. We saw one Red Spotted Newt; we hadn't seen any for the past week or so.

Prancer and Double B got to the shelter about an hour after us. We had hoped we would all meet up again after hiking over Mount Moosilauke. We are all planning on going to Lincoln, NH. The Tennessee crew came in after we had all gotten into our tents. There are five or six others tenting in this area tonight. Weather was okay today; it was foggy and damp this morning but by late afternoon there was sunshine. We hoped the weather would be good again tomorrow for crossing the 4000-foot Kinsman Mountains.

June 25, 2022 - We only hiked 4 miles today but it was up and over South Kinsman and North Kinsman Mountains, both over 4000 feet. We camped at Kinsman Pond Shelter on a big platform with Hound Dog and a guy in another tent who was on a weekend hike. Prancer and Double B also set up on a platform nearby. This is our first time staying at one of the campgrounds with a caretaker in New Hampshire. The caretaker monitored the campgrounds, collected fees and assigned tent sites. *We had been told the campsites can fill up on the weekends and we got there really early in the day and we're still lucky to find a place to set our tents.* Hopefully it wouldn't be this busy through the week. Lots of people are out on the trails on the weekends and it was Saturday. The hike today included more rock climbing which would have slowed us down but we only planned to hike the four miles because we were planning to go to Lincoln the next day. Prancer, Double B and

Hound Dog are going to Lincoln also. It would be nice to get good food, a hot shower and a bed for a couple of nights.

We went down by the lake near the shelter to get water and decided to sit by the lake and enjoy the view for a while. As we were looking at the beautiful blue sky with big white puffy clouds and of course admiring the reflections in the lake, we saw a glider plane. It flew around for several minutes and we were happy to have had the airshow. The lake was really clear and the water was very cold. There were a couple of people who jumped in and went swimming, they were braver than us. We were satisfied with just dipping our toes into the frigid water. *Cold water does not usually bother Roy, he will swim in the ocean a lot of times when I won't. But the water was even too cold for him.*

We heard about an experienced hiker who died a few days ago on Mount Washington. *According to what we found on the internet; he was caught in a fast-moving storm that moved through the White Mountains. The temperature dropped below freezing and it was raining/snowing with wind gusts up to 80 miles per hour. There was no cell phone service but the hiker was able to get a text to his wife and she notified authorities that he said he was too cold to move on. He was rescued but died several hours later after repeated resuscitation efforts failed. Several hikers had to be rescued that day according to the news reports.* This part of the trail is not to be taken lightly. We all really talked about not taking chances and being safe hiking through the White Mountains. Even in the summer this place could be dangerous. If in doubt a hiker should never gamble on the weather in the White Mountains, be prepared to turn around or better yet don't hike in the first place. News like this made us all stop and think about the multiple hazards of hiking the AT.

June 26, 2022 - We all hiked 8.8 miles that morning and arrived at a parking area on a highway near Lincoln, NH. We had reservations at Liberty Lodging and the owner picked us up at the trailhead. After we got checked in and showered all five of us got a ride to town. We went to a local outfitter for a few supplies. We ate at One Love restaurant before shopping for more supplies at the local grocery. I don't remember what we ate at the restaurant, but the food was very good. By the time we got back to the motel it was 6:00 p.m. Everyone said goodnight and retired to our rooms for the evening. We watched TV for a little while then crawled into a nice warm bed with real sheets and pillows.

June 27, 2022 - *Zero day #8.* The motel was set back off the main road, it was quiet and we slept well. We decided to take a zero-day due to rain. We were 74.7 miles from the finish. *I think we would both love to finish asap and get home to our kids, grandkids, and friends. We have been gone from home for four months today.* We had honey buns for breakfast and coffee in our room. The motel did a load of laundry for us and even folded it. I really liked it when we could get laundry done for us like that. We walked to Arnold's Diner (not the one in the show Happy Days) for lunch. Later in the afternoon we walked to the Irving Gas Station. *Each place was about a mile away in different directions. Even though there were days we didn't hike, we still walked several miles that didn't count toward the trail miles.* We had a big lunch of burgers and fries at the diner and they were excellent. *I don't think I got bad food in any restaurant on the trail, or maybe I was so hungry it didn't matter.*

I gave Roy another haircut as best I could with the tiny scissors I carried. We ate canned Chunky Soup we got from the gas station for supper and watched a movie. The weather was cooler and we really didn't need to go back to town so we were happy with staying in the room that evening.

Hound Dog has a ride scheduled for tomorrow morning to go on ahead to Pinkham Notch. He will be meeting his family on July 2. He is going to hike SOBO from Pinkham Notch instead of just waiting for them and logging zeros. The rest of us will continue NOBO on the trail from Lincoln.

June 28, 2022 - We said goodbye to Hound Dog that morning. He will be meeting his niece on July 2nd but will be hiking by himself until then. We are sure going to miss him. Hopefully we will cross paths with him again on the trail in a few days.

Prancer, Double B, Roy and I got back to the trail about 7:15 a.m. and hiked about 10 miles. We hiked over five 4000-foot mountains, Liberty, Haystack, Lincoln, Lafayette and Garfield; part of the trail was over the Franconia Ridge. *With the exception of Garfield, it strings the summits of these mountains together. The AT goes through what is called The Presidential Range in the White Mountains where the mountains are named for U.S. presidents and prominent public figures. These mountains are at 4000, 5000 and over 6000 feet elevation and the views are unbelievable.*

It was cold and windy with clouds moving through off and on. When we could see, the views were spectacular and I felt as though we were on top of the world. *The height of these mountains was no joke. I thought we had been on tall mountains before but this was indescribable.* The clouds cleared and the sun came out as we set up our tents. Prancer, Double B, Roy and I camped on a tent platform at the Garfield Ridge Campsite. We sure missed hiking with Hound Dog, it seemed like he should have his tent set close by. Everyone was tired after a long day of tough hiking and we crawled in our tents before dark. The Tennessee Crew came in a little bit after we got set up for the night. They camped on a platform a couple of spaces away from ours.

June 29, 2022 - One of the ladies hiking with the Tennessee Crew had hurt her knee and was going to try to walk out to the nearest road to seek medical care. I offered to use some KT tape to tape up her knee and she said she was willing to try it. I fixed her up best I could and hoped it would help her.

The hike involved some brutal downhills and it was extremely slow going. We stopped at the Galehead Hut and we "worked to eat" leftover breakfast by sweeping the floors. We also got one of our free baked goods that came with the camping permit we were required to purchase for New Hampshire. *In addition to camping areas the Appalachian Mountain Club (AMC) has eight huts set up in the White Mountains. They are around six to eight miles apart. Hikers can do work for stay or food if they are the first to ask. The cost to stay in the huts is well over $150 per night. We opted for the AMC campgrounds.* We had leftover oatmeal and coffee. The oatmeal was not great but it did provide us with extra calories. We were still hiking with Prancer and Double B. Prancer was not thrilled about stealth camping and wanted to stay at the Guyot

Shelter but it was about 0.6 miles off the trail so she decided to continue with us.

Prancer and Double B were with us when we were attacked by what we think was a Ptarmigan earlier in the day. We literally had to fight it off. Prancer and Double B made it through but the bird really got aggressive with me. Roy finally had to hit it with a hiking pole in order for us both to get around it. I don't think it was mortally injured but it was addled. It ceased the attack and allowed us to pass. *It reminded me of the one we had seen when we were out west but this one was even more aggressive.*

We stopped at Zealand Falls Hut, Prancer and Double B asked about work for stay and they were allowed to stay there for the night. There were only two people allowed to stay so we got fresh water there and continued to hike. We found a great stealth site about 0.3 miles down the trail. It was a big site with water nearby, there would have been enough room for Prancer and Double B if they had continued on with us. There was water nearby and we topped off our bottles. We had set up our tent and just barely gotten finished with our supper when it started to rain. Thankfully it was only one short shower, just enough to get our tent wet. It would be dry by morning.

We saw lots of gorgeous mountain views, it was warm, clear and the visibility was better than the day before. We hiked 10.21 miles today. We are 54.4 miles from the finish.

June 30, 2022 - First thing this morning we saw Spic and Span! The last time we saw him was when we crossed the bridge at the Hudson River in New York. He told us about trail magic being set up by one of his friends at Crawford Notch. Prancer and Double B passed us before we broke camp this morning. They were meeting Double B's uncle at Crawford Notch and were very excited to be getting off trail for a couple of days for some much-needed R&R.

I lost one of my Nike gloves today, I backtracked longer than I should have to try and find it to no avail. Darn Tough socks as gloves will have to do for the remainder of our journey.

We got to Crawford Notch and found the trail magic set up in the parking area. Hamburgers, hot dogs, chips, cokes, candy, pastries and lots more from Grouchy who set it all up for hikers. He had hiked on the AT earlier this year but had to leave the trail because of foot problems. We caught up to Prancer and Double B at the trail magic set up and got to tell them goodbye again before they left with Double B's uncle. *We would continue on the remainder of the journey by ourselves. We had really enjoyed getting to know Hound Dog, Prancer and Double B and we had all agreed to let each other know when we finished the trail.*

We had intended to hike to Webster Cliffs and camp there since there was supposed to be awesome sunsets from the area but we kept going. It was really too early in the day to stop. We continued to hike and made it to Mitzpah Hut/Nauman Campsites later that afternoon. We were going to ask about working for our stay but found out from a girl outside the hut she was already working for her stay. We checked in with the caretaker at the campsites and were assigned to a platform by ourselves. We set up our tent, ate some supper and crawled in for the evening. We had good weather all day and there were clear views of Mount Washington! *Of course, it towered over everything else around. We hoped it would be clear tomorrow too!*

We were pushing really hard to try and get to the finish, we were both more than ready to go home. We hiked 13.7 miles and up several near vertical rock climbs on the trail that afternoon and through yet more bogs. *We would continue on the trail from here without our tramily and we would sorely miss them.*

"The best views come after the toughest climbs." – Unknown

Chapter 38 - The Final Push

July 1, 2022 - We stopped at the Lake of the Clouds Hut before we got to Mt. Washington. We asked and were given pancakes and oatmeal. If you ask the staff about leftovers, they will usually give them to you if they have any. Lake of the Clouds Hut sits near a small lake. It's a unique site to see the small clear lake so high up in the mountains.

Believe it or not the weather on Mt. Washington was perfect. Granted it was cold (mid 50s) but it was clear and the visibility was awesome. We took note of the signage that said, "STOP, the area ahead has the worst weather in America. Many have died there from exposure. Even in the summer. Turn back now if the weather is bad." We got in line to get our picture with the sign on top of Mt. Washington. We have now gone as high as we can go in the White Mountains at 6288 feet elevation. Thank you, Lord, for the weather! The "hike" was a lot of rock climbing. We stopped at the visitor center and got an ice cream. Part of the visitor center was closed, probably because of Covid. There was a lot of weather monitoring equipment at the top of the mountain and we couldn't begin to imagine people actually staying here through all of the bad weather on the mountain but apparently, they do.

We saw several of the Cog Railway trains as we hiked near the tracks. It is a tradition with hikers to moon the railcar and the train engineer will throw coal at the hikers. It was pretty cold outside so we just wiggled our butts at the train and they all hollered at us and clapped anyway.

We got to the Madison Hut and kept going on the AT. In hindsight, we should have gone to the Valley View Campsite 0.6 miles off the trail. We had to follow trail markers that were piles of rocks called cairns, usually with a white rock on the top to signify the AT. I think we were tired and were so ready to push on to the finish that we didn't take into consideration the potential difficulty of the trail in the area. We were forced to stop and set up our tent at 5000 feet elevation which was above the tree line. The wind was getting too strong to hike, it was becoming foggier by the minute, visibility was nearly nonexistent and we were too far away to make it below the tree line before dark. We found an area at the edge of some small trees that was a little bit protected, so we set our tent there. It was probably the craziest tent set up anyone has ever done or will ever do. Our tent was on top of small plants, bushes and rocks and we really had a hard time trying to put our air mattresses in the tent where we could lie down. We actually tied the tent to small bushes on each side in order to help keep the wind from blowing it away. We decided we had to make it work and we just crawled in. It was after 8:00 p.m. when we stopped for the evening after hiking 12.5 miles.

We thought about the hiker who died recently on Mt. Washington. He apparently didn't have a tent with him and the temperature dropped much lower. With the conditions the way they were when he got caught in the weather a tent may not have helped him. We were glad we had carried all our supplies with us. We knew the temperature would be cold but probably not below freezing. We had our twenty-degree down sleeping bags and our down jackets in addition to our tent. We knew we would be fine, so we decided to shelter in place until the weather cleared. The wind gusted and it rained a little during the night but we were warm in our tent, dry, and had plenty of food and water. Sleep didn't come easy with the wind and the crazy tent set up. *I think both of us were concerned about the situation we were in at the time. I can say I was not truly afraid and I had faith that we would be alright until morning, we just had to give it some time for the weather to clear. The hardest thing to do was just wait knowing we only had 28.2 miles to go! We were too close to the finish to get in trouble now.*

July 2, 2022 - We awakened at 4:45 a.m., the wind was still strong and it was raining. After daylight we thought we heard hikers a couple of times but we were not sure until we clearly heard someone say, "I think it's this way". Roy got out and called out to them, but no one answered. I'm sure with the wind blowing loudly they probably couldn't hear. At this point we still couldn't see the mountains because of the fog. We just crawled back into the tent and hunkered down. Again, warm, dry, plenty of food and water, we were okay. We would wait. The weather finally broke about noon so we packed up and got going asap. *It is supposed to be illegal to camp above the tree line in the White Mountains and you're not supposed to squash the alpine plants. We were not camping. We were in survival mode.*

After we finally got going, we only hiked 2.3 miles which was 2500 feet downhill! Dropping over 1000 feet per mile made for an interesting descent and very slow going. We made it to the Osgood Tent Sites which is where we wanted to be the evening before when we were forced to stop. We decided to just stay when we got there and we put our tent on a platform. *I think we were both exhausted after the ordeal last night, neither of us slept very well and we were kicking ourselves for getting in the situation in the first place. When we stopped last night, we were 0.9 miles from the tree line and several good stealth campsites. In any other terrain we would have made it there well before dark. It took two hours that morning for us to cover that distance. There is no way we could have made it before dark and no way we could have made it in the dark. We did the right thing by staying where we did.* We were 25.9 miles from the finish.

When we got to the Osgood Tent Sites, I looked in the bear box to make sure it was clean before we put our stuff in it. I found a salami roll and a package of tortillas. There was no one else around. After we had been there for a while another couple came by us on their way to the water source. We asked if they had put anything in the bear box and they had not. There were several more campsites past us and we walked up that way to see if the food belonged to anyone else. There were more campsites but there were also more bear boxes. *A lot of times hikers will reconsider what they are packing and leave stuff that is too heavy. The salami roll and tortillas were definitely heavy, I certainly wouldn't have carried them.* After we were sure the stuff belonged to no one else there we decided to eat it for supper. It was pretty good. *I had almost forgotten but we also found a can of chicken breast in a bear box in the middle of nowhere with no one around a few weeks ago, we ate it too. Yes, we had become opportunistic feeders more than once during our hike.*

July 3, 2022 - We slept in and didn't get up until 6:30 a.m. We had been getting up around 5:30 or 6:00 a.m. at the latest. I guess we must have needed the rest. We hiked 10.8 miles up and over the Wildcat Mountains. The trail grapevine had said the wildcats were difficult but we didn't find them any worse than anything we had seen so far. There was a lot of climbing where we couldn't use our hiking poles.

We stopped before noon at the Pinkham Notch Visitors Center and got our $2.00 bowl of soup and bread. The soup was roasted potato and it was delicious. *The soup was another perk on the camping permit we purchased.* We also got ice cream, candy and peanuts. We saw Grumpy who did trail magic at Crawford Notch a couple of days ago. He had already made breakfast that morning for hikers. We were too late for his trail magic this time but we were fine with our soup and bread. We also saw a couple of younger hikers who said they hiked over Mt. Madison yesterday morning in the fog, it may have been them we heard while we were waiting for the weather to clear. We told them about having set our tent up there but they said they didn't see it. *I didn't know how they made it down that mountain in the fog. I sure didn't want to try it that morning.*

The trail seemed as though it was uphill most of the day, but there was a big downhill to the Carter Notch Hut. Of course, we were at lower elevations so there were several streams we crossed and lakes with beautiful reflections again. This was our last chance to get work for stay since it was the last hut in New Hampshire. *Hikers are told it is statistically unlikely to get to work for stay since there are so many hikers on the AT. But it doesn't hurt to ask.*

We got to the hut about 6:00 p.m. and I asked about the work for stay and they said yes! I was shocked but thrilled at the prospect of seeing what was so special about staying at the huts.

July 4, 2022 - Last night we ate bread, soup, salad, bowtie pasta, and dessert and it was all delicious. I noticed Roy was pushing the spinach from his soup to the side of the bowl. I encouraged him to try it and eat it because he needed the nutrition. *I told him the spinach is mostly a filler and takes on the flavor of*

276

the soup. I compared it to carrots in the soup I make at home that he eats, although he doesn't like carrots. I looked again a few minutes later and his soup bowl was clean, I guess it didn't taste bad after all. The dessert was some kind of caramel apple cake and it was delicious. Brittney was the one who made the dessert and she was really very sweet and friendly. There was another girl there who was her polar opposite, she sure wouldn't win Miss Congeniality. Our work consisted of washing part of a wall in the dining room which was not difficult. It was about 10 feet of the wall about 3 feet up from the floor where people had touched the wall with their shoes while sitting at the picnic style dining tables. It was a small price to pay for a good meal.

We set up our air mattresses and sleeping bags in the dining room and slept on the floor there after everyone turned in for the night, which was about 10:00 p.m. We were sure tired when we finally settled in for the night. We decided to get up and out of there early since Miss Congeniality was the first one up that morning and she didn't make us feel any more welcome than the evening before. We stopped on the trail to make coffee and have oatmeal not long after leaving the hut.

That day we hiked up and over Carter Dome, South, North and Middle Carter Mountains. We considered staying at a campsite for the night but it was only 1:30 p.m. We decided to push on, if we continued, we might just finish the trail.

The hiking was difficult but I think we were both running on adrenaline and excitement at the prospects of actually finishing the entire AT. A couple of more times we considered stopping to camp for the evening but we were so close and we had plenty of daylight so we just kept going.

We made it to the parking area at highway 2 near Gorham, New Hampshire about 7:00 p.m. *OMG! We were finished! I'm not sure either of us could believe it!* We did our own mini celebration about a mile from the finish and then again in front of the Rattle River Hostel where we stopped last year. We had made it! What a way to end the trail on July 4th! At this point I forgot about taking more pictures, all we could think about was getting a ride into town and planning the trip home.

After several phone calls we finally got a ride to the Gorham Motor Inn where we stayed last year before flying home. We of course got showers then went to find something to eat. It was getting late and several places were closed or closing by the time we arrived. I was after all a holiday. There were also still places closed due to Covid. We finally decided to just give up and eat at the McDonalds just up the street from the motel. We had clean clothes to wear and decided we could wait until we got home to do laundry. We went online and booked our bus ride from Gorham to Boston and our fight from Boston to Nashville for July 5th. There was no need to stay another night in New Hampshire when we could be on our way home. *We had finished the trail on July 4th, that would be another date that would be easy to remember. Oh, what a glorious feeling to finally be headed home.*

"If you know you are going home,
the journey is never too hard." - Angela Wood

Chapter 39 - There's No Place Like Home

July 5, 2022 - We got up about 5:30 a.m. and had coffee and pastries for breakfast. We packed up our stuff and got ready to catch the bus at the Circle K next to the motel. It was scheduled to leave at 7:50 a.m. and it left pretty close to that time. The bus traveled the same route through the White Mountains as when we rode it last fall. We got one last look at Mt. Washington and said goodbye to the AT. We arrived at the airport about 12:50 p.m. As we were walking through Boston-Logan International Airport I got a text that our connecting flight in Washington, D. C. was canceled. We went to the ticket counter and got our flight rescheduled; it was routed through Dallas/Fort Worth. We were originally supposed to have a connecting flight in Washington, D.C. *Ugh, we had to fly this route through Dallas/Fort Worth last time. Our flight was to leave an hour earlier but it didn't arrive in Nashville until 10:35 p.m. Here we go again, we won't be home until after midnight!* I texted Christi to tell her of the change in our flight plan since she and Jamie were going to pick us up.

We were riding in the tram at DFW and I saw Boston Rob from Survivor. He was wearing sunglasses and had a cap pulled down low. He saw me glance at him a couple of times. I just smiled at him and he smiled back. He had on a Patriots cap and jacket. I didn't call attention to him because he was trying to stay incognito and I didn't want to cause a scene he was trying to avoid. Roy told me he didn't see him and it probably wasn't him. I'm a big Survivor fan and have seen him on the show many times. *Just to refresh my memory about him, I looked him up online later. It was definitely him.*

We got to Nashville and picked up our packs from baggage claim. When we stepped outside the kids were waiting for us. Jamie, Christi, Autumn and Isaac all came to get us. They were amazed at how much weight we lost and how much we had changed. We stopped in Nashville somewhere for Autumn to use the restroom and Roy and I got big beers to celebrate! Jamie being the jokester he is said to Roy as he was approaching the checkout with two huge beer cans in his hands, "Don't ask me for any more money if you're going to just spend it on beer!" We all got a really good laugh out of that one. I believe the kids were really excited to see us and have us back in Kentucky. I know we were definitely glad to be back. We finally got home around 1:30 a.m., they dropped us off in our driveway and continued on to their home in Glasgow about 10 miles away. We got in the house and everything looked just like we left it. But it was going to take a couple of days to get used to being back in our home, sleeping in our own bed, driving instead of walking everywhere, taking a shower every day, drinking a pot of coffee every morning, seeing and talking with family, wearing real clothes (if we had any that fit), me wearing makeup and actually fixing my hair and using hair spray. Roy had lost 50 pounds and I had lost 40 pounds. We did need to put back on a few pounds, just not too much. It is amazing all the things we take for granted. I think we were both asleep that night before we got the covers pulled up. It took me a minute the next morning to realize I was at home and in my own bed.

Though hiking the AT was laborious we still tried to take time to stop along the way to admire this beautiful world God created for us. We enjoyed seeing the many sights along the trail, the unique and historic places, meeting interesting people and even challenging ourselves with the distances we traveled on foot each day or the mountains we climbed. There is no photo that can capture the beauty of the sights we saw and most of them would have to be committed to memory.

All the research we did before hiking prepared us well. But there was definitely nothing to prepare us for tolerating the weather and living outside for more than seven months. Nor did we realize the magnitude of the elevation gains and losses of the mountains we would traverse. These were things we had to experience for ourselves, looking at the maps just didn't prepare us.

We found there are a lot of everyday things people take for granted. A roof over your head, plenty of food to eat, clean cold drinking water, a warm bed, a shower, or a toilet were just a few of the things we all take for granted every day. You don't have any idea how much you miss these things until they are not readily available. Not having them sure made me appreciate them more.

Throughout the journey it also became very apparent to us there is no place like home and nothing like being with our family. We were so happy to finally be home.

I don't know what compels a person to hike long distances like the AT. But for some people I think it becomes an obsession. I believe my husband was obsessed with hiking the AT to completion and I was gradually convinced to hike with him. The mountains called him and I went along. For us, I don't know if it was determination or just plain stubbornness but we can say we hiked the entire Appalachian Trail.

"It always seems impossible until it's done."
- Nelson Mandela

EPILOGUE

We heard from our tramily members a little while after we returned home. Hound Dog climbed the summit at Katahdin and finished his AT hike on July 27. Prancer and Double B summited Katahdin on August 12th, then they went back to Harper's Ferry to hike SOBO to Springer Mountain, Georgia. They finished at Springer Mountain on November 6th. Wow, all five of us determined old farts beat the odds, one over 50, three over 60 and one over 70 all completed a thru hike of the AT! A bunch of determined older folks should never be underestimated. We are a lot tougher than you think.

My husband and I will still continue to hike backcountry trails. It will mainly be day hikes, but we may go on some short overnight trips. I don't think either of us want to tackle another long-distance hike like the AT, and hiking it once was enough. Besides, aren't we getting a little too old for this?

Fourteen States on the Appalachian Trail

2021 total mileage equals 2193.1 miles

Miles - State

78.1 - Georgia
226.6 - North Carolina/Tennessee
65.9 - Tennessee
551.1 - Virginia
4 - West Virginia
40.9 - Maryland
229.2 - Pennsylvania
72.4 - New Jersey
90 - New York
50.5- Connecticut
90.4 - Massachusetts
150.8 - Vermont
160.9 - New Hampshire
281.8 - Maine

Our Zero Hiking Days

3/23/2020 - Gatlinburg, Tennessee (rain)

8/16/2021 -Wilderness Edge Campground, Millinocket, Maine (exhaustion)

8/31/2021 - Lakeshore House, Monson, Maine (after the 100 Mile Wilderness)

9/05/2021 - The Sterling Inn, Caratunk, Maine

9/11/2021 - The Maine Roadhouse, Stratton, Maine

9/15/2021 - Reddington Stream Campsites (rain & wind)

3/12/2022 - Bland, VA (snow)

3/26/2022 - Daleville, VA (snow)

4/08/2022 - Waynesboro, VA (rain)

4/18/2022 - Front Royal, VA (rain)

5/01/2022 - Duncannon, PA (rain)

5/07/2022 - Port Clinton, PA (rain)

5/30/2022 - Great Barrington, MA (a much-needed break from the trail

6/27/2022 - Lincoln, NH (rain)

Lodging (*tenting with some facilities available)

2/27/2020 - Amicalola Falls State Park, Georgia
3/3/2020 - Seasons Inn, Blairsville, Georgia
3/7/2020 - Budget Inn, Hiawassee, Georgia
3/11/2020 - Budget Inn, Franklin, North Carolina
3/14/2020 - Nantahala Outdoor Center, Bryson City, North Carolina
3/17/2020 - Fontana Dam Resort, Tennessee
3/22/2020 - Econo Lodge, Gatlinburg, Tennessee
3/23/2020 - Econo Lodge, Gatlinburg, Tennessee
3/30/2020 - The Iron Horse, Hot Springs, North Carolina
8/14/2021 - *Wilderness Edge Campground, Millinocket, Maine
8/15/2021 - *Wilderness Edge Campground, Millinocket, Maine
8/16/2021 - *Wilderness Edge Campground, Millinocket, Maine
8/30/2021 - *Shaw's Hostel, Monson, Maine
8/31/2021 - Lakeshore House, Monson, Maine
9/4/2021 - *Three Rivers Trading Post, Caratunk, Maine
9/5/2021 - The Sterling Inn, Caratunk, Maine
9/10/2021 - The Maine Roadhouse Hostel, Stratton, Maine
9/11/2021 - The Maine Roadhouse Hostel, Stratton, Maine
9/17/2021 - The Saddleback Inn, Rangely, Maine
9/22/2021 - Pine Ellis Lodging, Andover, Maine
9/24/2021 - Mountain Valley Motel, Bethel, Maine
9/29/2021 - Gorham Motor Lodge, Gorham, New Hampshire
10/18/2021 - Motel 8, Erwin, Tennessee
10/23/2021 - Mountain Harbor Hostel, Roan Mountain, Tennessee
11/30/2021 - Travelers Inn, Elizabethton, Tennessee
3/05/2022 - Travel Inn, Marion, Virginia
3/11/2022 - The Big Walker Motel, Bland, Virginia
3/16/2022 - Angel's Rest Hiker Haven, Pearisburg, Virginia
3/25/2022 - Motel 8, Daleville, Virginia
3/26/2022 - Motel 8, Daleville, Virginia
3/28/2022 - Stanimal's Hostel, Glasgow, Virginia
4/07/2022 - Super 8, Waynesboro, Virginia
4/16/2022 - *Big Meadow Campground, Shenandoah National Park, Virginia

4/17/2022 - Super 8, Front Royal, Virginia
4/18/2022 - Super 8, Front Royal, Virginia
4/22/2022 - *Cross Trails Hostel, Maryland
4/25/2022 - Cobblestone Inn, Waynesboro, Virginia
4/30/2022 - The Doyle Hotel, Duncannon, Pennsylvania
5/01/2022 - The Doyle Hotel, Duncannon, Pennsylvania
5/06/2022 - *The Pavilion, Port Clinton, Pennsylvania
5/07/2022 - *The Pavilion, Port Clinton, Pennsylvania
5/11/2022 - The Gateway Motel, Wind Gap, Pennsylvania
5/15/2022 - *The Secret Shelter, Pennsylvania
5/17/2022 - Lake Lodging, Greenwood Lake, New York
5/29/2022 - Monument Motel, Great Barrington, Massachusetts
5/30/2022 - Monument Motel, Great Barrington, Massachusetts
6/03/2022 - *Father Toms Campsite, Cheshire, Massachusetts
6/06/2022 - Catamount Motel, Bennington, Vermont
6/12/2022 - Days Inn, Rutland, Vermont
6/18/2022 - Hanover Adventure Tours Hostel, Norwich, Vermont
6/22/2022 - *Hikers Welcome Hostel, Warren, New Hampshire
6/26/2022 - Mt. Liberty Lodging, Lincoln, New Hampshire
6/27/2022 - Mt. Liberty Lodging, Lincoln, New Hampshire
7/03/2022 - *Carter Notch Hut
7/04/2022 - Gorham Motor Lodge, Gorham, New Hampshire
7/05/2022 - Home - Glasgow, Kentucky

References

American Battlefield Trust (2023, February 9) Washington Inoculates Army - The Continental Army Battles Invisible Foe https://www.battlefields.org/learn/articles/washington-innoculates-army

Atlas Guides (2021, October 19) FarOut (App Version 11.0.2 (211122)) [mobile app]. App Store. https://faroutguides.com/guides/

Backpacker (2018, June 11) Cross the "Virginia Triple Crown" Off Your Hiking Bucket List https://www.backpacker.com/trips/virginia-tripe-crown/

Bears Den, Bluemont Virginia (2022, December 5) Welcome to Bears Den - An Official Hiker Hostel in Northern Virginia https://bearsdencenter.org/

Benavitch, David W. (1992, October 7) Oral History Interview with Taft Hughes https://www.nbatc.org/1992Interview.htm

Bloodhound (2018, December 13) Trail Angel Spotlight: Fresh Ground and his Leapfrog Cafe https://www.thetrek.co/appalachian-trail/trail-angel-spotlight-fresh-ground/

Bouchelle, Hugh (n.d.) Bluff Mountain and the Tragedy of Little Ottie Cline Powell https://lexingtonvirginia.com/outdoors/blog/bluff-mountain-and-the-tragedy-little-ottie-cline-powell

Darn Tough Official Site - Socks That Last Forever (2022, December9) https://darntough.com

Department of Land and Natural Resources, Hawaii.gov (2022, November 29)

https://dlnr.hawaii.gov/dsp/parks/oahu/diamond-head-state-monument

Explore Georgia - Amicalola Falls State Park & Lodge
https://www.exploregeorgia.org/dawsonville/outdoors-nature/state-parks/amicalola-falls-state-park-lodge

Henning, Herman G. (2014, May 30) Hiker Heaven: A break, a bed and a chunk of history await the weary at the Doyle Hotel
https://theburgnews.com/business/hiker-heaven-break-bead-chunk-history-await-weary-doyle-hotel

Hike to the Keffer Oak on the Appalachian Trail, Newport Virginia (2022, December 5) https://theoutboundcom/virginia/hiking/hike-to-the-keffer-oak-on-the-appalachian-trail/photos

Hiking in the Smokys (2023, February 6) Gregory Bald (via Gregory Bald Trail)
https://hikinginthesmokys.com/gregroy-bald-via-gregory-bald-trail/

HMdb.org The Historical Marker Database (2022, December 9) Lightning Guider Sleds https://www.hmdb.org/m.asp?m+19711

HMdb.org The Historical Marker Database (2023, February 9) Hempstead Huts
https:/www.hmdb.org/m.asp?m=208965

Hower, Stephanie (n.d.) Tom Oar: Mountain Man
https://citylifestyle.com/minneapolis-nm/articles/entertainment/tom-oar-mountain-man

jerseyislandholidays.com (2023, March 1) 59+ Hiking Industry Stastics for 2023

https://www.jerseyislandholidays.com/59-hiking-statistics/#chapter-5

Kentucky State Parks (2023, February 15) Cumberland Falls State Resort Park
https://stateparks.com/cumberland_falls_state_resort_park_in_kentucky.html

Kershner, Jim (2021, September 6) Apple Farming in Washington
https://www.historylink.org/File/21288

Madison, Erin (2016, June 23) Mountain Man of the Yaak
https://www.greatfallstribune.com/story/life/2016/06/23/moutain-man-yaak/86291304

Minnesota Museum of the Mississippi (2023, February 9) The 45th Parallel, Doc Grant's Restaurant, Rangely, Maine
https://www.nmnuseumofthems.org/45th/Rangeley.html

Mcncdmin (2017, April 2) Mitchell County Historical Society, The Cloudland Hotel, A Mammoth Landmark of Its Day
https://www.mitchellnchistory.org/2017/04/02/the-cloudland-hotel-a-mammoth-landmark-of-its-day/

National Park Reservations (2022, November 30) Overview of Paradise Inn
https://www.nationalparkreservations.com/lodge/paradise-inn/

Only In Your State (2019, May 3) The Rocky Waterfall Trail In Kentucky That Will Instantly Become Your Favorite
https://www.onlyinyourstate.com/kentucky/rocky-waterfall-trail-kentucky/

Ridge Trekker (2023, February 9) How long is the Appalachian Trail? - Breaking down the miles
https://ridgetrekker.com/how-long-is-the-appalachian-trail/

Ridge Trekker (2023, February 9) Elevation on the Appalachian Trail - Highest to Lowest Point
https://ridgetrekker.com/elevation-on-the-appalachian-trail/

Ross, Cindy (2016, October 28) "Poor Man's Country Club"- Frank Russo, the Port Clinton Barber, Shows us how to Live
https://cindyrosstraveler.com/2016/10/28/poor-mans-country-club-frank-russo-the-port-clintion-barber-shows-us-how-to-live/
Schneck, Marcus (2020, March 5) Man Who Hiked 2180 Mile Appalachian Trail 18 times headed to Hall of Fame
https://www.pennlive.com/life/2020/03/man-who-hiked-2180-mile-appalachian-trail-18-times-headed-to-hall-of-fame.htm/?outputType=amp

Sinonson, Amy (2022, June 20) Severely hypothermic hiker dies after rescue in "treacherous" conditions near Mt. Washington
https://amp.cnn.com/cnn/2022/06/20/20/us/hiker-rescue-mount-washington-new-hampshire/index.html

Skylis, Mary Beth (Mouse) (2022, June 3) Appalachian Trail Hiker Dies After Falling from McAfee Knob
https://www.outsideonline.com/outdoor-adventure/exploration-survival/appalachian-trail-death-mcafee-knob-paul-classen/

Suckkow, Alex (2023, January 5) Did you know Kentucky is one of the only places on Earth that had a regular moonbow?
https://www.wlky.com/amp/article/kentucky-moonbow-night-state-park-cumberland-falls/42407359

Visit My Smokies (2021, March 18) Learn About the Llamas that Take Supplies to Mount LeConte
https://www.visitmysmokies.com/blog/smoky-mountains/llamas-take-supplies-mount-leconte/

Wikipedia (2022, November 28) Civilian Conservation Corps
https://en.m.wikipedia.org/wiki/Civilian_Conservation_Corps

Wikipedia (2022, December 12) Dartmouth College
https://en.m.wikipedia.org/wiki/Dartmouth_College

Wikipedia (2023, February 9) Fisher (animal)
https://www.en.m.wikipedia.org/wiki/Fisher_(animal)

Wikipedia (2022, November 23) Hensley Settlement
https://en.wikipedia.org/wiki/Hensley_Settlement

Wikipedia (2023, February 11) Kalalau Trail
https://en.m.wikipedia.org/wiki/Kalalau_Trail

Wikipedia (2022, November 28) Mt. LeConte (Tennessee)
https://en.m.wikipedia.org/wiki/Mount_Le_Conte_(Tennessee)

Wikipedia (2022, November 30) Mount Washington
https://en.m.wikipedia.org/wiki/Mount_Washington

Wikipedia (2022, December 4) Audie Murphy
https://en.m.wikipedia.org/wiki/Audie_Murphy
Wikipedia (2022, December 12) Northeast Airlines Flight 946
https://en.m.wikipedia.org/wiki/Northeast_Airlines_Flight_946

About The Author

Angela James grew up on a small farm in southcentral Kentucky, as the youngest of four children she was always considered a tomboy, a daddy's girl and loved being outside. She has been married to her husband for twenty-nine years and they have a blended family of four grown children and eight treasured grandchildren. After her thirty-five-year career in healthcare she and her husband decided it was time to retire and hike the Appalachian Trail in 2020. Although she has considered writing a book for some time, this is her first published work. The idea to write this book started as a suggestion from a family member who was following her hiking adventures.

Made in the USA
Columbia, SC
27 September 2023

23500919R00165